A LIFE OF INTRIGUES

This book is dedicated to the memory
of my dear mother, a lovely lady
who believed in and lived by the principle:
'Give us courage, gaiety and the quiet mind'.
Her life was long and happy in consequence.

A LIFE OF INTRIGUES

Diana de Rosso

Lennard Publishing
1991

LENNARD PUBLISHING
a division of Lennard Associates Limited
Mackerye End
Harpenden
Herts AL5 5DR

British Library Cataloguing in Publication Data
Rosso, Diana de
A life of intrigues: the autobiography of Diana de Rosso.
1. Great Britain. Entertainments – Biographies
I. Title
791.092

ISBN 1 85291 091 7

First published 1991
© Diana de Rosso

Typeset in Monotype Sabon
Design by Forest Publication Services, Luton.
Cover design by Pocknell & Co.

Reproduced, printed and bound in Great Britain
by Butler & Tanner Ltd, Frome and London

Contents

But I have one talent, a wonderful thing –
Everyone listens when I start to sing!
Abba

Author's Note

I had never considered writing my life story, but after I had
written my biography of James Mason I was interviewed
about it on a number of radio programmes. On two of
them, Radio Oxford and Radio Brighton, it was suggested
that my own life was not without its interest as well.
In fora penny! I set about it.

What is written here is as true as I can make it. However,
in deference to the wishes of certain friends and colleagues,
I have suppressed or altered some dates and names. I have
done the same with others out of concern for the safety of
those who are still active in the cause of honour and
freedom, in places where these things are rare and precious.

Chapter One

Hélène

My mother had the greatest influence on my early years, not only as a parent, but as my best and closest friend throughout her life. I'm told that in general girls are supposed to favour their fathers, but in my case this wasn't so; an early instance of the generally contrary nature for which I was later to become notorious.

Mama was born in Chelsea on 18 December 1889, the second child of a Welsh-Irish mixture. The fire inherent in this combination was fanned by the characters of my grandparents, which resembled each other only in strength. Lloyd Spear-Morgan, my grandfather, was one of three brothers, and my grandmother, Dorothy Gatward had one sister. Both enjoyed conventional upbringings, though both belonged to families with some eccentric foibles.

Great Grandfather Morgan was greatly esteemed in Wales, serving as High Sheriff of Carmarthen, until at the age of seventy he flouted convention as spectacularly as can well be imagined. He married, with full Romany rites, a Gipsy girl of twenty. He was by then a widower of many years' standing, and had evaded many ladies with high hopes for themselves or their marriageable daughters. Tegfynydd wasn't a large estate, but the old man was still a substantial catch so that on several occasions his sons had been summoned back to Llanfellteg to rescue their father from some irksome female who had fallen victim to his charms and fortune.

Till then his eccentricities had been well known and fairly mild; they included writing on the flaps of envelopes to save paper. His three sons, who all attended Caius College, Cambridge, regarded them with affectionate if exasperated amusement, though they used to curse the meticulously numbered scraps that fluttered like leaves to the floor. Another oddity was Great Grandfather's aversion to having his hip-bath emptied after he had used it.

1

"It's a waste of good water," he would thunder at his valet and the other minions, who were there to empty part (only part) of a stone-cold bath and refill it with jugs of scalding water whenever he wanted to relax his aching arms and legs after a day's hunting and shooting.

If this was meanness, he made up for it by feeding his dogs and his livestock like kings: "And so they are," he would shout, throwing a leg of prime Welsh lamb to a favourite dog, "They're jewels - no arguments, no chatter, just loyalty and affection."

Grandfather Lloyd's brother Thomas was an expert on whippets, and kept several at Cambridge. He used to wager on them with fellow fanciers, and this, among other diversions, left no time at all for study, even when his allowance ran out. Then he would take to his bed until the next cheque arrived. Having decided to become a doctor he 'walked' Guy's Hospital for five years, but never passed a single examination. Ultimately he decided he was not cut out for a medical career, no doubt to the salvation of many lives.

My grandfather was also an occasional dipsomaniac, though he made genuine efforts to restrain his weakness for the bottle. He would implore my grandmother to meet him at his office to help him fight the cravings, but always in vain. Entirely against his own will he would employ the utmost deviousness to trick her, and set out for a prolonged binge in Wales. There he would book into a pub or hotel, usually in Saundersfoot. As a hotel resident he could get drinks served on a Sunday, while if he was in a pub where he was regarded as a friend he would spend the entire day bingeing in the back room. Sometimes his sleeping arrangements were less formal. It was not unknown for him to take a stroll in the country with a bottle for company and collapse under a hedgerow. These sessions often lasted for weeks on end, especially when he was joined by his brothers, ostensibly come to rescue him, but in truth there to roister with him for days at a time.

Always contrite, always swearing 'Never again', the three would return to their various homes, there to lead the lives of law-abiding, church-going pillars of the community, exemplars of the family motto, 'Fortitude and Prudence!' It must have been hell on earth for Grandmother, as she was a model lady of quality, perfectly groomed, beautifully mannered and a paragon of the domestic virtues. She abhorred all forms of indulgence and indiscipline, having fought that corner against a flighty mother who cared only for horses and ball gowns and damn the cost - for all that theirs was an impoverished county family. Education for girls was considered an extravagance, so inexpensive governesses of doubtful credentials were employed to ensure that etiquette and deportment were learned, for the only career open to young ladies of that generation was a Good Marriage.

Great Grandfather Morgan heartily approved of his son's marriage. Lloyd'ₛ choice was acceptable in every sense of the word, and to some extent redeemed the damage he himself had done to the Morgan name with his Romany. She had closed many doors against him. He was no longer invited to hunt balls, and if a fête was held on his estate, the County would not attend. Neither the birth of twin daughters nor the sudden death of his girl-bride from pneumonia had softened the hearts of the County against one of themselves who, in his position (which reflected on theirs), should have known better.

Great Grandfather Morgan and his brothers were all teetotal, having seen the effects of drink on their forebears, and had taken a lifelong pledge against it. Unfortunately, the next generation was disinclined to follow this fine example, and their drinking-bouts must surely have contributed to all their very early deaths. In every case tuberculosis, the scourge of the era, carried off the Morgan 'boys' in their early thirties, leaving behind young families to be brought up by their several widows.

Grandfather Lloyd was no businessman, being entirely too trusting, and believing that a gentleman's word was still his bond. He invested most of his capital in the brickyard of a partner less scrupulous than himself, retaining only a small income from his patrimony. Shortly after his death their company became insolvent, leaving my grandmother with two children to bring up and educate, very little money, and a stubborn determination to maintain herself and them in such style as was proper to the family traditions.

For her education my mother went to Somerville House in St Leonard's. It was a well-known small public school for girls, favoured by the German aristocracy including the von Bismarcks, but to Grandmother's disapproval she made no impression except in sporting activities. These were extensive, and very advanced for the time, including lawn tennis and cricket for girls. Mama was an excellent wicket-keeper. Uncle Howard went to Haileybury and Caius, determined to become a chartered accountant. I can only conjecture about how my grandmother managed to finance all this and make ends meet.

Mama's recollections of life on a shoestring were very amusing, nonetheless. On Sundays people were invited to tea in the drawing room, where the fire was never lit until well after lunch. It would be icy cold, even the chintz covers chilled the skin as you sat, so the order was given that Howard and Hélène stay in the room, stoke the fire, and above all, breathe!

"Breathe deeply, walk about, warm the air!"

Grandmother's order, which never failed to convulse both of them with laughter, allowed Mama to take refuge in playing the piano, and Uncle Howard in singing. They both had their father's love of music, and Mama's saddest memory recalls how when Grandfather Morgan lay dying he asked if an organ-grinder could be found to play under his window. Grandmother sent the maid to scour the streets, and his wish was granted. To the strains of a barrel organ he passed from this world aged thirty-three.

Grandmother lived as frugally as she could, saving every penny and wasting nothing. She kept a Spartan's eye on food. Breakfast, for instance, was three pieces of bread and butter and one small egg for each of the children, tea and an apple. Supper was again bread and butter, one sardine apiece, and whatever seasonable fruit was available.

Summer holidays were spent by the sea, generally in lodgings or at the invitation of the Hird-Morgans in Wales, near Tenby and Saundersfoot. This allowed Grandmother to let her own house, and make enough profit on the deal to pay her maidservant's annual wage, run a pony and trap, and pay a lad to look after the garden and stable. Elegance was her second nature, and by stitching and altering clothes she always managed to appear in the latest fashion.

Her hopes for her children were never realised, because they showed none of her reverence for learning, and had inherited their father's love of pleasure. Their interests were music, vaudeville, operetta, dancing, sport and (in a little while) flirting. My mother recalled how when they had been late at a party or a dance, a tap on the door at seven o'clock sharp would be accompanied by the few curt words, "Your bath is running - you can stay out all night to please yourself, now you can get up to please me."

No argument. If you lived in her home, you lived by her rules.

Once schooldays were over, and Uncle Howard safely at university, it was imperative that my mother find some work, of a type suitable for a young lady. But apart from being excellent at tennis and cricket, Mama had no obvious talents. On the other hand, as an eighteen-year-old with beautiful dark blue eyes, corn-coloured hair, a ravishing smile and a tiny waist, she turned all heads, leaving Grandmother proud but anxious.

"Hélène, if there was only a stone in the road, you'd start a flirtation with it!" she would admonish. Poor Grandmother, she was mortified at the insouciance of her children, whose single determination was to enjoy every aspect of life.

"If you came home and found me dead, you'd still go off to enjoy an evening of Gilbert and Sullivan! I know all you care about, either of you, is pleasure - I can just hear you saying, 'Poor Mama - but we can't do anything now, we'll do it when we come back!'"

There was truth in this, but despite the bitterness of Grandmother's words, Mama and Uncle Howard really loved her in their own way, though they shared neither her values nor her ideal of a happy life. Mama and Uncle Howard both had high hopes of her re-marrying - they felt it was time their single parent was free of the scrimping and saving and possible loneliness as they set about their own lives and careers. These generous hopes were thwarted; first by her sense of what was proper, which precluded taking on a man who might have interfered with their upbringing, or treated them unkindly.

Only when they were on the threshold of leaving home did she allow herself a suitor who, according to Mama, seemed ideal in every way. Yet even this paragon was unable to live up to Grandmother's standards. He ultimately incurred rejection when he blotted his copybook with an example of what she described as 'ungentlemanly behaviour'. This expression conjured up the most fearful lapses of taste, and indeed the abandonment (actual or attempted) of the most elementary propriety. Of course they were agog.

"Mother! What happened?"

"Tell us, Mother, what did Jack do?"

She turned a withering glance upon them. "I invited Jack to tea - to *tea*, mark you - and he was still sitting here at *six thirty*. My dears, I had to rise first and make my excuses - to tell a fib so as to be rid of him. I said I had to change for dinner as I was joining friends. Can you imagine a gentleman showing such a lack of finesse? I had noticed once or twice before that there was a certain sloppiness in his dress, and the flowers he brought with him today were not well chosen or wrapped. Quite impossible."

End of romance. The delinquent was crossed off her list, and no other suitor was ever considered.

As the years passed my mother often felt guilty, knowing that Grandmother had made so many sacrifices for her brother and herself, but their attitudes were so completely opposed that their affection was always clouded by a lack of understanding.

Work, for a young lady, offered a limited range in the first decade of the twentieth century, so when Mama decided to take a job with Belle Crystal, the well-known dancing teacher, Grandmother was beset with doubts about its propriety. Mama's primary efforts were to be directed to building up small classes in the north of England, and she must also be willing to call from door to door leaving a card detailing her fees, and the days she would be teaching in the neighbourhood. Not only must she undertake this hard grind, she must also be able to play at least one page of piano music to accompany each dance, which would include polka, waltz and the lancers. The pay was poor, barely one pound per week, but there were expenses for travel, board and lodging included. Mama, an enthusiast as always, was determined to make a success of the venture.

In this she succeeded, to her delight. With her gaiety, wit and beauty, her classes became very popular - and she never lost her love of the north of England and its people, whom she found to be warm-hearted, hospitable, and far less rigid in their views than those in the south. Belle Crystal had reason to congratulate herself on her choice of dancing mistress, and decided that Mama's talents would be even better employed in London. There her tact and charm would be appreciated by people of the professional class, especially men who had to be able to dance well so as to frequent society balls and meet suitable young ladies with large dowries.

To her regret Mama returned home and took up these duties under Belle's principal teacher, Mary Hadden. She was a very tall woman with a magnificent figure, a stentorian voice, and the sort of cockney accent called 'gorblimey', hardly heard any more. She combined them with a fascinatingly ugly face (it was like a squashed frog), and a heart of gold. Her detractors used to say that no one needed a clock in the Crystal Palace area, as the sound of Mary calling her classes to order kept time for the whole community.

She and Mama remained friends for life, and I remember her with great affection. She married during the First World War an officer and gentleman (and according to Mama a lazy ne'er-do-well) whom she doted on until his death in the early thirties. Her second husband was another of the same kind, and neither Mama nor I liked him much, but Mary saw the sun shine for his sake, so who were we to disagree?

Inevitably Mama's classes attracted an ever-increasing proportion of male pupils. They showered her with invitations to luncheons, dinners and parties, and she took up as many as she could, enjoying every minute of the day, working like a demon and playing no less hard. Solid, wealthy men, men struggling on the ladder, all vied with each other to create a good impression. Mama loved the attention, though she never took the compliments seriously. For her a posy of violets, a bus-ride or tea at Lyons Corner House were just as much fun as an expensive box of chocolates or toiletries, or a meal in a smart restaurant.

She also enjoyed her dancing for its own sake and kept it up until she was sixty. In later life she took lessons from Victor Sylvester, to maintain her high standards in general, and especially the timing and fluency of her pivot turns. Her vitality seemed endless, and she had no great wish to settle down. It worried my grandmother, who could see trouble ahead, as her admirers were a mixed lot. Then to her relief and delight Mama was wooed and (it seemed) won by Charles, a young Scotsman of impeccable breeding and social position. To Grandmother it seemed a romance made in Heaven. He was tall, fair-haired and handsome, and his family were whisky barons. He and Mama made a lovely couple, and when the banns for their marriage were first called in Paisley Abbey, Grandmother felt truly rewarded for all the effort she had put into guiding her children towards a proper and successful life.

Little did she know. One of Mama's pupils was a delicate, foreign-looking young man who was making a precarious living on the Stock Exchange. He was diffident, Jewish and almost penniless, and he was teased unmercifully by some of the better-off men in Mama's circle. Nonetheless, she found herself being drawn to his slight build, ivory complexion and honey-brown eyes. Mama remembered her little maid-of-all-work saying, "Oh Miss Hélène, he's so pale a gentleman, like a priest!" This impression was not entirely accurate. Isidore had already worked his way up from button-boy to independent speculator, and was in time to become a merchant banker in his own right. None of this was achieved by prayer - all was down to flair and nerve.

His mysterious background intrigued Mama, along with his silky black curls and his silver-knobbed cane. It wasn't much of a basis for romance, but she was hooked. Not only was this young man quite unlike any other she had met, she felt a need to protect him against the slights and sneers of his so-called friends, to which he never reacted with anger or embarrassment.

She had to tell poor Charles the engagement was off, she couldn't marry him feeling so full of doubts about their future. He, like the gentleman he was, withdrew, bewildered and hurt, leaving Grandmother outraged and furious at Mama. The introduction of Isidore Ostrer to the Spear-Morgan household added insult to the injury of the broken engagement. She was unable to contain her rage. "You might as well marry a black man - you will have no place in society, and no security for the future."

Her words fell on deaf ears, Mama was truly in love, and had no thought to money or position. In 1913 they were married, very inexpensively in a registry office, without so much as a photographer. She was twenty-three.

Uncle Howard took a more sanguine view of the Ostrers. He found them and their family life amusing, in an outlandish sort of way. It was as if he had been privileged to meet a family of aliens from Mars, though he was quick to tell his sister that no 'Jews, Turks or infidels' were going to enter society on his coat-tails. It was an unkind remark, yet not made maliciously. Even by the standards of his time he was a snob, and to him anyone who was not Welsh was of a lesser order - though to be pitied rather than blamed.

He was a very attractive personality, good-looking, witty and intelligent. Women loved him, but they soon came to bore him. Tea at the Ritz or Gunters, followed by an evening at the theatre with his latest conquest, could quickly turn to disaster, and when Grandmother taxed him with his unkindness and boorishness, he would fly off the handle: "Good God, Mother, what was I to do? The wretched girl gave me a headache. Of course I've dropped her - she's a silly, vapid, pretentious female."

At the outbreak of war he joined the First Welsh Border Regiment, and quickly won promotion to Captain. His men called him 'Captain Molly', on account of the way he fussed and fumed over their welfare. His 'boys', as he called them, were the love of his life, and he developed a maniacal hatred of Winston Churchill for what he saw as his failure of wisdom and foresight in the Gallipoli fiasco, where the soldiers, including Howard's, were mown down on the beaches or in the water as they staggered ashore under their heavy packs.

Shot through the head, Howard underwent several operations, but a fragment of the bullet was lodged too close to the brain to be removed. Consequently he had a tube in his head, and from time to time an abscess would form. Then he would collapse. When taken into the hospital for emergency treatment, he would always give his name as 'Captain Molly', rather than Spear-Morgan, which made it hard to check his medical history. This ultimately contributed to his death.

Patience was not among his virtues, and when the doctors warned him that in his condition he shouldn't drink, or if he must, only very moderately, he refused to listen. He preferred 'a short life but a gay one'. On a business trip to the Channel Islands he drank a great deal of whisky, and collapsed unconscious coming down the gangplank. No one had any idea what was the matter or how to treat him, and by the time the hospital had the details it was too late.

Another, and in effect the very last, of the Spear-Morgans was dead, for with Howard's death the family name died out. There remained only the Hird-Morgans, all ladies who remained spinsters apparently by choice.

Mama's marriage created a hiatus in Grandmother's life. She was always polite, but it was the beginning of a lifetime grudge against

Isidore Ostrer. She regarded him as totally alien, not without reason. His family were refugees from the Ukraine and spoke virtually no English. He and his sister and four brothers had been brought up in poverty in the east end of London. It was anathema; her only, beautiful, daughter throwing herself away, cutting herself off from the only society that mattered, and which decreed that one did not marry foreigners, certainly not Jews, and least of all Jews without income or background.

Mama took a different view of the matter, unwise though it was. The chasm between her and the Ostrers was unbridgeable, mainly through incompatibility of character. Gay, friendly, at ease in any sort of company, Mama was uninterested in money, success and ambition. She couldn't count, cook or sew, and how they managed in their first year or so of marriage defies imagining. They were in a house in Southend, rented for £1 per week and their only capital was £100 which Mama had saved. It was the cause of their first row, when she spent £5 of it on a pedigree Scots terrier. She loved animals, and had never lived in a household without dogs, cats, birds or preferably all three.

Isidore thought animals were unclean and carried germs, which amused Mama, but it was only one of their many conflicting views. He had shown himself willing to be cut off from his family if that was Mama's wish, but of course, she had no such desire. His parents, brothers and sister were all welcome in their house, and on the outbreak of war David, the eldest, moved in with his wife and two children until they found a place of their own.

A year after their marriage Mama miscarried of twin babies, to her profound emotional shock. She realised that what she wanted was children - far more than a husband, indeed, for domesticity without babies had few charms. She took on Mary, a young Irish Catholic maid who was to become a lifelong devotee, at five shillings a week. After the war Mary married a man who had lost a leg in it and bore him two children, whom she named Pamela, after Mama's first child, and Anthony after her last. She acted as nursemaid, kitchenmaid and general support when Pam was born in 1916, to be followed eighteen months later by Sheila, then Vivian. Finally Llewellyn was born, the family sorrow. He was most severely handicapped, and never had any prospect of life outside the sort of institution where he could receive constant care.

By now there was more money coming in, as the scope of Isidore's business widened, and he could speculate on a larger scale. The family moved to Broadstairs, where they employed a cook, housemaid and part-time gardener. When Mary left to join her husband, she was replaced by a children's nurse, Miss Thomas. It was there, at East

Hornden on the Esplanade, that the trouble to come manifested itself for the first time.

Isidore was beginning to make his name in business, and Mama was finding their life together less and less congenial. She felt closer to her brothers-in-law, Mark and Maurice, mainly because of Isidore's tendency to let work take precedence over his family. Mark was a special favourite of Mama's, a jolly, genial fellow, full of wit and enjoyment of life. Maurice, the youngest of the Ostrer boys was spoilt and conceited, but a marvellous ballroom dancer. He and Mama used to spend a lot of time together, and they won many competitions. After I was born Maurice was to show his true character. He said he had always disliked and resented Mama for having married his brother, who would surely otherwise have taken a suitable Jewish girl, and raised his family in the Orthodox tradition. Whether this or his previous appearance of friendship was a lie, I still don't know, and it surely doesn't matter. Either way, it says all one needs to know about Maurice.

By the end of the First World War Mama was exhausted. She had had too many and too difficult pregnancies, the war itself (including Uncle Howard's headwound) had been a strain, then there had been the Black Flu (also known as Spanish Influenza). She and Grandmother needed a break from routine, so they took a short holiday together at St Malo. There by pure chance she met the man who was to become my father.

Count Louis de Rosso was eldest son and heir-apparent to his father, who had settled in France for his health (and the gambling). The family was old, and could claim connections with the houses of Savoy and Aosta - which made them third cousins of Kings Victor-Emmanuel and Umberto. The Palazzo di Rosso in Turin is still extant. Neither he nor my mother had really come to St Malo in search of more than a holiday romance, but the attraction and sudden passion they felt for each other led not only to the pregnancy, but to a longing to be together.

Back in England, Mama told Isidore everything as soon as she realised she was pregnant. They discussed divorce, and began to set it in motion. The only stumbling-block was Isidore's ultimatum: all the children must remain with him, including the unborn latest that would in due course become myself. Mama refused to agree to this, so proceedings went into abeyance.

I was born in August 1921. Here, to Isidore's chagrin, was a fair-haired, green-eyed child, in contrast to the dark babies he had grown used to. Meanwhile my father, who had been kept informed about both the pregnancy and the on-off divorce, had not been idle. I was only a few weeks old when he went to Rome to petition for, and receive, dispensation from the Church, and to register my birth as his natural daughter - just in case Isidore should try to make good his threat to claim and keep all the offspring of his marriage, legitimate or not.

Isidore's reason for this remains obscure. While he claimed (through his lawyers) that he was simply unwilling for any child to bear the stigma of bastardy through any action of his, my mother claimed that his threat was only an expression of spite. Doubtless the truth lies somewhere in between, and is more complex. It certainly had nothing to do with the religious difference; Isidore neither believed in nor practised the Faith.

The problems of the next two years are too tedious and lengthy to record. Not only did Isidore accuse my mother of conducting affairs with every Tom, Dick or Harry she met, he involved the wonderful local Doctor Raven, who attended the whole household, by saying that he was also one of her lovers. Apart from the professional slur, he and his family were personal friends; Mama took great exception to the suggestion that she had abused their trust in such a common fashion.

The question of divorce was re-opened, and this time Mama was adamant. She wanted her freedom, she loved her children, but she could no longer live with Isidore. She was under heavy pressure, but no one at this stage had given a thought to the law, as manifested in the person of the King's Proctor. This powerful figure would allow no petition to go forward until Isidore could present new evidence of adultery with someone other than the previous co-respondent, whose wrongdoing he had accepted and forgiven if not condoned - i.e., by continuing to live, ostensibly as man and wife, under the same roof as Mama.

Mama had no option but to go on living with Isidore, as if she had left he could have described it as desertion. This would have weakened her position enormously. She would have been in danger of losing not only the case but access to her children.

There was no evidence to call, and on this legal point a long battle ensued. Mama's lawyers refused point-blank to ease the situation by bringing forward a name and proof of adultery, which would have meant a quick ending to the marriage, because Isidore had still refused to define her rights to the children, or to offer maintenance of any sort. He would only reiterate that it would be 'generous'.

'Not enough,' the lawyers said: this could mean as little as £200 a year, no recompense for a lady who had produced a child or a miscarriage annually, and had maintained the matrimonial home on a shoestring for the complainant and others of his family. The vexed question of custody of the children was also of paramount importance, and neither was prepared either to yield or to take on a weak position by further admitted adultery.

Over the years Isidore's finances had improved, so that conditions in the home were now comfortable. Mama had no idea, until her solicitors told her, that her husband was a very rich man. Unknown to her, he had made several coups on the market, and while she and the staff had been running the home in a very modest style, Isidore and his brothers had been living a rich life in London on their secret wealth.

During the court battle Mama received, for the very first time, presents of furs and jewellery, all of which she must return, as they might otherwise be construed as bribes to secure her acquiescence in court. In any event, she had never taken much interest in such things, but when agreement was finally reached she found that she was allowed to keep them as a peace-offering. She was later to divide these gifts among her daughters. She wanted none of them for herself, and she had a stock answer for friends who thought her mad to give up such a rich man without a proper settlement: "Maybe he is a millionaire, once or twice over, but now I am free and have peace of mind. That is worth a fortune to me."

Apart from the presents and promises from Isidore, Mama had to endure coarse innuendo, insults, and prolonged cross-examination in the witness box, for this was no polite, arranged divorce. It was a pillory, in which she must fight for the right to her children.

In the early 1920s, it was the accepted practice that the gentleman took the blame so that the proceedings should take the minimum time and arouse the minimum interest. He might suffer censorious comment, and might be required to resign from some of the more old-fashioned clubs, but that was all. A gentleman was free to act the bounder from time to time, but a lady was not. She was immediately thrown beyond the pale of decency, she became a scarlet woman, a Jezebel, if not actually a whore.

For Grandmother it was a time of unalloyed misery. She must see her daughter branded an unfit mother, hear the sniggers and jokes of a gossip-hungry public, and the barely-veiled contempt of the sarcastic opposing counsel turned the knife in the wound. What had been an armed truce with the Ostrers developed into open enmity. Uncle Howard gave moral support to his mother and sister, but the terrible head-wound he had suffered at Gallipoli sometimes prevented him from being in court.

The next development after the divorce surprised everyone. A friendship developed between the formerly-married couple, which had been markedly absent for a long time. He now saw only her best qualities, and wished they had never parted. Mama, by contrast, was thrilled to be free, but was now able to feel a sympathy and understanding towards Isidore which had not been possible during their long legal battle.

Later I was to realise that Mama was well aware of the hostility my father's family showed her. A non-Catholic, a divorcée with four children by her first husband, a foreigner - unacceptable on all counts. I've no doubt that her lack of a fortune was even less to their liking. Old Italian families are very conservative about dowries.

In any event, Mama was now on her own, with a small monthly allowance from Isidore on condition that she did not marry her other lover, a certain Englishman to whom she was giving almost as much devotion as my father, but had no intention of living with. He, as it happens, was heavily involved with the woman whom he was later to marry, but who was at that time nursing a very sick husband and bringing up two sons. Here was another example of Mama's extraordinary ability to retain the affection of her lovers. In later years he would visit us in France, arousing no less fury in Louis than Isidore did. We continued to meet him occasionally up until 1960, when he settled permanently on Jersey; Mama's affairs were truly only ever ended by death.

For my grandmother the death of Uncle Howard coming so soon after the disgrace of the divorce had a devastating effect. She had always been delicate, but now it seemed as though a light had gone out. She was still a forceful and irascible character, but her son was dead, her daughter was embarking on a life without order or design, and she no longer had any *raison d'être*. As for having so many grandchildren, it seemed to Grandmother that such breeding bordered on the plebeian. Pregnancy was to be regulated by whatever means came to hand, abstinence being best. Mama agreed to differ over this. For her a large family meant fulfilment, and if this meant that the children had different fathers, so be it.

I suppose that even today Mama's morals would be considered a trifle louche. Certainly, she never pretended to be virtuous, or tried to keep her affairs hidden. She loved all her lovers, and remained friends with them throughout her life, which says something both for the choices she made and the sort of relationships she enjoyed. Even my father (who I must admit loathed Isidore) came to understand and accept that Mama when 'abroad' would be unable to resist a flirtation.

"Some things with you, *Chérie*, can't be helped."

I pondered these words for many years. What couldn't be helped? It took me a while to work it out. Men could never resist my mother. She was a beautiful woman, and it owed very little to artifice, but I don't think it was just her looks that attracted - she possessed a vitality and natural charm that confounded her critics. Love was a gift, to enjoy and fulfil, and literally until her final illness I never saw her really dispirited or downcast.

She knew sorrow, as we all must know it, but her optimism shone through all the misfortunes (whether of her own making or not) of her long life, and she faced them with a smile. She was a butterfly, flitting from flower to flower, lovely to behold, gentle and without guile.

Chapter Two

Childhood

My first few years were divided between France and England, sometimes with my half-sisters and brothers, but mainly in Menton, with my younger half-brother, Anthony. We children were brought up to take no shame in the fact that though we shared the same mother, our paternal lines were quite different and incompatible.

There were compensations to being the smallest, and almost the youngest of Mama's brood. It was a chaotic and busy household, where I could often be overlooked. Nothing could have suited me better - I liked being alone and free to enjoy my dreamworld, which I peopled with animals, rather than children or fairies, and certainly no adults.

The first home I remember was Villa La Cuse, which had a wonderful garden falling in terraces down to the sea. It had been planned and stocked by a retired English couple, so that the flowers I remember best are those I later found in England. There were herbaceous borders of lupins, golden-rod, delphiniums, nasturtiums, lavender, roses, lilies, carnations and peonies. Add to these the scent of mimosa, wisteria, lilac and the wild broom found on the Côte, and you'll have some idea of the sheer beauty which overwhelmed me. There was the hum of bees, the flutter of butterflies, and (joy of joys!) lizards and frogs in abundance. I used to carry these in my pockets to my 'own' tiny patch of garden, which was overgrown with a shady pepper tree and a sunken pool made from an old *évier*, the shallow washing sink of a traditional French kitchen. There my frogs and toads could bathe in comfort, and the wild birds come to drink after their dust-baths.

Mama suffered a very serious illness in this villa. It was peritonitis, associated with the miscarriage of a seven-month foetus, which I suppose could easily have been saved nowadays, but almost killed her. He survived long enough to be christened Michel Christian, and is buried at Menton. I remember how Pam, Sheila, Vivian and I sat outside

15

the door waiting for the doctor to come and tell us that she was over the crisis and would soon be well again. It's difficult to recall our exact emotions at this time. Pam was the eldest and probably suffered most, as she must have been most aware of the danger we would be in if we lost our mother, but I know we all shed tears and hugged each other. Her condition had given rise to real anxiety - I can still remember my father's red-rimmed eyes as he set out for Mass to pray for her recovery.

Shortly after this we moved to Villa Hilde, my father's original intention. La Cuse was really too big, requiring a full-time gardener and at least two maids. Hilde also had a lovely garden, though it was wilder than the one at La Cuse. There was a wall round it, with iron railings at the top, and it had views of the Garavan Tennis Club from the back, and Menton, with the harbour and the church of St. Michel, from the front. The church looked especially impressive, rising steeply from the stark, grey houses of the old town.

I had been attending the convent school for infants from the age of three. Now, at six, I came under the short-sighted eyes of old Sister Geneviève, who rarely noticed my frequent unofficial absences.

Each morning our cook, Palmyrra, accompanied me to the school gates before going about her business at the food market. I would then make my way to the chapel, where I would light a candle and pray to Jesus to forgive me for dodging my classes. Reassured by the love and compassion on the statue's face, I would slip stealthily away home to collect my tiny chocolate-coloured donkey and take her into the hills. There I could enjoy my own thoughts, and talk to the working people and soldiers in the local dialect.

Her name was Cocotte, and her stable was an old hut half hidden from the villa by oleander and tangerine trees. She wasn't much bigger than a large dog, and had been rescued by my mother from some very rough people who had brought her, along with some other donkeys and mules, to the annual carnival. There they had offered rides to children, and had kept on whacking the poor ill-fed creatures as long as the money kept flowing. Mama's Celtic blood had burst forth in a furious tirade of fractured French which she turned on the illiterate fairground people. To placate *la dame anglaise*, they offered to sell her Cocotte at a ludicrously low price, which is how I became the proud possessor of the first love of my life.

I coveted every animal I saw, with what in retrospect seems an abnormal passion, though at the time it struck me as in no way unusual that I should wish to collect lizards, frogs, mice, dogs, bats, cats and anything else I came across for my menagerie. Every creature was fascinating, so that I could never understand why humans, allegedly cast in the image of God, were so ugly and noisy, whereas animals, especially the baby ones, were so perfectly beautiful. How exquisite was my tortoise-shell kitten, Minou, while by contrast, how very red and squashy-looking was my baby brother!

In fact, he was to improve, becoming a golden-curled, sweet-faced cherub with huge blue eyes, but it seemed to take a very long time. As for myself -

"That child is a gypsy!" Henrietta, our housemaid, would yell to the cook or the gardener. "It's a disgrace - no shoes, no proper clothes, no hat. Mark my words, she'll get sunstroke!"

Nor was the old witch wrong. In the summer of 1927, having spent the whole of one afternoon on the quayside barefoot and hatless with the fishermen 'helping them mend their nets', I came home with a sick headache, and badly burned on the back of my neck and shoulders. The sun and the salt air had combined to give me a week of misery.

Both my parents were fair, though Mama tanned easily and beautifully to the colour of the brown buttered eggs. But I was pale, and quick to turn an unbecoming red. To my father the sun was Public Enemy Number One. He thought the English were lunatics to disport themselves in such a way. Why should they wish to achieve the colour of the black people on whom they looked down so openly?

Fortunately my blisters and fever spared me from interrogation about how I had come by my heatstroke - at least until Sister Geneviève called to enquire after my health. "Such a long absence from lessons," she breathed to my astonished parent, "So many weeks. Mother Barbara feared it must be serious."

I was undone. My otherwise pleasant convalescence concluded with my suffering a long and bitter harangue from my father. "And if you ever do it again," he threatened, knowing my achilles heel, "I shall sell that little mule."

"Cocotte is a donkey, not a mule, Papa, and anyway it's not her fault."

"Don't argue. You have played truant, told lies."

"No, Papa, I didn't lie. Nobody asked me."

"We asked you about school!"

"And I told you it was the same, which it is. I asked God every morning to forgive my absence, and he accepted my reasons."

"Don't blaspheme. You need to spend more time on your knees, and less time with that mule."

End of conversation. Adults were so contrary. But Papa's ill-temper was fleeting, and a good dinner soothed his nerves, while the prospect of an evening at the Casino pushed most other matters out of his mind. Mama was always far more reasonable. She explained how wrong it was to miss school, and how much worse to pretend I was in class when in fact I was wandering among the hills and olive groves, alone with Cocotte.

"Not alone. Richelieu (our dog) comes with me. Minou is in my lunch basket, and sometimes Capucine and Cricrack are in my pockets."

"Lizards, frogs, cats, dogs and tortoises - whatever! You must promise to attend the Convent, then after lessons you can take the animals up to the hills if you wish. You realise that your father is very cross."

"Are you very cross, Mama?"

She hugged me close and her lovely blue eyes twinkled, "I don't wish to be, darling, but you mustn't do it. If you play truant again I may have to be really angry."

That was enough. I loved my parents, Mama in particular. She never complained about my menagerie, or said that animals carried germs, or were smelly, as many of her friends did. I had already noticed that none of mine smelt as bad as the people in the market, or even the ones at the tennis club after several sets of violent exercise, sweaty and horrible. Mama said people only 'perspired', but I couldn't see the difference. In fact, a sweaty horse smells much better than a sweaty man.

"I promise to be good and go to school, Mama, and I will ask God to forgive me for having upset you and Papa."

She kissed me, and I was blissful. I could hardly wait to go to the kitchen and whip some apples and carrots while cook wasn't looking. Then I could rush off and tell Cocotte of our new routine.

On occasions I remember hearing Papa lamenting, "I despair of that child of yours! Why does she swear?"

It was true, my language was often ripe. I picked the words up from listening to the Alpine Chasseurs, shouting at their mules as they ambled into the forts above the town. Phrases such as *amerdeur*, *Éspèce de couillon* or (worst of all) *Éspèce de con* filled the air. I found the sounds rather musical, and they became a part of my vocabulary long before I understood their meaning.

"And why does she argue, why does she always contradict?"

I didn't - always - but I was inquisitive. I listened to what grown-ups said, and if I didn't understand, I asked for an explanation - surely normal for a six-year-old.

"Do you never swear, Papa?"

"Don't be cheeky - you need more discipline, my girl, and less freedom."

Even at that young age I was a cause for concern to him. His sister's daughters, my cousins Gabriella and Denise were far less troublesome, conforming to the accepted Franco-Italian mould. They played with dolls, appeared primped out in pretty dresses, and were altogether little ladies. Not I. Poor Papa. Short-haired and barefoot for preference, his daughter went in tatty clothes to her favourite places - the market, the harbour and the hill forts. I loved the old Mentonaise women in their black dresses, the men in their customary blue overalls tending the olive groves or herding sheep and goats on the upper slopes near St. Agnes. My people were the fisherfolk on the quayside, the coachmen (they would be cab-drivers now) awaiting fares in their fiacres, and I felt at home with them, babbling in the local patois. Mentonaise insults the ears of a purist French-speaker, but it came quite naturally to me. It came just as naturally to my father, incidentally, though he would never allow me to address him in what he termed a bastard tongue.

My only complaint as a child concerned the emphasis my father placed on food and drink. He was a gourmet, and made Sunday lunches a nightmare as he gravely considered the rival attractions of lobster at Chez Renaud, or the perfect hors d'oevres at Le Chèvre d'Or, or the famed desserts and view from Le Château de Madrid etc., etc. He had about twelve favourite restaurants, each with its peculiar speciality. I was expected to share this enthusiasm in true continental fashion, but I found the whole business thoroughly boring. My idea of the perfect quick meal was bread and butter, fruit juice, and an occasional *Chocolat Liègeois* or alternatively a mixed salad and a glass of milk, but the household was geared to Papa's regime of a four-course luncheon and a five-course dinner, served with suitable wines, liqueurs and coffee. When his best friends were invited, the menu must be very special indeed.

I cursed with special (if silent) vehemence if the Hussons were coming. That meant an even longer meal, and listening to Marjorie's complaints. She was English, but had married a French hotelier and given him four children. She was very tall, with a beautiful body which she maintained with an incessant rearguard action against the years. She used diets, exercise, massage, beauty treatments, and daily visits to her hairdresser and dressmaker. This regime had done wonders for her looks, but it so absorbed her life as to be her only topic of conversation apart from her health. If she felt that her husband's attention was wandering she would feign faintness, and demand that Georges feel her pulse and her brow. It was a blessing all round that by her time 'the vapours' had lost

their vogue as a feminine malady, nonetheless, Georges would sometimes call her 'a phlegmatic Englishwoman' when she refused to have
a row - generally over her expensive tastes.

"I will kill myself," he would rage.

"*Comme tu me fait le théâtre!*" ("Such melodrama you lay on for me!")
she would reply, infuriating him even more.

Nevertheless, he was immensely proud of her looks and her chic, and
in her own selfish way I suppose she cared for him.

She claimed to find life in Menton staid and limiting. To her the tennis
club, the bridge club, cocktail parties, gala nights at the Casino were all
occasions for new clothes, but rarely for meeting new people. There
were plenty of 'tourists', but were they of suitable status? Mostly not.
But those whose status was acceptable consorted only with the cream
of the British colony - which did not include anyone who had shown
such poor taste as to marry a foreigner.

Life in a small, conventional French town offered limited excitement:
no theatres, few concerts, few, if any, wild parties. She did not belong
to the English society of the day, and found the French (as she often said)
"so bourgeois, Hélène, so provincial."

She had previously borne two daughters to a notorious Englishman,
whose love of life and convenience had led him to maintain three
mistresses in the same block of flats near Marylebone Road in London,
which he financed by his marriage to a wealthy but long-suffering lady
on the Côte. He was a prolific begetter, and considered one of the best-
looking men of his day. By the time I knew him he was well into middle
age, but still handsome in a florid, fleshy way.

We would see him quite often, eating in the Bec Fin in Monte Carlo,
very tall, impeccably turned out, with a wonderful head of white hair
and matching moustache. I think he went to the Bec as much for the
charm and beauty of the owner as the food, but nor was my father averse
to holding her hand a little longer than was entirely necessary, much to
Mama's amusement. She was receiving similar glances from male
diners, and appreciated them openly enough.

Apart from the Hussons, my parents' closest friends were Charlie and
Alice Duranger, a brother and sister who lived like a very loving married
couple, to great scandal among the respectable citizens of Menton. They
had inherited their parents' hotel, the Astoria, which they converted into
flats. These yielded a very good income, which they devoted to good
living. Then came my father's partner in the Agence Amarante estate
agency, M. Courreger and his wife. He was a large, genial man whom
I greatly liked, and who always kept a few Pierrot Gourmand lollipops

for me. He used to sit in his office ceaselessly twiddling his hair, while she, a small bird-like woman, constantly nagged him to stop. Ultimately, while I was in England, this drove the poor man to a mental breakdown. He had to be taken to a *maison de repos*, which got him away from her.

Mama's group were mainly Englishwomen, some married to Frenchmen, others looking for husbands of substance, and preferably British. I have sour memories of only two of them from my blissful youth. They were both Englishwomen, Dolly Knight and Mona Garrett, and they both strongly disapproved of the freedom I enjoyed, and which led to antics which might have embarrassed a lesser woman than Mama. I recall two incidents which especially annoyed both of them, and Dolly in particular.

I had taken up the habit of joining the coachmen on their boxes, when they had fares, and if, as often happened, the fiacre went along the promenade I would be allowed to take the 'ribbons' (as the reins were called) and send the horses at a spanking trot down the road, passing the smartest bars, such as Willi's, the Rendezvous and Helios.

Invariably Mama would be enjoying a little pre-lunch get-together in one of them, over aperitifs and *amuse gueules*, (little pieces of cheese, olives and anchovy canapés). I would drive past yelling, "*Mamam, regarde moi!*" leaving her friends to avert their gaze from such a little ragamuffin.

Mona would exclaim loudly, "Hélène, don't tell me you allow Diana to drive with the coachmen - it's not safe."

"No dear," Mama would say, deliberately misunderstanding her, "probably not, but she's a mite safer driving with them than on her own." Nevertheless, she would admonish me later about safety and being careful, while my father took me to task about my lack of respect for his wishes. As he had never actually forbidden me to ride or drive, I felt he had failed to make his wishes clear.

Dolly and I simply did not like each other.

Apart from the Alpine Chasseurs I enjoyed mixing with the Senegalese troops who visited from time to time. They were like large, uncouth children, and quite shameless about relieving their bladders at the roadside. I saw nothing strange about this until one especially huge fellow dropped his pants completely, surprising me with the sight of his nakedness and all-over blackness. I recounted this incident to Mama and Dolly, who was shocked to the core.

"Hélène, how can you allow this child to mix with such creatures? She'll be abused, mark my words - it's disgusting, niggers behaving like that.

They're savages - you must stop her from going into the hills."

"They mean no harm Dolly," Mama replied unruffled. "Diana knows the officers in charge, and they see that she's safe."

"She'll be contaminated. No child should see sights like that."

Stupid woman! I saw plenty of half-clothed bodies on the beach, even in those days, and a bum was a bum, whatever its colour. Many years later I remained unrepentant after insulting Dolly as 'a narrow-minded twit, all barge-arse and dairy', a description I had borrowed from a horseman friend, and very apt for Dolly - a tall, large-bosomed, wide-hipped lady who disapproved of everything and everyone on principle, and was also very jealous of Mama's success with men. That they remained friends for so long I can only put down to Mama's good nature.

The Ostrer divorce had cast a shadow on the lives of my half-siblings, but not on mine. I remained unaware of the disapproval my mother suffered from some sections of Menton society, and of the ill-feeling my father's family had towards her. Later on I realised that though they always welcomed me, they totally refused to acknowledge her existence, or to mention by name a divorced Protestant, burdened with several children, whose life had caused a public scandal, if only in an English court. In this connection, I must in fairness say that this was partly Papa's fault; he took the line of least resistance. It was also partly Mama's. She refused point blank to contemplate another marriage, and remained á la main gauche by choice. Religion played no part in her life, though she tried to instil in us the qualities of fair play, kindness and tolerance, for their own sakes.

My brother Anthony was beginning to grow up by this time, if that's the right expression. From the moment he could toddle he was a monster. His angelic face masked a devil's temper, and he had a short way with nurses and governesses. Dressed in his white sailor suit, he would roll under the benches along the seafront until whoever had nominal charge of him agreed to take him where he wanted.

"Cap Martin," or "The Boulevard," he would order, and having gained his point would become charming and cooperative.

Liquor fascinated him from infancy, and it mattered little what dregs were to be found in cocktail or liqueur glasses, he would pick up each in turn and savour the last drops. One day he decided that the half inch of wine and water offered him at lunch was insufficient, so he scuttled to the kitchen clutching his throat and telling Palmyrra, "I'm thirsty, give me a drop of wine." How many drops it took to slake his thirst we never found out, but at tea-time our German governess rang for the doctor.

"Master Tony is feverish, very hot, red in the face and keeps falling off his chair."

Dr Didier attended to him. He enjoyed practising his excellent English on Mama, and always arrived very promptly.

"*Chère Madame*," he began, "do not be alarmed." He smiled benignly. "The little lad is sleeping comfortably, he is suffering from too much wine. In short, I have to tell you, your little boy is drunk. *Ce n'est pas serieux*."

How Mama laughed - her wicked baby, a boozy Morgan in the making - but the kitchen was firmly told that in future if Master Tony was thirsty he should only be given fruit juice or Evian water. Tony was undeterred; throughout his young life his interest in finishing whatever alcohol was available remained undiminished, and the Rendezvous Bar and Helios were his haunts from an early age.

I never realised that our family was not as others. Schooling in France was straightforward enough, work, work and more work! Home for lunch, and at weekends out for Sunday lunch and dinner. There were lovely visits to La Turbie, over the Italian border to La Mortala, San Remo, Vence, Eze, Nice, and Monte Carlo. I would sit in the garden of the Cafe de Paris with Amos, the latest Scottish terrier. He was quite a celebrity, having won every *Medaille d'Or* obtainable at dog shows on the Côte, but now, having a weak heart, had acquired a taste for a noggin of brandy, sugar and warm milk.

"It perks him up," Mama would say, fondly watching him lap up this pick-me-up, but on one occasion she overdid the booze so that he passed out. In tears she awaited the verdict of the vet, M. Calvin, who pronounced, "Madame, you have an inebriated Scotch terrier. He is not ill, only drunk."

We danced like lunatics for the joy of this good news, and M. Calvin could only shake his head, reinforcing his view that *les Anglais sont fous*.

We loved Amos, though I admit he had one antisocial habit. If we failed to include him on an outing, he would make a nest of the clothes on either my bed or Mama's where he would void his bladder. Nor was this from need, for he was always taken for a little 'lift leg', and our balconies were freely available. It was reprisal, and recognised as such by my father, who would be furious. Mama never permitted any punishment for Amos beyond a grumble, which left him unrepentant and undeterred.

He disgraced himself in another way with Rosalie Clarke, a close friend of Mama's. She was a very pretty, fragile-looking Englishwoman, living in Menton with her mother, and according to Papa, husband-hunting - an activity for which he always professed scorn.

"Papa, why should they come to France for husbands?" I enquired. "Are there not enough men in England?"

Mama would explain how the terrible First World War had left many young girls with a dearth of acceptable prospects.

"But Frenchmen died in the war too, Mama."

I couldn't understand even when Mama told me that well-connected girls often went to India hoping to meet young army officers (who were very acceptable). This long journey into the unknown was presumably reserved for young ladies with dowries or very good backgrounds. (In fact this was not entirely the case. The other sort were vulgarly referred to as the Fishing Fleet.) I wondered if Rosalie Clarke's background was not sufficiently 'suitable', and if not, why not? She had studied at the Royal College of Music. It was all very confusing.

Amos evidently had ideas on the subject, for he reacted very markedly when she played violin while Mama accompanied her on the piano. These sessions set him howling, with ecstasy, Mama maintained, but I disagreed, reserving my sympathy for the dog.

In fact Rosalie married a dashing young French army captain in the early thirties, to the annoyance of certain local mothers.

"You won't try hawking me around, will you Mama?" I thought the whole idea too frightful to contemplate.

"No darling, of course not - anyway, somehow I feel it won't be necessary," Mama laughed, and though I didn't understand why, I felt reassured.

Even after so bitter a divorce, Isidore seemed incapable of severing all ties with his ex-wife. In fact, for several years he seemed determined to try to win her back to him, much to the disgust of my father. He would arrive in Menton complete with Rolls Royce, chauffeur, Pam, Sheila and Vivian, and take up residence in the Imperial Hotel, just a few blocks from our new home, an apartment in the centre of town, more convenient for Papa's office. We had moved there in 1930, and it was much more to Mama's liking than Garavan.

I missed the garden and the creatures, but as school and travel claimed more and more of my time, I adapted easily, like most children. My dear little Cocotte had been pensioned off to our cook's small-holding, and I was able to visit her quite frequently. I spent summer holidays in England now, and quite often part of the winter in Switzerland.

Much to my parents' relief I began to dress more carefully, keep my clothes better, and show signs of joining the human race, rather than identifying only with animals. I also enjoyed having my brothers and sisters around, even if their visits acted as a disruptive influence on our household.

Only my father seemed infuriated by these visitations, which made for many a snide remark, and added nothing to Mama's reputation, though I knew nothing of that. I got on well with my half-brothers and sisters, and we enjoyed each others' company, though our only mutual interest was Mama. Pam was already well aware of her beauty, and the effect it could have. Much to Mama's amusement she would commandeer the Rolls and chauffeur to buzz off with whichever admirer was currently in favour, well away from her father's scrutiny.

On these occasions Isidore would drive around town in a fiacre, a small, delicate-looking man, with his face powdered against the sun, but otherwise looking like some oriental potentate. The Mentonais made fun of him, particularly as he insisted that he could speak French, when in fact he could scarcely string two words together.

Vivian enjoyed tennis, and Sheila, a very pretty, petite girl, was amenable to the daily routine, and always considerate to her hosts when she stayed with us.

Between Isidore and myself there was a tangible antipathy, though he tried to disguise it. I, childlike, was less able to hide my feelings, and this led to constraint and embarrassment when, in an effort to show interest, he would take me out to tea at the Engadine or Bosio's patisserie. He was inordinately greedy, which he disguised transparently with a wish that I should 'enjoy myself' at these sessions. He would order plates of *Mille Feuilles*, *Eclairs aux Chocolat*, *Marie Louises*, *Mont Blancs*, which he ate with gusto, while pressing me to 'have another'.

Like most children I had a healthy appetite, but in France we were not encouraged to gorge on sweets or rich cakes: one gateau, and a bon-bon from time to time, was enough, and though meals at home were lavish, they were very well balanced, with plenty of vegetables, salads, fruit and bread. We wolfed down masses of baguettes, followed by mandarins, bananas and pears. A tiny piece of bitter chocolate on dry bread was a treat, but Isidore went well over the top.

It was worse when he insisted on taking us to the smart Monte Carlo Sporting Club swimming pool. I dreaded these occasions, as luncheon was *de rigueur*, and very different from the way we ate by choice. We spent most of our time in the water, and would eat wonderful meals of fruit and salad under shady umbrellas on the terrace or beside the pool. Perhaps we would have an ice cream or a gateau before we left. Not so for Isidore. He would sit beside Mama and order a vast array of dishes which no one in a hundred years could have got through, and then mess each one about, tasting a scrap here and a morsel there, finally leaving far more than he ate.

I found it rather disgusting, and I was aware of the reactions from other tables as dish after dish came and went from ours. There were contemptuous looks, whispers behind hands, and occasionally a remark, pitched loud enough to be overheard and extremely unflattering, but of course, wasted on Isidore with his non-existent French. I hated being associated with the gluttony and conspicuous waste on show, but when I taxed Mama with his behaviour, she always tried to defend him.

"He's known great deprivation and poverty, Diana - it's only now that he can indulge himself. He's like a child, he wants everything he sees, just to try it. Remember, darling, none of us is perfect, and be charitable. After all, he doesn't come very often, only when he's lonely."

I can't claim to have discovered 'charity', I just breathed a sigh of relief when he went back to London.

Sheila spent more time with us than Pam or Vivian, and I enjoyed her company. I don't know how she felt towards my father - I think feelings were guarded on both sides. She must have wondered about Mama's involvements with men other than Isidore, but she never brought the issue up.

My father had distinct reservations about the whole Ostrer family, but he never showed his resentment to the young people. On one occasion I remember him saying to my mother, "*Chérie*, they are all your children, and I welcome them for that reason."

Was he one of nature's long-suffering victims? There were times when I thought he must be, as Mama's 'romances' became more obvious to me. I discovered in due course that even my brother Anthony was no more my full brother than any of the others. He was the result of a whirlwind affair with a very distinguished Englishman, known for his excessive appetite for women and gambling (and whose name, even now, I am not going to divulge). His background was aristocratic but impoverished, and he married for money, trading his name for financial security. Yet I could never find fault with Mama - the joyous gaiety that governed her life was infectious, she wanted everyone to be happy, to be friends, to enjoy the moment and have no regrets.

Although I felt more French than English, I was drawn to England. The weather, despised by so many, suited my temperament, while the absence of horses on the Côte made life irksome, though the town had many attractions. I adored funerals, for instance, with their banked flowers and black horses with matching plumes, so much so that Mama gave strict instructions to all the main florists that I must not be allowed to order wreaths. The same order had to be given to Clothilde's in Wigmore Street, a glorious shop owned by the wonderful mezzo soprano Conchita Supervia. I had without thinking ordered a wreath of red and white carnations to be sent to one of Mama's friends who was in hospital. I meant no harm, though I had been told to order a bouquet, but the wreaths were so much more beautiful.

Mea culpa, on that occasion, as on many before and since.

Mama had a unique way of dealing with recalcitrant children. Never losing her temper, she would patiently explain the rights and wrongs of my actions, discuss my arguments, and leave me happy and secure. According to her, I never gave a day's trouble, and was perfectly behaved. The local priests would have disagreed. I had a habit of arguing with them, questioning their right to interpret the laws of God, even accusing them of preying on the fears of common mortals ...

"And I suppose you have no fear of offending God?" asked my sternest critic, Father Bernard. My invariable reply only angered him further.

"I speak to God every day, Father, and I believe He loves me - I would never offer Him offence, but neither will I fear Him."

Bearing in mind my tender age, and my devout Catholic father, it was immediately assumed that my mother's immoral influence was giving rise to these heretical expressions. Not so: I loved attending Mass, with its colour, incense, choir and candles. They appealed to my sense of theatre. But if I felt the need to contemplate or speak to the Almighty, or the *Sainte Vierge*, I found an empty, silent church the place to worship and confess my sins - directly to that statue that from early childhood had always seemed so full of compassion and loving-kindness. I never left a church without feeling uplifted and forgiven for my shortcomings, though one particular incident will remain in my mind forever.

We were staying in Le Touquet in a charming villa called Sunnyside. Once again Mama had been persuaded to chaperone the children while Isidore was away on business, and though Papa was none too pleased, he knew my mother enjoyed the cooler weather there. I was even happier, as riding conditions were excellent, with shady forests and long beaches and good horses to ride.

We introduced our own serpent into this Eden, or Pam did, but we all cooperated. Her idea was to supplement our sweet ration by stealing from a stall in the market owned and run by a huge, bearded, barrel-chested man. The plan was that the three English-speaking youngsters should divert the attention of the owner, while I, the smallest, would grab a handful of his revolting sticky bon-bons and run like hell. We didn't really want the beastly things, but it would be fun.

Or it should have been. I muffed it, grabbing the sweets and immediately tripping over. I was caught by the man and (much worse) his shrew of a wife who should have been knitting beneath the guillotine with her fellow *tricoteuses*. What a row! The obscenities heaped on my head showed me only too plainly how little I had learned from the Alpine Chasseurs. The vocabulary was much the same, but the venom was something new. Moreover, it was being directed not at a male, but at me. I was threatened with the police, and made to empty my pockets, which contained a good ten times the value of the skinflints' poisonous goodies.

Later, confessing the incident to the Seigneur, I felt for the first time that his face was grave and remote, giving no comfort. From this small and unimportant event I decided that it was possible to be good without being smug, kind without being stupid - lessons I retained long after childhood was over.

This is not to deny that my good intentions came to nothing too often to recount, and we cost Mama a really enjoyable holiday romance. As always, there was an endless procession of charming men falling at her feet (and hoping to sweep her off them). She had met the latest at the Le Touquet Casino, and he invited her to cocktails tête-à-tête. We 'performing crabs', as she termed us, were instructed to remain at the villa, where lunch would be provided, until she came back. That was fine by me, as I'd planned to go riding that afternoon, but Pam, already quite sophisticated, had other ideas.

"We all know where Mummy will be going," she said confidently. "We'll order a fiacre and drive there to see who she's meeting."

Great! We piled into the fiacre, and clip-clopped our way to the smartest bar-restaurant in town, where the elegant went to display their latest clothes and conquests. Horrid little brats that we were, we found ourselves a nice table on the terrace, opposite Mama and her suitor. She didn't see us at first, but we forced ourselves on her attention with whoops and cries of Mummy! and Mama! Then we swarmed like bees from our table to hers, carrying our drinks. There our furious and discomfited parent had no option but to introduce us to a surprised and chagrined man.

Whatever may have transpired later I know not, but he took it very well, paying for our drinks, and buying us ice cream sundaes. He contrived to make polite conversation until Mama, seething with anger, took us home to receive such an ear-bashing as is hardly to be forgotten.

"You ill-mannered horde of locusts!" She really was angry. "How dare you disobey me - I was so ashamed! You gobbled up the olives, the canapés, the crisps, as though you were starving, and then ice cream and drinks. You should go without food for a day - little beasts!"

I know she blamed Pam for the incident, and I suppose that without her it would not have occurred. I doubt that Sheila would have instigated such an outing, and I most certainly would not. Vivian and Pam were definitely ringleaders by nature, but I don't think they had malicious intentions.

Mama felt otherwise, so gloom and despondency fell on the household. She had a way of making you feel ashamed while saying nothing. In fact, her silence was the worst part of her displeasure. She would reply politely to anything directed at her, but conversation and laughter were *non est*.

One period that I particularly enjoyed was when in 1927 Isidore was forced to extend a business trip to the United States and prevailed upon Mama to take over Sipton, his lovely house in Lyminge, Kent. He had rented it to be near to Beachborough Park, which was Vivian's school while Pam and Sheila had a series of teachers at home. Grandmama settled herself into the household, having little faith in Mama's capacity to maintain order among a staff of eight indoor and six outdoor servants, excluding Anthony's, a Swiss nurse, complete with ample lap and shaggy moustache.

Oddity that I was, I found a boon companion in George the cowman, who had charge of the small herd of Jerseys. He was kindly and soft-spoken, and very lame from a war wound. I identified so completely with him that I adopted a sympathetic limp, which I found very difficult to discard, even under my Grandmother's eagle eye.

The head gardener, a Mr Coleman, was an absolute Tartar. He kept all the fruit cages under lock and key, and to discourage us from scrumping he turned a newly-farrowed sow and her litter into the orchard, believing we would be scared of her. Silly man! We made a hole in the hedge and enticed her through it by capturing the tiniest piglet, and showing the sow how to get out and retrieve it. She and her squealing brood thoroughly enjoyed a rampage through the vegetable garden.

Mama never enjoyed her stay at Sipton. The weeping trees, the mist that rolled over the surrounding acres, for me spelt mystery and wonder, but for her only depression, and a sense of isolation. The house was old, and very large. It had a haunted room that had been sealed for ages, and an armoury that was my constant delight. I liked to imagine the men of bygone eras riding out to war in their clanking gear. It was easy to drop out of sight among the different wings of the place, which was a further bonus. George had plenty of lovely stories (true or false? I don't know) about the owner, while Miss Abbott, the housekeeper, never tired of extolling his saintly virtues.

She was a most formidable woman, with a terrific sniff for anything that displeased her. She took no nonsense from the household, except the butler, for whom she had more than a sneaking admiration; he responded by drinking the cellar dry in Isidore's absence.

Grandmama, straight-backed and disapproving, added greatly to Mama's distress at having to serve as watchdog for so long. To relieve the monotony she sometimes managed to escape to Folkestone with Marian Chappell, Vivian's headmaster's wife, a woman of outstanding charm and beauty. She, like Mama, was constantly falling unwisely in love, and had another great weakness - a love of gambling that meant she was always broke. Whatever they did on their sprees, I know it raised Mama's spirits considerably. She was never one to grouse or grumble, though I once found her in the study watching the rain pouring down, with matching tears running down her cheeks. I was shaken - my lovely mother, weeping! Was she ill?

"No child, I'm fine, but how I long to see the sun shining, and hear a roulette wheel clicking!"

Pam and Sheila also found the country dreary, and couldn't wait to return to London. Only I missed the solitude, and talking with the staff, who let me cross the boundary of the green baize door and enjoy cook's teas, which were more plentiful than those served in the drawing room when Grandmama was in charge.

To grace that table, I must be clean, tidy and primped up, so it wasn't my choice. Even so, there were occasions when for the sake of politeness I must change my garments and attend. She had a knack of making me feel shy and tongue-tied, as I advanced under her steely eye.

"You may take two." Her cool smile would accompany this invitation, as my hand hovered over the plate of bread and butter or sandwiches, crustless, minute and tempting. In the kitchen, or in the nursery with Anthony, a plateful would disappear in a flash, but in the drawing room proper decorum must be observed.

Grandmother's stern view of the niceties caused friction on many occasions. Mama would arrive home nearer 5 p.m. than the appointed hour of 4.15 or 4.30, to find Grandmama sitting there, tray before her, cake stands loaded with cook's most delicious offerings, but not having eaten or even poured, for herself or me (starving after a hike across the pasture).

"Mother, why on earth didn't you start without me?" Mama would wail, and the sharp retort was always the same.

"This is your house, my dear, I am a guest."

Some guest! She was a permanent feature during all our time at Lyminge, and a very regular visitor wherever we happened to be.

My father, always very courteous to women, once remarked that he felt obliged to defer to her on every issue, so as to retain her favour. Oddly enough, she showed a genuine liking for him, though it was coloured with a patronising attitude.

"He's a very charming man, Hélène." I heard her say quite often, "particularly considering he is a foreigner. And he is a gentleman."

It used to infuriate me. Papa was not a 'foreigner' in France, Grandmama was, even though, unlike most of the British visitors, she struggled to speak a precise and grammatical French. She, not he, was the interloper in our midst, and anyway, what did that make me? A kind of half-breed?

Later on I could laugh at such attitudes. I encountered plenty of them in the war years, and insularity is as common in France as in England. But then I had still to learn that Chauvinism derives from M. Chauvin.

In retrospect I see my grandmother for the remarkable woman she was - elegant, strong-willed and reliable. Her world was governed by strict rules, and those who infringed them, by deviating from the clear path of duty and responsibility, earned her scorn. This even applied to Mama at times, on account of her *laissez-faire* attitude that Grandmama could never condone.

Grandmama also took a very dim view of an incident which took place on the hunting field. I had attended only one previous meet, when I had found the chase exhilarating, and as no fox had been killed, my conscience was hypocritically suppressed. My love of animals was on this occasion outweighed by my love of excitement, and when I was offered another opportunity, I jumped at it, even though my 'job' was to ride Peppermint, a bad-tempered, flea-bitten old grey who was to be second horse for her lady owner. I was to hack around, and when she changed horses, ride her first hunter back to the stables. The hunt met at Sipton, and I asked one of the whips if I could follow him.

"If you can keep up, alright, but if you fall off, I'll not stop to pick you up."

I had no intention of falling off, and for all her faults, Peppermint was fast and sure-footed. Shortly before we reached our agreed meeting point, we saw a single horseman galloping towards us. The whip shouted something I couldn't catch and moved off swiftly - to intercept what he recognised as a bolting horse, I learned later. Too late. The animal went for a gap in the hedge, swerved suddenly, scrambled a jump and came down, shooting the rider over its head.

I was soon on the scene, hoping to catch hold of the horse as it got to its feet and (I must admit) to see what had happened to the horseman, who lay quite still.

"Is he hurt?" I asked.

"He's dead," the whip replied bluntly. "Broken his neck. Now, girl, can you ride for help? Go carefully, the pack aren't far away, bring a couple of men back."

I set Peppermint off at a lick, and caught up quickly with the main group to gasp out my message. The Hunt Secretary, meaning to be kind, told me to stay put, but not likely! I was determined to go back for another peep.

"He looked quite happy, Granny," I recounted. "He didn't seem dead, just asleep in a funny way."

My grandmother was not amused. Apart from taking the view that a child of my age should not have seen a dead body, she was disturbed by my interest and lack of awe. She also felt that I showed a singular lack of respect in describing how it happened.

"I was worried for the horse, Granny, he went right over, poor bugger."

The last straw! Such a word, how dare I use such language!

George the cowman often used to say, with tender concern when a calf was due, "Poor little bugger, he's not long for this world," so what harm was done? I really did find adults difficult to fathom.

That was the end of my fox-hunting days, though I did some drag-hunting later. Our stay at Sipton was over, and our bags packed for the return home.

But where was home? France, my father, the beauties of the Côte, my school friends, Amos, all these were part of me, but so were the sights and smells of the English countryside. Whenever we arrived at Dover or Folkestone to spend a few months avoiding the hottest period in the south of France, Mama would open the train windows as soon as our journey began and say, "Now children, breathe, breathe deeply this lovely air."

And she was right. Nothing could compare with the sweet smell of fresh-mown grass, the apple orchards, even the Channel had an aroma of its own, fresh and bracing after the Mediterranean.

They say home is where the heart is; mine was always in two places, but as long as Mama was there, everywhere was joyful.

Chapter Three

Adolescence

According to Mama I inherited a number of Morgan qualities, including a tendency to find people in general boring and tedious. My distaste extended to gossip, chit-chat, and discussion of the personal shortcomings of third parties not present. I wasn't even a film fan, and hated sunbathing, picnics *en famille* and the long dreary meals which gave such pleasure to my father.

As a very small girl I had been slightly confused as to whom I should regard as my real father, but by the age of nine I had decided that Papa Isidore (or Pup, as he preferred to be called) was no longer in contention. My father's name was Louis, and so I called him, much to his amusement. Isidore became and remained I.O., though Mama always referred to him as 'Mephi', short for Mephistopheles.

Our home life was tranquil, and I can remember very few angry words spoken by Mama, who had learned Grandmama's technique of icy silence. Louis was otherwise. His view was that women should look pretty, show an interest in clothes, marriage and the home, and leave politics, religion and philosophy to the men, who were physically equipped to understand them.

Poor man! I know how he suffered as his only daughter became first a hoyden of a child, then a rebellious teenager, and now seemed to be heading for spinsterhood.

"*Sukon*," (a pet name for Mama) he would exclaim, "*Diana deviendra une vieille fille, elle n'est pas convenable*." ("Diana will become an old maid. She does not conform.")

He blamed the time I had spent in England for the apparent lack of Latin fire in my blood. "You are of the fish race," was the worst insult he could muster when I had infuriated him, usually by criticising the Church. The idea of Confession, in particular, was repugnant to me.

By the time I was sixteen, I had decided that I wanted no one, priest or otherwise, interceding on my behalf. It was a simplistic attitude, which I hadn't taken up to annoy him, though that's what it did. He could not satisfy my questioning, and the angrier he got over my 'lack of respect', the deeper I probed. I rejected what I regarded as dogma - man-made rules demanding obedience without question.

Louis's faith was very important to him; I never knew him miss Confession or Mass, or fail to observe Saints' days or the Edicts of the Church. He had gone to the length of getting special dispensation from Rome to live with Mama, as he had acknowledged me as his child, and was seeing that I was brought up in the Faith. Mama, by contrast, was not at all religious, but unlike many church-goers she was compassionate and tolerant. Her life-style incurred much vilification, but she never reacted with malice or anger.

She understood my longing to work with horses, and allowed me to leave school at fourteen (the lowest legal age at that time), but first she made me agree to spend a year or so at an English boarding school. She wanted me to learn to appreciate my home through absence and to see how well I could cope away from the family. She chose Tudor Hall and at twelve I went there as a boarder. It was run by a marvellous Irish lady called Mrs Kelleher. She divided the school into two competing houses, York and Lancaster (which was mine), so that the girls should learn a competitive spirit and the rudiments of *esprit de corps*, especially as misdemeanours counted against the House as a whole. Her three daughters were all extremely pretty as well as intelligent. The youngest, Denise, was awaiting her place at Medical School and became my best friend, so my two years at Tudor Hall sped past, leaving me with many happy memories.

I was introduced to the English theatre, and will never forget John Gielgud in 'Richard of Bordeaux', nor the terrifying performance of Emlyn Williams in 'Night Must Fall'. Then there was my first sight of Malcolm Sargent at the Albert Hall, a full-scale pageant of Hiawatha. There and then I fell in love with his coat-tails and his saturnine features (in that order). I attended Wimbledon, the Aldershot Tattoo, point-to-points, a National Hunt meeting and a day at Ascot during my last term. Did I get any work done? Not a lot, apart from reading, drawing, piano and (Hell on Earth) Greek dancing. Imagine a number of schoolgirls, all of different ages and sizes, lumbering around barefoot in pastel-coloured tunics. This took place in the gym, where the floor creaked at every movement, and the echo amplified every sound. Miss Cowley the music teacher played the piano, with agony etched on her face, while we plunged gracelessly and unwillingly around, and only coincidentally in time. A ludicrously inappropriate activity for someone whose mind was filled with 'The General Stud Book', 'Horse and Hound', and 'La Vie Hippique'.

As I was from France, my standard of education was presumed to be advanced, so I was able to satisfy my teachers and take advantage of (as Mrs Kelleher called it) 'a broader view of the Arts and Creative Pursuits, very necessary to gels if they were to take their place in Society'. I also found I could earn enough money for an extra riding lesson each week by doing all the French translations for my classmates, but unfortunately, our Mademoiselle noted the exceptional improvement in her pupils. One unhappy day she reversed the order of each girl's text, and listened with mock horror to the stumbling, unprepared homework. I got a rocket, a mark against my House, and removal from further French classes.

Because schooldays in England were such fun, I learned to be less prejudiced against the British, whose demeanour in France and Switzerland often brought discredit on the standards of their homeland: snobbish, brash, and given to saying loudly that they only lived in France because brandy and servants were so cheap. I was also coming to realise that Mama was *persona non grata* with some of the English colony, which offended me even more than my realisation that the French and English held quite opposite views of what happened in history. I still clung to the French version, having made Napoleon my hero for many years. 'Perfidious Albion' was only banished from my mind when Hitler launched his onslaught on this resilient island.

My French, History and Literature offset my abysmal Mathematics. Our teacher, a very butch lady, asked Mrs Kelleher to remove me from her class because (this is a verbatim quote) "I simply cannot stand looking at Diana's blank expression."

It was true. Try as I might, algebra and its attendant subjects were beyond me. I could add, subtract and multiply (just). Beyond that my brain went dead. As there were no more than ten girls in any class, there was nowhere for me to hide from the cold, stern eyes that bored into mine as I frantically searched for an answer to a question.

Ultimately (and indirectly) I got my revenge over her. She responded to the crush which she inspired in one of the sixth-formers, whom I will call only Daphne. Daphne told Miss Kelleher that she was going to visit her beloved parents for the weekend (which was permitted) and the two caught the train for London and a weekend of another kind of love entirely. Unfortunately for them, her parents chose that Friday evening to ring her. Miss Kelleher replied that she was on her way, and they could expect her shortly, so the subterfuge was rapidly exposed. Next day the two were caught *flagrante* in the Strand Hotel, and both were expelled in disgrace.

Mrs Kelleher suggested that I spend more time studying the subjects where I had some chance of making progress. Hallelujah! For hours on end I was allowed to read Dickens, who had awakened my interest more than any writer. I studied 'Henry V', and took the title role in the end of term play (the paradoxical bonus that my powerful soprano gained me), but I actually fell in love with Shakespeare's tragic heroes - Othello, Hamlet, Richard III and Macbeth.

Drawing was another interest, and until I arrived at Tudor Hall, where I took tuition under a Professor Kell from the Slade, I believed I was rather good at painting and sketching. Consequently my first class with him was a disaster. He was a thin, elderly man, and took only eight pupils from the school, two of whom were very good.

"What are you good at?" Mr Kell drawled.

"Horses, in particular," I said with brimming confidence.

"Good, draw me one that I may assess you," he said in the even and friendly tones of one who has set a trap for vanity. I still failed to see my danger.

"Is this a horse?" he asked, in shocked unbelief when I was finished. He held my piece of paper in two fingers as if it might contaminate him, and, most horrid of all, pinned the wretched offering on the board (to the accompaniment of titters from the other seven) so that all could benefit while he itemised its failings.

They went on for a long time, while my face crimsoned and my temper rose. Even worse than the laughter of my classmates, I could see exactly what he meant.

"Where are this creature's blood, its muscles, its sinews?" he asked rhetorically, adding more gently, "You see, my dear, animals, plants, whatever, must *breathe*, be alive, move. You must be able to feel their movement, touch them."

I realised that he was right, and I must learn from scratch. Everything I had drawn so far had been two-dimensional - animals for which it was impossible to imagine any insides. I buckled down to being taught, and if that meant devoting a whole term to perspective studies of cubes and cones, so be it. So it was, and I came to enjoy every session.

Mr Kell was a diabetic, on a strict regime, so he ate alone in Mrs Kelleher's private dining room. His pupils waited on him, carrying his trays in and out, according to a rota.

I remember how he looked at me on my first duty. His eyes twinkled as he said, "I hope you have not put powdered glass in my food! Not that I would blame you - I was harsh, I know, but I saw you had talent, but a lot to unlearn."

I could have kissed him. To be told I had some talent was marvellous, particularly as this old man had shown me he was an artist of immense skill, whose landscape paintings were quite beautiful. To adapt his own words, the countryside was alive, you could feel and touch the leaves, the trees and whatever else was alive in the picture.

In fact my 'talent' was small, but I took enormous pleasure in seeing how much Mr Kell had been able to improve my drawing. He showed me what to look for, in nature and in colour, and afterwards I was grateful to him for having opened my eyes.

With the years I had grown into quite a graceful, pretty girl. I noticed a change in Louis's attitude. I was no longer 'Mama's child', but 'his daughter'! This was not to last. The animals, including dear Cocotte, who lived through till 1938, were still my prime interest, though not all those who had shared my childhood survived. I belonged with them, I understood their needs, their moods; boys, dances, pretty clothes were all very well in their place, but they stood well below my creatures. I wanted to go back to England, and become a female stable-lad. I can still remember Louis's outrage as I told him of this wish.

For a northern Italian aristocrat, it was the last straw. He flung his hands in the air, and overnight I reverted from 'my daughter' to 'your child - heavens above, a circus girl!'

"Not a circus, Louis, a stable."

"Do not argue!" his temper erupted, and I beat a hasty retreat, quietly mumbling, "Please God, let him win at roulette tonight!"

So much always depended on the whims of the Sporting Club in Monte Carlo. Yet even I was surprised when my mother said, "Your father has agreed that you spend a year in England, darling."

Oh, my lovely, clever, adorable mother! "You did it, you changed his mind, I love you!"

"Calm down, it was the Casino that sparked off his change of heart."

"He won?"

Mama looked at me and smiled mysteriously, "No, sweetie, he lost. I think he felt ashamed."

"Of losing?"

"Good Lord, no! That is quite usual. No, I think he felt that you should be free to choose your own life. He disapproves, but, as he says, you are an oddity."

Horse mania still dominated my life. Just to observe the brilliant horsemasters of my youth was a joy; Talbot Ponsonby, Santini, D'Inzeo snr, Captain Hance, Sam Marsh, Lady Wright, Mrs Oscar Muntz and others all contributed to my yearning to achieve a special prominence in their world. I was determined to compete with these famous names for the very highest honours.

Mrs Muntz was a quite remarkable lady, tiny and straight-backed, and I owe her a debt of gratitude. I met her on a riding holiday, when Mama, Anthony and I went to the Moorland Links Hotel at Yelverton after the Bath and West Counties Show. She invited me to visit her stud, where she questioned me at length about the sort of show horse I was seeking.

The stud groom showed me some magnificent stock, virtually all sired by the wonderful stallion Love Song, and I was sure my paltry savings would never be adequate to purchase anything of hers. I cringed inwardly when she asked me directly what I could pay.

A weak croak of "Fifty pounds," slipped out, and a knowing smile hovered on her lips.

"I'll strike a bargain with you," she said. I waited, and she continued, "Because you haven't once used the word I simply abhor, I'll let you have the little iron-grey mare you saw in the paddock. She's worth a great deal more, but we sold her as a two-year-old, and bought her back a year later, having been told she was being very badly treated. No one has sat on her since, and she's been turned out for a year. If you can manage her, she's yours for £50 and I'll pay the carriage. But ..."

I was sitting, open-mouthed with delight and astonishment, as Mrs Muntz continued, "But, I want a written guarantee that if you cannot cope with her, you will have her put down. I don't want her handed on to just anyone."

The deal was struck, and I was the proud owner of a lovely little grey mare of 14.2 hands. As I left, I took courage in both hands: "Mrs Muntz, may I ask what is the word I didn't use?"

She looked at me with a glint of amusement in her eyes, "Wizard," she said.

I could never have uttered the expression, as living mostly in France, I had never heard it used before. In grateful deference to Mrs Muntz, I have never taken it up. Breathing a 'thank you, God', I went home to tell Mama of my good fortune.

Now that I knew of it, I heard several people using 'wizard' to describe a variety of good things, and shuddered each time. I might have picked it up, and lost Astrid, my first show pony.

My mother's amours remained quite mysterious to me. She and my father lived happily together when we were in Menton, and in England I was not much concerned with a very charming and good-looking Englishman who danced attendance on her, and seemed to have known her for many years. Surprise, surprise! He was indeed an old flame, who had courted Mama before, during and after her divorce, even chasing her as far as Menton, to the disgusted rage of my jealous father.

He was married by then, but Mama was still the great love of his life. I found him pleasant enough, but was still naive enough to be unaware that extramarital affairs were a frequent aspect of Mama's life. She was permanently in love with someone, though not always the same 'someone', by any means.

My eyes were opened somewhat in Switzerland, when an Englishman, Catholic and married, began to lay siege to Mama with the full battery of Old World Charm - what one might call a gentle but purposeful walk down the romantic path. He was mad about skating, so after dinner and a couple of dances fatigue would set in. Far from objecting, Mama always encouraged Dickie to 'get off early and be fresh for the following day'. There had to be a reason for this solicitude, and in fact it was a most delightful Swiss called Paul Nessler, manager of the Belvedere Hotel, very convenient for the Silberhorn, where we were staying.

Paul's duties left him free to dance through the hotels and night clubs until the small hours, which he did with Mama, so that early mornings were not for her. Anthony and I would be off enjoying ourselves in the mountains until after lunch, when Mama would join us to skate or *luge*. This is a sort of open toboggan for one person, who lies feet first on his back or (for the more daring) head first on his stomach. Then we could enjoy tea dances in ski clothes, followed by a bath and a change into formal wear, then dinner. Miss Launer, who owned the Silberhorn, organised entertainments in the hotel, fancy dress parties, dancing, games, etc., but Mama would often suggest that I ease Dickie towards his bedroom on the pretext that sporting activities had tired us all out.

I cottoned on fairly quickly, and shared many a giggle with Mama when she crept back into our own bedroom in the small hours. "Sorry darling, did I wake you? Go back to sleep." She would kiss me, and I would breathe in the perfume that was part of her.

"Did you have a good time?" I always asked.

"Lovely, absolutely lovely. Paul's a dream."

Oh Mama, how many dreams did you enjoy through that carefree time? Quite a few, I think.

I suppose we all have certain special childhood associations having to do with clothes and smells. Mama always had an aura of delicate Lanvin perfume, whereas Marjorie Husson favoured the tangy *Ma Griffe*. What struck me as a youngster was her unbecoming flowerpot hats, and her odd, drop-waisted dresses. I vowed that when I was grown up, these were two modes that would never grace my wardrobe, and this may have been the first stirring of my dress-sense, such as it was.

Unaware of the never-ending changes of fashion, I rarely admired the clothes of the late twenties and early thirties, although on the Côte the colours were eye-catching and rather splendid. The sun and climate formed a background that generally favoured a constant display of new gowns, especially at the *soirées de gala*, where the women vied with each other to display the newest and most fashionable evening dresses. Black tie was *de rigueur* for these occasions, and for the Monte Carlo Opera, where I suffered a salutary lesson in humility.

It was in the opera season of 1936-37 that Mama decided it was time for me to attend in long dress for the first time. It was a lovely confection of sea-green tulle, very simple in design, but with the colour chosen to match my eyes perfectly. I probably looked like a gawky schoolgirl, but I felt like a reigning beauty when I finally joined Mama and Sheila on the steps of Palais Viale to find Louis waiting in our fine big Fiat, with its special Lalique Eagle's head emblem.

"*Incroyable, incroyable*," he kept repeating to Mama, "*une vrai beauté*." Never had I heard such praise from him.

We swept into the Opera House, but only the three of us. My father, because of his growing deafness, had decided that Roulette had more allure than 'La Traviata'.

As the lights went up after the first act we rose to leave the auditorium, and as I did so I found myself eye-to-eye with an incredibly handsome man, middle-aged to be sure, but gorgeous in his sash and a chestful of medals. As he smiled and followed us into the foyer, I turned, prepared to give him the full benefit of my lovely dress and matching eyes. Instead, I found myself gently set aside, as he turned his full attention on Mama. Bending low to kiss her hand with diplomatic panache, he proceeded to chat to her and ignore me until the bell rang for the second act.

Sheila and I had a great giggle together in the back of the car going home, despite sharp warning glances from Mama, who was obviously not going to recount the whole of the evening's events to Louis. The handsome stranger was a Swedish ambassador, currently acting as aide-de-camp to King Gustav on his annual visit to the Côte. He was an inveterate flirt, and the prettiest girls were always invited to join his table or play tennis, which was his great hobby until well into his seventies.

Mama had made a series of assignations with her Swedish admirer, and for the next few days she asked Sheila and me not to walk past Louis's office during the afternoon, but to take tea at Bosio before going home.

"You see, darlings, I've told Louis that we're all going to Monte after lunch. So ..."

No more was needed - we understood. We couldn't be in two places at once, and nor could she. As Sheila and I loved playing bezique together, it was no hardship to present a united front, and Bosio cakes were just as good as at the Engadine pâtisserie near Louis's office in the Avenue Thiers.

Before my schooldays were over, Pam, Sheila and Vivian left Isidore's flat. There were several reasons, mainly Isidore's intention to re-marry, which caused his children some concern, as the lady was not to their liking. I knew that Isidore had little time for anything but business, and though there were servants and every luxury at Park Street, there was little companionship or guidance for young people about to step into adult life.

Pam, performing as Pam Ostrer, had landed a part opposite Conrad Veidt in the film of 'Jew Suss', playing his daughter, a very good start, but she never had a great career as an actress. However, she soon had a young camerman, Roy Kellino, madly in love with her. Nothing new about that! Pam was lovely and lively - slim, dark, witty, and quite as flirtatious as Mama - as her constant string of admirers bore witness.

I think Isidore was surprised by her sudden decision to marry Roy, but it suited him. She and Sheila had been sharing a flat in New Cavendish Street, while Vivian had moved into Reeves Mews behind Grosvenor House and started to train for work on the Stock Exchange. Once Pam married they must have separate apartments, and Isidore took adjoining flats for them in Dorset House, Marylebone Road.

I always enjoyed visiting them. Pam was a comedienne, who kept us all laughing, while Sheila was sweet, gentle, and always concerned for others. We used to call her 'Auntie', which sounds very uncomplimentary, but was meant affectionately. It was at Dorset House that I met James Mason, who was later to become Pam's second husband. He was making his way in the theatre then, though he already had a few film parts behind him. He had met Pam on the set with Roy, and was already determined to have her, come Hell, high water or husband.

Sheila had always had plenty of friends, though fewer admirers than Pam. Now she secured a job in Wardour Street, as dogsbody to C.M. Wolfe, the film director, and Sasha the photographer, who used her to fetch and carry. She began to blossom forth in other ways, and published two books of poetry before war broke out 'The Lenci Madonna', and 'Like a Flower'.

She attracted a number of young men, several of them attached to the 601 Auxiliary Squadron of London. Richard Shaw, the Commanding Officer, was particularly smitten, and Mama had great hopes of an engagement, but it was not to be. On one of her visits to us at Menton Sheila fell completely under the spell of the infamous Mario Valfleur, who had leeched off women for many years as a *gigolo de luxe*. He was certainly a remarkable physical specimen - tall, hawk-faced, well-knit, impeccably and expensively dressed. I had already reached the conclusion that someone else must have paid for his clothes for he was phenomenally mean.

As a child I had frequented Helios and Willi's Bar, where I used to have an orange juice under an umbrella, away from the sun. Valfleur would often turn up for an aperitif, and if he was alone we would play dice. I always won (dice is more a game of skill than it looks, or Valfleur realised), so I used to make him settle up by paying for my drink. It delighted me to see him squirm with genuine pain as he put money on the table, the more so as he was in a no-win situation; he could never have demanded that a little girl buy a drink for him! I teased him unmercifully.

"I've no change," was his bleated opening gambit.

"You've plenty of notes," I would reply, and watch him peel one off the wad that crammed his wallet. He carried a lot of gold as well - watch, cigarette case, lighter, rings - all gifts from female victims, or so Louis said.

Louis was horrified to hear that Sheila was meeting this roué, fearing for her youth and inexperience. Our unflappable Mama pointed out with unassailable logic that their romance could not possibly last, as Sheila had far too little money. Valfleur might dally for a short while, but once it meant putting his hand in his pocket, he'd be off like a shot. So it proved, indeed. An American lady who had been contributing to his upkeep arrived on the Côte, and he followed the dollars.

Sheila was a little saddened by this, but soon found herself being courted by a very acceptable Frenchman, Roger Guillovin, whose father was a well-known hotelier. He wanted to marry her, and would, I'm sure have made a very good husband for her - kind and protective. But as we bucketed back and forth across the Channel it was difficult to sustain a close relationship. He faded from the picture.

Meanwhile, Mama, who loved music, had persuaded me to take singing lessons. I would join her at the piano, and sing whatever she played, generally something from a Novello musical, or a ballad of the time. I was especially found of 'Catari', a song made famous by the Corsican tenor Tino Rossi. Grace Moore's 'One Night of Love' was another favourite, and Mama would always laugh as I breathed passion into the lyrics, though with no direct experience of the subject.

"Darling, why not take up singing? You have a lovely voice, and a second string might come in useful later."

She knew my first string was a riding career, but she beguiled me into agreement, while Louis positively beamed approval at this belated manifestation of a ladylike ambition. He was already suffering from the deafness that was to mar his later life, but he insisted on taking me to the Opera at Monte Carlo to hear 'Madame Butterfly', and later to hear a performance by the magnificent, never to be forgotten, Eva Turner in 'Turandot' at La Scala, Milan.

In those days opera was like church - gorgeous, mystical, dramatic - but it had little influence on my long-term intentions. Nonetheless, I owed my parents a compromise. If for much of the year I could ride and show horses, surely for a shorter period I could do the decent thing and please them by taking up singing! Moreover, I had some talent, and began to enjoy the praise it earned.

Louise Edvina, a famous singer of her day and a relative by one of her three marriages (I'm not sure which) lived in Cannes, so lessons were no problem. She said my voice was unusually developed for my age, with an extensive range and plenty of volume. I suspect it was the reward of emulating the shouts of Alpine Chasseurs, though I never told her this. I found the vocalise, which ran to scales, Ricci cadenzas and the like, tedious, but the actual process of singing was exhilarating, and I studied intermittently for a couple of years.

I suspect my parents hoped that even this late, Nature would intercede to lead me into more girlish pursuits, such as make-up, dances and the male of the species, supplanting stallions, mares, foals and their attendant smells of manure, leather and sweat. Fat chance! I enjoyed it all, but I was determined to learn about stable routine so that I could start and run my own little outfit.

My opportunity came soon after my last school term. A local riding school was short-handed, and offered me a job at £1 per week, hours unspecified. I was to be general dogsbody, but with the marvellous bonus of being allowed to ride the boss's own hunter at the local shows. He was a great bright bay of 16.2 hands who had cleared the boards and won many championships. I was so thrilled by this prospect that I never asked what my duties would be, though I could guess well enough;

mucking out the boxes and stalls, staggering under the weight of heavy buckets, hauling bales of straw and hay, grooming and strapping three horses, feeding them, cleaning tack.

It made for a long heavy day, for although I had riding experience, it was my groom who did most of the heavy work. Now I had a full-time job and my own horses to school. How was I to fit it all in and be ready to attend the shows?

That summer passed in a daze. I never seemed to have enough sleep, I reeled from stable to stable and home, where I collapsed in my dirty jodhpurs, hardly seeing Mama's wrinkled nose as I fell through the door.

"A bath for you, darling," were her first words, "and then bed - Hilda will bring you some food."

I knew she was worried, and not just about the workload. She was nervous of horses, and had seen me thrown a few times, which was worse for her than for me. I knew that none of my knocks had been serious so far - just a few cracked bones - and I tried to allay her fears, but with little success.

I never told her of my initiation at the livery stables. Two horrid lads, foul-mouthed and foul-mannered, had ordered me (in the absence of the owner) to clean out a drain. The smell was appalling, and the filth indescribable. I suspect they had bunged it up for my special benefit, because later I overheard them promising themselves to 'get rid of Miss La-di-da' before long. They were to be disillusioned! My flow of invective was not confined to French or Italian, and while I couldn't match them they still got quite a shock when I turned it on them.

Unfortunately, my habitual instinct in these matters led me to adopt much of their own language, which was heavily laced with 'bloody', 'bugger', 'fuckin'', and 'bleedin''. It was done to no purpose, and I joined in only to join their 'club'. Everyone swore endlessly, and without constraint - it meant nothing, but it was ugly. Inevitably, I aired it in my long-suffering Mama's drawing room.

"You cannot come in here, Diana, and spill such words like confetti! I won't have it. If you persist, you will be fined sixpence for each offence. I have prepared a swear box."

The loss of my first precious week's wages came as a shock, particularly as it left me without sufficient to pay for my usual meal of egg and chips on several occasions. But the owner of the café, who shoved piles of chips and cups of tea at us, was an angel of mercy, and allowed me to run up credit to the princely sum of five shillings. Meanwhile, I soon learned to control my wayward tongue in the comfort of my own home.

After a day or so we became 'lads' together, following one incident that caused general merriment at the stables, and when I recounted it at home.

Cleaning tack is a tough business. In my day, steel bits had to be washed, dried and rubbed hard with a pad made of chain mail. The saddles presented no problem until I asked the head lad what preparation he used.

"Saddle soap and elbow grease," he replied.

Fine. I knew about saddle soap, but where did they keep the other stuff?

Idiot that I was, I hunted high and low for the unknown container, while the saddle soap that I had already applied caked and hardened. Near to tears, I timidly approached the boss and asked if he could help. His incredulous expression, and roar of laughter, left me crimson with embarrassment, as he explained in precise terms what was meant. It took me a long time to live that down.

I later discovered that sending the greenhorn for elbow grease is a traditional April Fool joke. It was not April First, but I suspect they realised what had gone wrong and were laughing up their sleeves.

A milestone in my horsey period was the start of what was to have been a setpiece in the Show Season calendar. The war put paid to it, but the first Hundred Mile Ride held in England gave my brother and me a most exciting and rewarding few days. We were the youngest competitors, with Tony on his pony Bayard, my groom, Beckley, on my grey, Astrid, and myself on my much-loved old Onyx. She was a mare I had bought from the RSPCA for £7.10s.0d, including an old saddle and bridle, a case of unwitting neglect. When she came to me she was such a bundle of bones that, rather than let her be seen as she was, we led her from the station to our stables covered in blankets, bandaged on legs and tail, with knee caps and a hood. I'm sure passers-by must have thought we had a prize thoroughbred under all those wraps; had they seen her condition, they might have attacked us for cruelty.

Fortunately loving care brought out the remarkable-looking lady in her, without an ounce of malice, though a very difficult ride. She won many hearts as we set out from Canterbury on the two-and-a-half day trek to Eastbourne, where the County Show was to crown the event. Every night and morning a vet checked our mounts to see that they were fit and sound, and every rider had to undertake the care, feeding and grooming of his or her own horse. We loved every minute of it, though by the end of the day we were more than ready for bath and bed.

Our long-suffering mother met up with us on the way, the Hillman Hawk packed with riding equipment, show saddles, and food for our evening meals. Luckily for her she had a radio to while away the long hours on the road, though perhaps her driving made them more exciting than they should have been. In fact, I often wondered how Mama avoided an accident when driving, because more often than not she would forget she was in England, and curse 'those stupid people on the wrong side of the road'. Possibly they saw her hurtle towards them in her massive vehicle, and decided that discretion was the better part of valour, enhancing her belief that she had right of way.

A story she liked to tell, and which amused me, was that driving Anthony to school she had once remarked to him that she looked forward to the time when she was an old lady, and he could drive her.

"Of course, Mama, with the greatest pleasure, but won't you be dead when I'm grown up?"

Once we had arrived we had half a day to rest the animals, and prepare for three days of showing, hack, handy hunter and jumping classes. We washed Onyx in Reckitt's Blue, to give her an eye-dazzling whiteness, and her tail, plaited overnight, flowed in waves like a beautiful girl's hair. Astrid's mane was plaited, Bayard's quarters 'diamonded' with brush and sponge, a tedious process but producing a marvellous effect. Finally Anthony and I got into our best gear, with gloves, stocks and canes.

It was Beckley who made it all possible - a groom in a million, soft-spoken, with a soothing manner that horses responded to immediately. He oozed confidence, and I never saw him looking less than immaculate. His boots shone, and all his clothes, whether for work or show, were spotless. We put it down to his cavalry training, but he also taught me the value of keeping horses happy in their work, and healthy with careful feeding. Each horse had a different diet, suited to its size, age and temperament, but the quality was always the best - hay and straw, mashes, mineral salts, home-crushed oats, hand-cut chaff. Beckley swore they were the keys to maintaining condition, and our horses were bursting out of their skins with vitality. It certainly paid off. We brought home prizes or rosettes in nearly every class, and commemorative medals to treasure.

There was one more exciting event that summer. I had taken Onyx to be shod on several occasions to a particular smithy. She was well into her twenties by then, and her hooves needed special attention that only an exceptional farrier could give. As he worked he remarked that a 'painter fellow' in the big house opposite had left a message asking me to call when I next visited. I had heard that he was a famous man, and duly presented myself.

His wife, a tiny little lady, explained that her husband liked her to take photographs of his subjects, since he was no longer young and wished to keep sittings to a minimum. "Would you like to sit for him? He wants to paint you on your white horse."

I didn't like to say Onyx was a grey, only white with age, so I happily agreed to pose, and went home bursting with pride and delight. "Mama, Walter Sickert has asked me to sit for him - isn't it exciting?"

It was, but 'pride cometh before a fall', though not literally on this occasion. In Sickert's big walled garden I sat bareback on Onyx, bent slightly forward over her neck. Only after a couple of visits did I think to ask the great painter why he had chosen me.

He looked surprised, then gave me the blunt truth, "It was your horse, not you who took my eye - such a lovely creature, those big, dark eyes, the blue whiteness of the coat!" He must have seen my crestfallen expression, for he added, "And you and the animal seem as one, you sat on her as though you were part of her - like a young centaur."

It was some comfort for being the lesser part of a package deal, but I did have an affinity with horses, and it had been recognised.

Some time later I attended an exhibition of his works, and there I saw the finished painting, 'Girl on a Horse'. Mama would have bought it, had she not been stony broke. It went to a gentleman called Henry Lessore, and I admire his taste. Regardless of my contribution, I can honestly say that Onyx looked perfectly beautiful.

While I was growing up in my own way, Mama was enjoying herself in hers. Peter Coke, a young English friend of ours from the South of France who had become an actor, spent a season or so at the Margate Repertory Theatre before getting a part in the West End. He and James Mason were to play together in Dodie Smith's 'Bonnet over the Windmill', and became close friends, proving how small the world can be. Peter subsequently became very well known and successful, playing Paul Temple in the many radio series. His play 'Breath of Spring' was a smash hit as well.

To our delight Peter was invited to make a guest appearance in Margate, and Mama insisted that he stay with us for the run of the play (which was only a few weeks, in fact), but he brought us all a great deal of enjoyment, leading to lasting friendship. Peter had charming and entirely natural manners, as well as vitality and fun, and he was like a son to Mama and a brother to me. He introduced us to the local Theatre Club, and all the company, which was run rather autocratically by Pat Nye, a lady famous for her lovely speaking voice and rather square figure. Other members included the redhead Daphne Rye, who was married to Roland Culver, whose cat-imitations have never been bettered. He was to become quite a star, and had a long career, now carried on by his son, Michael Culver.

The young juvenile lead, temporarily displaced by Peter, was Dennis Edwards, another lifelong friend. Like many actors he was quiet and retiring offstage, but he had a lovely turn of phrase, and was very attractive. He was also very poor, and fighting to maintain his standards on a salary which barely kept him fed and clothed. He impressed Mama tremendously, not only with his talents, but with the grit he showed in the management of his life.

She knew he must watch every penny, but even if it meant walking miles to save a bus fare he would never visit without a tiny gift, such as a bunch of violets, a few chocolates, or a special cake of soap. It was very touching, and we all grew very attached to him.

I was still only fifteen, but my particular boyfriend at that time was Ronnie Belasco, a golfing blue from Cambridge whose father owned 'Old Moore's Almanack'. He did his best to interest me in golf, but I could never see any point in hitting a tiny white ball and walking after it. We agreed to differ about this, though I almost changed my mind when I met one of his friends from the university team. Johnnie Hanson Lawson was absolutely gorgeous, but he never so much as blinked at me - or any of the other girls who were ready to swoon at his feet. His whole life was dedicated to becoming a champion. I hadn't quite reached the swooning stage, but it was the first time any man left me feeling weak at the knees. Till then I had accepted whatever adulation might come my way as my due, and had seen no reason to give anything in return.

The pleasure of growing older! I wasn't very keen on the feeling - I always liked to think I was in control of the situation, with people or horses, and I fear I took out my ill temper on Ronnie, and Alfie, another would-be suitor. Altogether, I would be glad to return to Menton. Summer had been exhausting.

Mama was torn between France and England, where she had more real friends and all her relatives. My favourite was Aunt Christine, a tiny woman of four foot nothing who had to have all her chair legs cut down so that her feet would touch the floor. She had bought a touring company and played Shakespeare all over England. Her cottage near Buntingford had a traditional cottage garden, crowded and overgrown, but full of colour and perfume. The only drawback to her cottage was the pair of fat spaniels who pre-empted the only comfortable chairs. They would wait until you were about to sit down, then rush past you and plonk themselves down, and loll out their glistening pink tongues, with laughter in their eyes.

"We call them Keith and Prowse," Aunt Christine proudly proclaimed.

"You want the best seats? We have them!" She loved those two brutes, and no one was allowed to disturb them, though on a couple of occasions I managed to lure them off their seats and sink into the upholstery myself.

Christine's sister Elsie was completely different, a delicate, reticent woman with an exquisite voice, pure and sexless as a choirboy's. She had studied music and singing, but her natural reserve made a public career impossible. She only sang in choirs, where she took solo parts in 'The Creation', 'The Messiah', 'Elijah' and many Bach cantatas.

She was witty as well, never unkind but always funny. She travelled extensively, and her favourite city was Vienna. It was there that she surprised all her relatives by entering for, and winning, the prestigious La Scala award for fencing. The Morgans, Spear and Hird, were unusually and diversely talented. Even so, I wondered what my mother meant when she sometimes shook her head over me and asked why I, of all her children, had inherited all the eccentricities of her forebears.

Back in Menton life was very different. There was always a definite routine to be observed, and much less freedom. Louis's days were governed by his office, his meals and his gambling (not necessarily in that order). Menton was a gay little provincial town in those days, with Cannes, Nice and Monte Carlo nearby to offer more entertainment. Mama adored dancing and tennis, so what with the dressmaker, the milliner, the hairdresser etc. all needing to be fitted in between tennis matches, dances, gala nights at various casinos, and the Battles of Flowers that took place all along the Côte, her life was full of activity.

One of my daily duties was to help a lady from the RSPCA to hunt up the stray cats and see them fed. They were poor interbred creatures, thin as rails, flea-ridden, and often rickety. We would stagger from the butcher in the market laden with scraps of meat and offal (some of it horse, to my distress), containers of milk, and water. We took it to the old town, and the unkempt gardens where the wretched animals congregated, and put food down. Then we waited to see how many appeared. A ravenous army descended on it, and we would try to note if any were too injured or too ill to fend for themselves. If so, we would alert a local vet, who set up cages to capture and destroy the poor frightened animals. I think I shed more tears over those unwanted cats than for anything else until the Second World War.

I was being courted quite seriously by a young hotel-owner. He told my parents he had watched me growing up, and fallen in love with me even before I left school. Louis approved of him; he was twenty-four, and a man of the world, he said. All his other credentials were more than satisfactory: well-established, hard-working, good family background. An especially sensible match to bring to heel a girl with such odd ideas as Diana! Mama held other views.

I was not to consider any attachment until I had really grown up. My temperament was slightly unusual, with my love of solitude and reading. I had little genuine interest in 'good times', and although I enjoyed the company of men, it was mainly because I found the topics of female conversation - clothes, hair-dos, cosmetics - profoundly tedious. I liked older people, and identified more easily with them than with my own generation. Mama felt I was mentally well ahead of my age, but physically immature.

Nevertheless, I enjoyed being squired by a good-looking man, who possessed the added attraction of a lovely Lancia sports car. Moreover, he was extremely correct - no liberties were taken or attempted, and on one occasion, when Louis asked if I was pleased with my *jeune homme*, I told him how much I appreciated his perfect behaviour.

"I should think so, *mon Dieu!* He intends to marry you," was his astonishing reply. It was news to me, and highly unwelcome. A charming escort, yes; a future husband, no way! in the blunt American idiom.

I always had to laugh at the anxious look on Papa's face whenever we were about to leave Menton.

"Sukon," he would begin his appeal, "Do you owe any accounts?"

"Good God, are we going to have an inquest?" Mama would sound quite cross.

"*Non Chérie*, of course not, but I prefer to know, in case anyone should ask."

"Pay them. Whoever or whatever - if they say I owe them, I do." Mama would launch into a list of those to whom she *might* be indebted. "Madame Charlotte, my hats; Madame Mangin, my dressmaker; Michel, the hairdresser; Barberis, the wine merchant; the Engadine (Swiss patisserie) for *vacherins* (a delicious meringue concoction); the Quincaillier (hardware shop); the florist, Helios Bar, the Mayfair bar, Rumpelmeyers, the Epicerie, the butcher," etc., etc.

Poor Papa! What with her debts and his gambling, no wonder we always looked to see if he'd sold the furniture when we were away! Most of it had been bought at Boucheron's in Paris, and was very expensive, but somehow he managed to survive the cash crises which were never far away, and our home remained intact.

As did our debts.

Chapter Four

1939

The morning of 3 September 1939 found me in a tranquil and optimistic mood. I had just celebrated my eighteenth birthday, life was good, and my future rosy - I thought.

My birthday meant I was now free to enter all the adult classes at the international horse shows. Junior classes and graded honours were all very well, but at eighteen I could see myself competing at the highest level - and winning, naturally. In retrospect this was not a very realistic assumption. My horses, bought on the cheap, were all well bred, but their low prices reflected defects. They were all somewhat troublesome, due to bad handling and ill-treatment by previous owners.

Then came the terrible news, with its solemn rendition of 'God Save the King', which moved my mother to tears. It was the first time I had ever seen her really distressed, and I realised with a shock that for her and her generation the horror of war was a dreadful reality. They remembered the carnage of the First World War in the measured tones of Neville Chamberlain, confessing that there would not, after all, be 'peace in our time'.

A bare twenty years had passed since the Armistice; T.S. Eliot's *entre deux guerres* that Robert Graves was shortly to call 'the long weekend', during which I had been born and grown up. For Mama, remembering her dead brother, for Beckley, injured among the dead and dying horses for whom he had shed helpless tears, for Bennett, our gardener, proud to have served as a Private of the Buffs in the 'War to end all Wars', the horror was all still fresh.

My thoughts were mainly for my mother, and how she would react, but I had grave anxiety for my father as well. He was from a well-known Italian family, which meant that the Blackshirts had demanded his respect and support. They had had to make do with his open contempt and rejection, in retaliation for which they had stripped him of his passport, property and citizenship. Unlike his brothers he had not sought French papers, and therein lay the danger. For many years Mussolini had been demanding the return of Corsica and the Côte, which according to him, were naturally part of Italy. 'Nice, Nice,' the border guards would yell to anyone in earshot, but all they got in response was a contemptuous shrug from the French customs officials and guards on 'our' side of the crossing.

The likelihood of conflict over this issue had been a source of apprehension throughout my childhood, and on more than one occasion the great hill-fort guns had locked sights with their enemies across the border, while troops from the barracks at Carnolés would be moved swiftly up the mountains.

The locals reacted to these scares by burying their silver, hiding their money, and drinking their cellars. 'Leave nothing for those scavengers!' was their attitude, and Louis's. He hid his First World War medals, and swilled the finest cognacs and champagnes, careless of expense and his liver alike. Of course, once the crisis was over there would be gloomy looks and nasty hangovers, but since the Blackshirts hadn't come, they had gained no booty. Even so, I knew from an early age how politics could enrage, and mar peaceful co-existence. In the south Colonel de la Roc's Fascist *Cagoulards* (hooded men) were a force to be reckoned with, their fiery crosses in the Alpes Maritime a trade-mark to be admired or derided according to one's sympathies. At that time their principal activity was harassment, and fierce talk at political meetings.

There was division among my friends - Socialists, Fascists, Corsican non-conformists and Communists were all to be found in Menton, and their voices rose to crescendo with the elections. There would be fights in bars and *estaminets*, often quite serious ones, and I well remember myself aged sixteen repeating one of my father's opinions to a friend who was in the French navy. "Tell your father to keep quiet. He's no Frenchman, just a bloody Italian," was the scornful reply.

It shocked me deeply, as I had always regarded Louis as French, if not by blood at least in spirit. He loved France, and believed whole-heartedly in *Liberté, Egalité, Fraternité* and all that *La Belle France* stood for. I could hardly believe that he was identified with Mussolini's mobsters.

On such occasions Grandmama's words came back to haunt me; Louis was a foreigner to her, and worse than that, he was a foreigner to my friends - the people with whom I'd been to school, visited the cinema and dances, and even my first *boîte de nuit*. What would the future hold for him now? Without a passport he would be a stateless alien wherever he went. It had never crossed my mind before, but now the French might intern him. Perhaps he could join us in England, but would the British welcome an Italian?

When the French and British navies entered the port on their goodwill visits, we townsfolk were invited to enjoy the hospitality of the fleet. The British were far the jolliest as far as I, a teenager, was concerned. I found them less formal than their French counterparts, and I think everyone looked forward to a few hours among officers and men of His Majesty's Navy.

The French were naturally extremely proud of the *Force Navale*; in their uniforms they looked just as splendid as the British, and the food and drink aboard the French vessels were deemed to be better than that provided by *La Flotte Anglaise*, but I cared nothing for such things. It was the sheer size and majesty of the ships that fascinated me, and the chivalry with which everyone was greeted. Neither French nor English set my father apart as a foreigner.

What a stupid girl! From 1939 I was to learn many unpalatable lessons, growing up in what the real world was becoming. Many of Mama's relatives were naval men, and through them I grew to understand better that people are conditioned by education, upbringing and (sad to say) prejudice. It colours the minds and responses of all races.

My mother had experienced this as a schoolgirl, when she had formed close friendships with two German girls - a von Bismarck and a von Schwerine, both from famous military families. Bitter wartime propaganda caused a rift between them, leaving understanding and affection to wither. The rise of the Nazis did little to offset suspicion and distrust of Germany among those who had suffered after 1914.

I tried not to burden Mama with my fears for Louis; she had enough of her own. I had never seen her show such emotion, it was as if a cloud had descended on her. She acknowledged that she was afraid of invasion, of armies, of air-raids, which I found extraordinary. The declaration of war presaged no immediate catastrophe, though planes from Manston Aerodrome bumbled about more frequently, and there was plenty of jingoistic talk in the air. My young English boyfriends, rather laid-back undergraduate types, were all for joining up immediately, and I, galvanised with a kind of moral fervour, decided to offer my services to whomsoever might be unwise enough to accept them.

Mama tried to channel my enthusiasm into calmer waters. "Darling, you can't do anything much, you don't drive yet. I don't think horses will play much part this time, thank God!"

I would have none of it. "I speak languages, I could learn anything."

I found she was right soon enough. My confidence soon ran out, and

I began to put my head in order. First, in view of Mama's fears, a house by the sea was not the best place, and nearby Manston only added to the anxiety. My father very wisely advised us to stay calm and not think of returning to France until Hitler's next move was disclosed. The news of Poland's defeat, and the ruthlessness of the attacks on her cities and civilian population made us accept this decision without much argument. To this we could add the dire warnings of some Czech friends who had seen the force and cruelty of Nazi troops at close quarters.

"Be warned, they will destroy the whole of Europe," they said. As several of the Czechs had seen service, their views were to be respected, though typically, Mama had formed an attachment for one particularly charming fellow from the Sudetenland, Walter Ritter. He was small and dark, with an infectious gaiety except when he spoke of the Panzer divisions, and used the unfamiliar term 'Blitzkrieg'.

"Diana, it is an awesome sight, tanks by the hundred, bombs raining down, a scene from Dante's *Inferno* - I know."

I wondered how he knew, since he had left Prague virtually as soon as Hitler moved into his country, but of course, all Germany's victims had seen at first hand the efficiency of the Nazi war machine. The Czech government in exile was not idle meanwhile, and battalions were formed to fight alongside the British when the time came. Meanwhile Walter comforted Mama, and Sheila began what looked like quite a serious romance with Leo, one of his friends. I liked them both, they were amusing, educated and very well-mannered.

These were Grandmama's criteria for approval. She had died shortly before war broke out, and I was glad she would be spared the upheaval, the opening of old wounds, and the greater intrusiveness of public officials. She could not have coped with them in her delicate and fretful old age. Nonetheless, as one always does, I wished I had been nicer to her, more willing to visit than I had been, less obviously impatient to be away. All too late.

Sheila's love-life took a sudden turn for the worse, leaving Leo heartbroken. Mama had grave doubts over her new choice of future husband. He was a Canadian RAF pilot, and originally a penfriend. Their relationship had grown from the letters, and led them to marry in June 1940.

Bill Thompson was a great athlete, and a cup-winning runner, which naturally impressed me. I valued trophies and rosettes, and Bill's Canadian and Airforce cups were bigger than mine. Mama had reservations because she felt that Sheila was too gentle and sweet-natured to cope with someone she suspected of being a bit of a bully. She was never one to interfere or cause scenes, so she tried coaxing and advising, but in the frenetic atmosphere of 1939, Sheila dug her heels in, and the marriage was arranged.

Meanwhile I suffered another ugly shock. We had no money! Our great problem had always been that Mama had no idea of how to manage it. If she had £1,000, she would spend it ten times over, and was constantly being sent for by the utterly charming manager of Barclay's Bank, Menton, M. Viale. He would begin sternly, but, like every other man, always finished by patting her shoulder and sympathising with her difficulties. Papa was little help; an inveterate gambler, his fortunes were as unpredictable as Mama's arithmetic, yet strangely enough, the household had always run smoothly. We lived comfortably and well, with the best of food, drink and servants, in France and England, so that when I was old enough to appreciate our financial predicament, the shock was considerable.

We had always had a house by the sea in Thanet, a mews flat in London, a holiday in Switzerland etc., so to wake up to the realities of life at the age of eighteen, just as Hitler's War was starting, left me gasping with amazement and filled with anxiety.

There was a mountain of debts, Mama's small income was already pledged for several years ahead, what was to be done? Muggins Diana was as clueless as usual, the subject had never come up. We spent what was needed, always had. Now, suddenly, there was nothing to spend, but a 'small' staff to pay, a flat in London and two cars to maintain, to say nothing of sundry animals. Mama went to the bank, and this time I accompanied her. Now there was no charming, indulgent M. Viale, but a hard-bitten, sober-sided Briton, gloomily perusing the pile of papers on his desk, which he quite evidently understood as we did not.

"Well, what do you suggest?" Mama had done her best to explain the chaos, but the bank manager's understanding of accountancy had stood him in poor stead among the tangles of our family tree, wherein Isidore was hopelessly confused with my father and an old flame of Mama's who had undertaken the doomed endeavour of guiding her finances into safer waters.

We reeled out of Barclay's with one definite piece of advice (well, order, actually) 'Sell your house'. More easily said than done; it was by the sea and near an RAF station - not good selling points with war just declared. Solicitors and accountants were called in, and some kind of order asserted itself. A buyer was found, and our lovely home vanished.

There was really no alternative, and in a sense I was glad to get Mama away from an area which might become dangerous, and of which she was becoming nervous. London seemed an unwise choice for us. It was the period of 'wait and see', so we took an old coaching inn, Bear Lane

House, in Ashwell, Hertfordshire, where we moved with our Chow dogs, cats and an Irish maid who had had charge of the London flat. Dear Kitty Dever was as wayward a creature as can be imagined, temperamental, irrational, but a wonderful cook and stiff with traditional Irish charm. She was susceptible to it herself, being married to a very handsome ne'er-do-well, who had hopped back to Eire with their two daughters for 'safe keeping' with his family. "He's a useless varmint," Kitty said stoically, but to give him his due, after a short absence he returned to England and joined the army.

To my horror and disgust, no sooner were we in our new home than an uncle and aunt descended on us. They too had left their house on the North Foreland, not because of financial pressure, but because in Uncle Mac's view the place might well become a first line of defence against the Nazi hordes who he was quite certain could and would overrun Europe at will.

"Bloody Frenchmen won't fight," he would mutter, and in reaction I became more French daily, muttering abuse about unwanted guests in French to Mama. I was genuinely insulted. How dare he criticise those countries which faced the onslaught, while sitting safe in England with the sea to protect him, and not even caring to stay in earshot of that!

Poor Mama, she must have had a trying time, with me grousing, Kitty eating all the bacon and butter she could get, Aunt Ethel grumbling about the cold and draughts, Uncle Mac grumbling about everything. They had returned after years in Africa, with its abundant servants, where 'sundowners' and bridge parties had been their ruling passions. Ethel was so used to calling for her personal servant, Mombashu, to pick up her paper that making her own bed constituted a major disaster.

Worse was to follow. In the late winter my half-brother Vivian landed on the doorstep with his wife Judy, an American ex-showgirl, and their infant son, Carl. Why they came was a mystery that I never penetrated. I think his choice of wife must have angered Isidore Ostrer so that they were not on speaking terms, but Mama, generous-hearted as ever, took them in and made them welcome.

I was not amused. The house was large enough, but they were all so lazy, Mama was worn out with shopping, gardening, and supervising this much expanded household, Kitty was threatening to leave, while all they did was sit on their bottoms, playing cards, grizzling and waiting for the next meal. Mac missed his golf, Ethel missed the African sun, Vivian was morose, Judy was understandably bored, and the baby wailed at every opportunity.

Our finances were still rock-bottom, the sale of the house had only dented our huge debt, and worst of all, I had been forced to dispose of the horses. In violation of the letter, though not the spirit, of my promise to Mrs Muntz, I had sold Astrid to a wonderful retirement home nearby. My dear, and by now very old Onyx, had to be put down, as she was suffering from leg trouble and needed constant care, Anthony's Bayard had gone to a family we knew in Ashford, and Silverdale Canaletto, my best mount, had been returned to his original breeder on the understanding that I should have him back within a few months once the war ended.

To live without horses was to live with a constant dull pain. I missed their feel as I groomed them, their little nickers of pleasure when I entered their boxes, and worst of all, I missed riding across country at speed, feeling the wind and rain on my face, taking fences and hedges as they came. I hated the country without them, and spent my days planning to get work of some kind, preferably in a stables. But I couldn't leave Mama to the mercy of that household of drones - I had to get rid of them first.

My father was still undecided what to do; if Hitler didn't overrun France, we could return, but if he did there was little doubt that Mussolini would cross the border and occupy Menton. He asked us to remain in safety until the 'Phoney War' developed into either a quick peace or real conflict. Meanwhile, Kitty gave her notice. "It's no use, Miss Diana, I'm not here to wait on them hand and foot. They're eating us out of house and home - Madam should tell them to leave. Anyway, I'm back to Ireland."

That was Catastrophe Number 1. With only a slightly nutty lady helper from the village to lend a hand, I could see myself becoming a domestic. Not bloody likely! Nor would I let my beautiful mother wear herself out ministering to a handful of selfish parasites who did nothing but carp about expense and the lack of their favourite food and drink. They acted so helpless, though I knew they were only useless. But for the same reason, Mama felt guilty at insisting that they find places for themselves. It was easier to stay with us, being catered for and waited on.

"We'll contribute, Hélène dear, it will be a little extra for you."

Ha! Not the way they ate, and certainly not helpful towards our heating costs. Always cold, always shivering, my suggestions that they warm themselves up by work in the garden or help in the house were never well received.

Catastrophe Number 2 followed quickly. My Chows, who had never seen sheep before, moved into a flock and panicked them. They weren't vicious, just interested, but the sheep were not to know. Irate farmers called, usually two at a time, and threatened to shoot my adored Joss and Togo. I promised they would never harm the stupid creatures, but it was no use.

"Give us a chance, and we'll shoot the buggers."

This monstrously enhanced my inherent dislike of the English, and I wept for France.

"Darling, we'll go back." Mama had also come to the end of her tether. She longed for a life of theatre, dances and flirtations; for the Côte; and maybe, somewhere near the foot of the list, my father. "Meanwhile, sweetie, we'll return to London. I hate the country, and the sound of planes droning overhead at night is driving me mad."

Blessed Mama! But how would she cope if London were attacked? She was still afraid of aeroplanes, how would bombs affect her? I didn't know, and to be truthful, at this stage I didn't care. If France must wait, let's head for London.

There were two more blows to fall concurrently. My dogs got out on their own, and shifted another flock. On this occasion one sheep died of exhaustion or fear, and one was actually bitten. It was a death sentence. My two black beauties had always been free to roam at will, follow me on horseback or ramble on their own at Kingsgate, now they had to be kept on the chain. A kindly vet suggested that I have them put down.

"It's quite painless, my dear, and it's for the best. Once dogs are known to molest stock they're done for. Yours will get blamed for everything that goes wrong. Chows are not popular at the best of times - it's their blue tongues, probably." He was right, I knew, though my dogs were the gentlest of creatures, used to freedom and no longer young.

I went about the house red-eyed and puffy-faced from copious tears until the dread day came. Anthony was home from his Jesuit-run public school, Beaumont, and he, Mama and I fed the barbiturate pills wrapped in the Chows' favourite food and watched and waited until they fell into deep sleep. It was an agony to see them wobble drunkenly as their legs gradually gave way, but mercifully they knew nothing. They were at home with us, caressed and petted until the end came.

Anthony helped me bury them in the garden near their favourite spot, and I can't say which of us was the more miserable. We had lost many other animals during my eighteen years, and I suppose we shed tears over all of them, but the passing of Joss and Togo crystallised my already dissatisfied thoughts. I could no longer stay in Ashwell. We would go to London in preparation for our return to Menton. I took the decision out of Mama's hands.

France fell in June 1940, and my hopes with her. The enormity of events in Europe hit me all at once. Mama seemed unable to grasp that the Nazis were the overlords of Europe, and Britain must be their next objective. For my part, the thought of shifting my obnoxious relatives' arses off their comfortable berths buoyed me up.

They only capitulated when we gave our date for returning to the London flat. Within two weeks of that they were gone, and soon so were we. We arrived in London just in time for the beginning of the Battle of Britain. Our flat was nearly opposite Madame Tussaud's, and a landmine falling nearby blew in our windows, filled my bedroom with soot and dirt, left us without heat or light, and in general gave us a taste of what was to follow.

It happened too quickly for me to feel scared, but I wondered what effect it might have on Mama. In fact she took it very well. "Not so bad, darling. Now I've seen what can happen I feel better. We'll survive, come what may."

From then on the war took on a new dimension for Mama - London was quite recklessly gay. Theatres, clubs, cinemas, dances - all went on, regardless of alerts, raids, inconveniences of all kinds, rationing, queues, gas cut-offs, power cuts, blown-out windows. So what! Life and love abounded, and I began to understand better my father's words, 'Some things with you, *Chérie*, can't be helped!'

Wartime London offered numerous opportunities for Mama's romances, which blossomed in the hedonistic fatalism of the blitz. I was less happy. I knew we were still in the direst financial straits, and I wanted to work - at anything, provided it paid. Mama was not in favour of this. She said I was too inexperienced of life and the world, but the real reason was that she enjoyed having me at home. Anthony had left Beaumont School and was working on a farm near Cambridge, and I suspected Mama felt the need of one of us for company. Sheila had gone with Bill, Pam and James had moved to Beaconsfield, and I, who had always been closest to her, was an anchor. In her heart, and indeed in her head, she was younger than I, the perfect optimist.

But I was now nineteen, and had no excuse not to work. What was I to do? I had my own answer. I would become a singer, and follow in the steps of another relative, the famous Louise Edvina, noted performer with Chaliapin and Jean de Reske. I had in fact enjoyed learning my arias, if not the interminable solfeggios that formed the bulk of my tuition, and in London it was easy to find a voice teacher. I remembered that Pam and James had spoken highly of a Welshman called Gwynne Davies, whose wife, Josie Fearon, had been the chosen partner of the great Richard Tauber in 'Land of Smiles'. To my pleasure I found that he lived in Chiltern Street, literally five minutes' walk from our flat.

I went hotfoot to our first appointment, bringing with me Mama's favourite song, 'Sing, Joyous Bird', and my own, 'O del mio amato ben'.

He greeted me with enthusiasm, and asked if I had any operatic arias at my command. Indeed I had - four, to be precise. 'Caro nome' from 'Rigoletto', the Waltz Song from 'Juliette', the Mad Scene from 'Hamlet', and the first big aria from 'Lucia di Lammermoor'.

With the courage of profound ignorance I warbled my way through Juliette's music, and was clasped and kissed profusely by the solid figure of my future teacher. "Sheer genius, girl, a new Melba, wait, I'll call my wife, she must hear you."

And so on. Josie was a fabulous lady, no longer young by then, but with flaming red hair, heavy make-up, and all the signs of having been a great beauty in her time, and having known it. Dutifully I performed for her, then left them to discuss with Mama tuition terms, and what hopes of engagements I might reasonably entertain.

Of course, it was not so simple as I had thought, but quite soon I found a *répétiteur* at Weekes' Studios in Hanover Square with whom I could practise my art. She was a tiny little lady called Florence Jones, to whom I owe my first engagement. She could whack out a tremendous volume for her size, which gave me comfort, surrounding my soaring soprano like an orchestra. It also covered a multitude of sins which had to be corrected later, but at the time I felt set fair to conquer the world.

In fact things were moving very fast. I was offered an audition to sing two leading roles in Dublin, and from this invitation sprang my introduction to opera, and from that to another, very different role, in the shadowy world of Intelligence.

Chapter Five

Début

What should the phrase 'Intelligence Service' conjure up? Seedy, down-at-heel men who drink too much? Furtive, bowler-hatted civil servants with unmentionable private lives? Beautiful girls with stilettos in their stocking tops?

To me it signified nothing whatever. I had never entertained the faintest preconception of spies and counter-spies, although since 1936 I had been very interested in the political aspects of totalitarian states (the word is Mussolini's coinage), where the Security Services played an important, not to say frightening part in all aspects of government. My introduction to the complexities of wartime Intelligence came about in a very unexpected manner, as I suppose it did for many.

I knew two Czech brothers, naturalised Frenchmen, who had lived in Paris until 1940 running their small textile company. They were members of SOKOL, a Czech organisation offering fitness and gymnastic training, and as such perfectly placed to provide cover for underground cells. They introduced me to Colonel Moravec, who I was later to learn headed one of the best Intelligence services of the day, and was regarded as the ideal spymaster. In his office I was introduced successively to Major Pollak, Colonel Stanislaw Gano of the Polish Deuxiéme Bureau, and ultimately to Colonel Marian Utnik, who ran the Sixiéme.

A girlfriend of mine, Elvira Kwiatkowska, was an Italian married to a Polish officer, and after several visits to the Polish Hearth Club in Exhibition Road, and even more frequent and enjoyable luncheons at Rubens Hotel, the Polish HQ, Elvira confided to me that her husband had heard rumours that I was about to be recruited into the Polish Intelligence Network. In fact she was well off the mark. I was becoming a regular visitor to Rubens, where the meals were always excellent, and I loved the elegance of the Polish manners. I really took a fancy to hand-kissing. I also attended the club in Hanover Street opposite Weekes' Studios, which the improbably-named Pole Johnny Mills ran for his compatriots, where I had laughed to overhear a query: was I working for Polish Security, or a spy for the Italians?

Incredible nonsense - at this time the closest I came to anything approaching 'Security' was at the Report and Control centre near Baker Street, where I tried to make myself useful to a Civil Defence Unit by manning a telephone switchboard, none too efficiently I fear.

I was flattered when Major Pollak began to pay me attention. He was aged about forty, obviously intelligent, and very knowledgeable about opera, but I totally misconstrued his interest, which was neither romantic nor artistic. He was in search of recruits for his Service, and rapidly rejected me as unsuitable. Nonetheless, through him I met a very special Pole whom I knew as Anton Szymanski, though he had several aliases and code-names, and my subsequent visits to the club and the HQ were romantically motivated. It was my first personal attempt at a sexual relationship, but sadly nothing came of it. He was parachuted back into Poland, with tragic results for himself and many other Resistance people.

The Nazis were formidable foes, not least in the field of security. The *Abwehr*, the Military Intelligence Wing of the armed forces, was highly proficient, while the Gestapo had their *Abteilung* organisation to operate outside Germany. Both had far more experience than SIS or the French *Bureau Centrale de Renseignements et d'Action*.

I saw plenty of my Czech friends, and my circle rapidly became quite cosmopolitan, including Dutch, Canadian, French, Polish, Czech, British and Yugoslav. One Yugoslav in particular became a close friend. Dusko Popov was a double agent of immense talent and courage, who worked for both the British (who code-named him 'Tricycle') and for the *Abwehr*.

I became involved because I was flattered by the attentions of several middle-aged men. The thought of spying was exciting, the more so as I had no idea of what it would entail. I was further swayed by my desire to be of use to the French, who I felt were unappreciated and put down by the English. I still had little time for the English in 1940.

I had several friends among the Free French, who had been serving in the French Navy or Air Force before the war began. Charles de la Haye and Victor Audrin were my closest naval friends, and I missed them both very much when their duties took them away, though I met Charles again after the war, when he took command of the Atlantic Fleet. He was a wonderful-looking man, tall, white-haired at thirty, blue-eyed, and with a deep, dark, Charles Boyer voice. His wife and daughters had gone to Canada, and I fear Charles broke many hearts during the war years, but he was not the sort to mislead a lady about his intentions, honourable or not.

Among themselves their relationships were often rather strained, as many naval men felt that Admiral Muselier deserved their allegiance more than the austere and uncompromising General de Gaulle. As the Free French kept a very good table I would often join my friends there for a *bon repas*, and see the great general, who sometimes ate with us. No special dishes for him, no special wines. He was not a man to inspire affection, though he prided himself on being treated as any other member of his forces. The animosity subsided in due course, but he never achieved a very easy relationship with certain of his officers.

This was not the case with Captain André Dewavrin, his Chief of Intelligence, the legendary 'Colonel Passy'. This was a code-name, taken as were many others from a Paris Metro station, and to me he was always the archetypal espionage chief - just as he emerges in his own books: very right-wing, totally ruthless, and utterly charming.

The spymasters carried awesome responsibilities. If they made mistakes, their agents in the field, even ones as brilliant as Tricycle, could be doomed. It was essential that there should be perfect trust between them, and when, as sometimes happened, this was lacking the consequences could be very nasty.

To an extent the attitude to the French resistance epitomises an official line. Field Marshall Montgomery, later Viscount Montgomery of Alamein, respected them neither as individuals nor as a fighting force. He took the view that the Wehrmacht had every right to attack and shoot Resistance fighters, who were irregular, ununiformed troops in armed conflict with them, and that reprisals against their bases and civilian back-ups were acceptable. He likened them to the Sinn Fein of 1921, against whom he had fought as a Brigade Major, and applied the same standards.

My part in this deadly game was never to be anything but a very small one, yet at this point I was being considered by two very important officers as a possible 'post-bag'. One was Colonel Passy, the other an Englishman whom I regard to this day as one of the finest spymasters of all time. He has come in for some very heavy personal criticism, some of it justified, but nonetheless I believe Claude Dansey displayed all the qualities that justified his long career and great reputation.

Certainly he had his defects; he was harsh, even brutal towards some people who, in his opinion, were not up to scratch. He would rather see an agent killed than have an operation or network jeopardised. With him, it was 'when in doubt, act'. He had neither sentiment nor conscience, nor could the world of Intelligence afford fainthearts. He knew it accommodated traitors, who must be rooted out where possible and dealt with for what they were. Colonel Dansey epitomised the service - a patriot, a cynic, disliked by many, yet there were many others who held him in deep affection and would willingly have died for him.

He was in principle against using women as field agents, but this was an aspect of his gallantry, not contempt. He was always courteous and thoughtful in his dealings with them, and held many of the wartime heroines in the highest regard. He realised, perhaps more immediately than other spymasters who used women very successfully, that many of them would in the nature of things end their lives under torture or in the concentration camps. He had no wish to find himself in a position where he must sacrifice one. War was man's work.

His attitude was traditional in the Service. Colonel David Henderson's very first Official Intelligence Manual, published in April 1904, has this to say about women as agents:

When women are employed as Secret Service Agents, the probability of success and the difficulty of administration are alike increased - women are frequently very skilful at eliciting information, they require no disguise; if attractive they are likely to be welcome everywhere and may be able to seduce from their loyalty those whose assistance or indiscretion may be of use. On the other hand, they are variable, easily offended, seldom sufficiently reticent and apt to be reckless. Their treatment requires the most watchful discretion. Usually they will work more consistently for a person than for a principle and a lover in the Intelligence Corps makes a useful intermediary.

Claude Dansey opposed the formation of SOE, which he felt would conflict with the 'legitimate' Intelligence departments, and believed that through lack of training and ill-considered action it wasted many gallant lives. I was never in a position to say, but I do know that many brave people gave their lives for our liberty. May they never be forgotten!

One aspect I could never understand was the mutual and fierce dislike between Claude Dansey and Colonel Valentine Vivian. Dissimilar attitudes and temperaments may have accounted for it to a degree, but the undisguised contempt of Dansey for a close associate bordered on open war. Perhaps it was partly because Vivian was technically Dansey's superior, being in overall charge of Security and Counterespionage, but Dansey certainly won the contest of wills, leaving Vivian uncertain as to his duties, and his capacity to see them through.

Both held the rank of colonel, and both were Deputy Directors of SIS under 'C' (Sir Stuart Menzies), but Dansey had all the influence over his Chief, and Vivian was naturally jealous.

I, on the outer fringes of this hierarchy, never heard anything unpleasant about Vivian from anyone - quite the opposite. Yet I heard plenty of severe criticism, sometimes combined with openly expressed hatred, directed at Dansey's actions and methods. Those who supported him were just as loud in their loyalty and admiration. Consider these quotes:

Claude Dansey was an utter shit - corrupt, incompetent, but with a certain low cunning.

Hugh Trevor-Roper

Claude Dansey was the only true professional in MI6. The others at the top were all second-rate minds.

Malcolm Muggeridge

Take your choice. I personally found Dansey kindly and courteous. Against the faults which are laid to his door must be set the intelligence and courage he displayed throughout a long career spanning the Boer War until he died in harness during the Second World War. In my limited but professional view, he and the almost equally legendary Colonel Passy were both top-class men in their chosen field.

One marvellous character who seems always to have remained in the background was Colonel John Bevan of the Joint Planning Staff. He was Chief of the powerful London Controlling Section, and his name put the fear of God into many of his less able contributors, but in wartime there is little margin for error. He certainly had no time for fools or bunglers, and when you consider the immense complexity of the relationships between sections, from M1 to M14, and the rivalry between them, it is not surprising that ill-feeling arose.

I fell quite unwittingly and by chance into this maelstrom. My future comings and goings were made possible solely as a result of being in contact with people seeking useful runners. My training was minimal, but so were my duties - I had no wireless to operate, no codes to encipher or crack. All I had to do was make a few journeys and keep in touch with the prescribed people. The 'need to know' (or need not to know) governed my war years, and whatever service I could give, I gave most willingly. I was enjoying every minute.

Luckily I was never considered for field work, or the hazardous role of heroine. I had a single useful attribute - I could travel without arousing suspicion. A singer could go to work in Madrid, Stockholm, Berne, Geneva, Lisbon, and most of all Dublin. There were several airfields from which one could fly from England to Europe, including Filton and Poole, but the Irish Free State was neutral, which made it a useful point of departure. That was to be my main destination, since from there I could set out for the other places with far less hassle than from England.

In fact my first visit there was bona fide. The opera season offered me my début as a prima donna.

During my first week there I met the acting French Consul, a delightful naval man who had been left in charge without notice when his superior decamped for Vichy. I was still desperately homesick for France, the more so from the shameful knowledge that with the capitulation the Vichy government was openly collaborating with the Nazis. It was wonderful to spend a few hours with 'real' Frenchmen, smelling their Gauloises and Gitanes, and listening to their conversation, though at this point I knew very little about the Resistance units preparing to carry out their war against the occupying forces.

As time passed, and my circle of friends broadened, I got to know more about the Maquis and the Partisan movements in Europe. The Poles had their guerilla groups 'Monika' and 'Bardsea' working already. I think they became a section of SOE, under Major Antoni Zdnojewski, who was parachuted into France in July 1942 to take over command of the group.

I learned about the spy networks in neutral countries as well. The Swiss seemed to have the most notorious groups working in their borders, but they were extremely strict when dealing with any breach of neutrality, understandably considering the size of their country, and its position. The Spaniards and the Portuguese were strict as well, though for the opposite reason. Franco was pro-Axis, Salazar sympathetic to fellow Fascist governments, while the Swedes were ambivalent. Their neutrality was absolute, but I always felt that they were simply businessmen, unmoved by political ideals, and mainly concerned to maintain the status quo.

The unfortunate French Consul in Dublin was very tempted to make himself available to London, but his wife and child were in Paris, and he feared for their safety if he did. Nevertheless, he had some quite useful information, and during his time in Ireland I gleaned a number of interesting snippets from him, which I passed to Colonel Passy to make such use of as he could.

Travel was never comfortable, and there was always the risk of one's plane being attacked, though I never suffered that unpleasantness. My bugbear was the Irish Channel. What a crossing! The sea has never had much charm for me except to look at, and the Holyhead to Dun-Laoghaire trips certainly added to my dislike and fear of the water. The boats were all old, and creaked and groaned endlessly, many people were sick, drunk, or both as we pitched, rolled and yawed our way across. The only redeeming feature was the welcome of the lights after the blackout in England.

The procedures before disembarkation were much less hospitable. Customs officers came aboard, and all the passengers must line up to face one across a little table and give a full account of themselves, and their reasons for coming to Ireland. It was an unwelcome delay before I could stand on dry land, and enjoy the comfort of the Gresham, Shelbourne or Hibernian Hotel. I used them all, and was thoroughly pampered every time.

I was extremely lucky to get two leading roles so early, and with so little repertoire. I had been working with Florence Jones in London, looking for openings. Prospects were bleak, as we pored over 'The Stage': ENSA and CEMA had yet to get off the ground, and there was no shortage of seasoned talent. Then Florence suggested that I sing for Tommasini, one of her clients, a well-known baritone who had made a fine career in Italy, though he was Canadian by birth.

"You will find him charming, and I know he can help you find a job."

"What shall I sing?"

"'Caro Nome', and Ophelia's mad scene."

Florence took charge, and the audition was arranged. With shaking knees I attended the great Tommasini's flat in South Street, carrying my music and with tiny Florence pushing me from behind. It was a lovely apartment, very opulent and luxurious, and he was a charming man - not young, but still handsome and very kindly. He took time to put me at my ease before I sang at the fine Bechstein, and received my efforts with rapture.

I was the answer to his prayers, 'They' would snap me up immediately, and he would arrange for me to sing at the Wigmore for 'Them' - a set of names which meant nothing to me whatsoever.

Dutifully I performed, and before I could draw breath there were Tommasini, Arthur Hammond and two Irishmen in the green room with a fabulous offer - £60 per performance, travel and hotel expenses to Dublin, costume allowance, and the parts of Gilda in 'Rigoletto' and Lucia in 'Lucia de Lammermoor'. The latter had last been performed in Dublin by the great Luisa Tetrazzini. It was to be the culmination of the season, and I was to be a star.

Did I know the roles? "Yes," I said. Then I hurtled giddily to HMV in Oxford Street, where I bought the full recorded versions in two huge sets of 78s. For 'Rigoletto' I had the HMV set, with Lina Pagliughi as Gilda, for Lucia the Columbia set with Mercedes Capsir. For two weeks I listened to them day and night, until I knew not only my own part but everyone else's as well. I also bought scores, partly for the sake of appearances, as I couldn't read music, having learnt to play the piano and sing purely by ear. I could tell if the notes were going up or down, and that was it.

It was only because I was so utterly ignorant of the technical difficulties that I could, without fear, copy the cadenzas of the great Galli Curci, Melba, Tetrazzini, Toti dal Monti and the rest.

I enjoyed the pyrotechnics, for I had the range to cope with any scale, and once my ears were attuned, I could hear the piece played a dozen times or so, then let the sheer excitement carry me through. Surprisingly, no one spotted my lack of musical understanding. I was young, pretty and foreign, which covered the lot.

I silently blessed the leader of one orchestra whom I heard talking to a group of the chorus. "You must remember, she may not understand English too well, so if she looks lost, just speak quietly and slowly. And don't forget, she's not used to our Irish brogues."

My blank looks were genuine. I had no idea what the producer and conductor meant when they used the terms of my new profession - upstage, downstage, the rake, side entrance left, were directions I often misunderstood, as were such coded messages as "*Portando*, back to 25, *ritenuto* and *piano*, please - *fila di voce, sostenuto,* Diana, *per favore.*"

I was simply confused, but the gods smiled on me, and the performances went without a hitch - almost! The tenor singing Edgardo to my Lucia lost his voice, and became known, cruelly, as 'The Phantom of the Opera'. In fact, very bravely, he agreed to walk the role, mime it, and leave me to take up his part in the duets. The reason for this was that his understudy had got stage fright, and lost his own voice in sympathy. That house, and every subsequent performance, had been sold out well in advance, and the conductor and company director literally begged me to bear the extra strain and go on.

They need not have worried - I was so completely unaware of the pitfalls that if need be I'd have offered to sing his part in its entirety - I knew it backwards. The only real loss to the ensembles was the lack of a tenor voice in the sextet, but this caused me no anxiety. Not only was I hailed as a heroine for battling against such odds, I gained the bonus of bringing the curtain down on Lucia's mad scene, which is normally followed by her funeral cortège and a passionate aria from the tenor as he kills himself. I had all the glory, and the audience was wildly enthusiastic.

We had a central staircase on that set, and I practised falling day after day, until I managed a really spectacular collapse, my long hair in disarray, and my bloodstained white dress lying around my body like the wings of a wounded butterfly. I was especially thrilled because my final note, an E in Alt, had come off with ease, and allowed me to sustain it effortlessly. The flowers, the applause, it was all wonderful, even the critics noticed only my talent, my youth, and the silvery quality of my voice (the brickbats were to come at a later stage of my career).

Dear Christy Reddin, a patron of the opera who had done all he could to make my stay in Dublin happy and comfortable, played a typical trick on me on the first night of 'Rigoletto'. He came to my dressing room at the end of the second act to tell me solemnly that my mother was in tears. I was stunned, until Christy laughed at my horrified face and hugged me to him.

"You silly girl, she's crying with happiness - everyone is talking about you - the purity of your voice, and the sweetness of its tone - your appearance, so young, so innocent - your Mama is overjoyed."

Panic over. But I remembered it was Christy who, when hearing that a very young singer had been discovered for the title roles, had sent a cryptic telegram to London suggesting that all the artists leave their crutches at Holyhead. I had been annoyed at the time, because most of my colleagues were certainly mature, it was wartime, and young artists were quite hard to find.

Among my fellow singers was the tenor Heddle Nash, whose artistry was equal to Tito Schipa's. His recordings are still played today. He had a thrilling voice as Romeo or Rodolpho, and his diction in any language was perfection, as was his elegance on stage. I have to admit, though, that seeing him in his dressing room for the first time was a bit of a shock. No longer young, a little flabby round the middle, sitting in his long-johns with half his make-up off, he looked a sorry Romeo, but the voice was still there, and he was as kind as he was talented.

My introduction to opera was coloured throughout by kindness and support from the other, experienced singers. I only realised later how easy it would have been for them to spoil my chances to shine, instead of which they nursed me through some quite momentous weeks, and unselfishly enhanced my performances, possibly to the detriment of their own. Being young I received far more attention, far less criticism, and far more adulation than I deserved. Christy had a soft spot for me as well, and entertained lavishly on my behalf, arranging broadcasts and concerts. He was determined to have me back in Ireland as soon as possible, not knowing that I would have other reasons for coming.

A further pleasure that I enjoyed in my first season was to meet Count John MacCormack, whose rendering of 'The Snowy-breasted Pearl' or 'My Lagan Love' always brought tears to my eyes. Though he was already ill he made a point of coming to hear me, and came backstage to talk to me.

"You have a beautiful voice and much talent - I would hope you have an advisor equal to it, my dear girl."

When I told him that I was looking for a coach because I knew nothing about musical theory, he recommended Spencer Clay, who became my guide and mentor until his death, long after the war. I could never repay Count John for his good advice, and I mourned his passing. Spencer had worked not only with MacCormack, but with Joseph Hislop and Frederick Harvey. I owed my development as a recitalist entirely to his musical influence.

Another star who crossed my path that season was Margherita Sheridan, who had won all hearts at La Scala before the war, and inevitably been christened 'The Irish Nightingale'. In those days it was very difficult for a non-Italian to become established in the Verdi and Puccini repertoires, but 'La Sheridana' made a brilliant Butterfly, and I will never forget her 'Ancora un passo via'.

When she came to hear my Lucia she arrived a little late, just as I had begun my first aria, 'Regnava nel silenzio'. There was a noticeable, and quite intentional, commotion as she took her seat, but I had been forewarned, and didn't allow it to distract me. When the curtain fell at the end of the first act, I could hear her calling "Bis, Bis," as she applauded, so after bowing to the audience I made a point of directing my gaze to the Irish Nightingale's box, and dropping her a deep curtsey. From that moment on we were friends, and she gave me many valuable tips for my tours of Italy after the war.

One of my favourite arias was the 'Willow Song' from 'Otello', and Margherita shaped and honed my singing of this lovely piece. She was kindness itself, critical but constructive. I never stayed in Dublin without seeing her, and we had a lot of fun and good meals together, usually at Jammet's famous restaurant.

Another incident during my 'Lucia' was luckier, and rather more disconcerting. It came during the scene where I tell my lady-in-waiting (sung by Ceinwen Reynolds) of my terrible dream of blood in the fountain before which we are now sitting, myself on the bench, she at my feet. The second half of the aria shows a change of mood, and I moved down towards the footlights, to sing about my love for Edguardo.

My lady-in-waiting should join me there towards the end of the cabaletta, to point to the wings and announce the arrival of my beloved. As the finale was approaching I turned to see my companion still heaped on the stage, making vain attempts to rise. She was jerking up and down, and I began to panic - was she ill?

Fortunately, just as my last high note left me, I felt a flurry of movement and breathed a sigh of relief. Ceinwen was at my side, and all proceeded according to the programme. After the curtain fell I enquired what had happened.

Ceinwen, near to tears, explained that her heel had caught in the tapes of her crinoline, and she had been unable to free herself. "I feared that my crinoline would crumple around my feet if I tried to break the tapes," she wailed, "but I was frantic, and eventually I managed to free myself. It was ghastly."

It was certainly a night of incidents, but it ended in a personal triumph.

But the greatest event of my début season was my mother's arrival in Dublin, at great risk to herself. She had applied for a travel visa to accompany me, but had been refused on security grounds. Her journey was not considered 'necessary', and even after several interviews and applications, the answer was still no. My brother canvassed for her, even to the extent of having dinner with Anthony Eden - no small achievement for a sixteen-year-old boy, even one with the influence of his natural father to back his own intrinsic address. Eden lent a sympathetic ear, but, rightly, felt himself unable to break the rules of his own Civil Service.

Mama was undaunted. Without telling me she approached an Irish friend living in England, and they exchanged passports. She packed a few nice clothes, and chose some dowdy ones for the journey. My brother bought a dark 'Charlady's front' hairpiece from Nathan, the theatrical costumier, so as to match Kitty's passport photo. With no make-up, and a piece of cotton wool up her nose, she became Kitty Doyle of Dundalk.

Even so, wartime travel was no picnic. She had to go past Police (civilian and military) as well as Customs, and all three scrutinised her travel documents very carefully indeed, while loudspeakers relayed dire warnings about the penalties for making false statements etc.

My first inkling of her plot was when the switchboard at the Gresham rang late one evening to say that I had a visitor who insisted on speaking to me. I had recently received a telegram from her, saying 'UP THE WELSH STOP DONT WORRY ABOUT ANYTHING', but I had assumed this was only encouragement for my first night as Gilda in two days. Now a little voice on the phone announced, "Darling, it's me," and for a moment I thought I was dreaming.

"Where are you?" I asked stupidly.

"Downstairs, darling, they won't let me up until you say so."

I gave instructions, and in no time at all Mama stood before me, dark-haired, in a battered felt hat, carrying a country basket. Behind her stood the night porter, with two badly scuffed suitcases. Fortunately I had a double room and private bathroom, so I rang room service for sandwiches and a pot of tea. Then I could give Mama my full, if still incredulous, attention.

Off came the wiglet, her nose returned to its normal size, and she set aside the dreary garments for the homeward journey. "I wasn't going to let your début take place without me sitting in a box near the stage."

I could have wept with the delight of seeing her, and my fears for her return trip, when she must run the same gauntlet, had not yet arisen.

To my amazement, when the following day I told the hotel that Mrs Doyle was to be my guest, they showed no surprise at seeing a smashing blonde lady appear instead of the shabbily-dressed woman from last night, nor did the director of the opera want to know how my mother had appeared, like a genie from a bottle. "It's God's will, my dear, God's will."

Maybe so, and it certainly raised my spirits, and allayed my first-night nerves. I was determined to sing my heart out for Mama's sake, if not my own. Gilda was her favourite among my parts, and I confess to shedding real tears in my death scene, when I tell my father that 'Lassu in cielo' (There in Heaven my mother waits for me). My eyeblack ran down my cheeks (waterproof mascara had yet to be invented), so I took my first curtain call looking very odd indeed.

I asked Mama if she'd been apprehensive during her journey, and she said her only trouble had been filling the necessary forms on disembarkation. How to spell Dun-Laoghaire, pronounced Dunleary? To have written Kingstown would have given her away as British, so she sidled up to an elderly and rather drunk Irishman, and in the heavy stage brogue of an ashamed illiterate, asked him to help her fill in the form.

"To be sure I will, me darlin'," he had replied in the same dialect. "Home to your family, I'll be sure," he added, and leered into her basket. "You'd not have a drop of tea to spare?"

Tea was hard to come by in Ireland, but my cleverclogs Mama had saved a few ounces from our ration as presents for Irish friends. One of these most precious gifts passed into his grubby outstretched hands, but it was a fair price. With her entry form in order, she was safe and sound with me.

The return to England was a nightmare that left me shaken and drained, but not so Mama. She breezed through Customs, Immigration and Police without turning a hair, acting the Irish country lady with a quip here and there, laughing and chatting to all and sundry. I tried to keep an eye on her in case trouble arose, though it's difficult to see what I could have done to help. "Never again, darling Mama, never try anything like it again," I begged, and she agreed. Even so, I'm glad it was never put to the test, as she was allowed to travel to Dublin on several subsequent occasions, though never further than that.

Typically, Mama 'fell in love' on another visit to Dublin. Once again I was singing Gilda, and the principal tenor decided to back out at the last minute, leaving us with an inadequate understudy for the Duke of Mantua.

We were desperate, which suited Alfred O'Shea, an Irish tenor much admired by Nellie Melba, now long retired because of too great a fondness for the hard stuff, which made him recalcitrant on stage. Be that as it may, we enticed him to come and discuss fees with our director. He was utterly charming on that occasion, and better still, intensely knowledgeable about opera. Even so, I think it was Mama who finally persuaded him.

I saw their eyes lock, and after that there was no doubt that he would sign the contract. He had a stipulation, however; we must sing in Italian, as he knew no roles in English, and in any case disapproved of translations. Fine for me; I always found Italian far easier to sing, and up till now had always performed in original languages. On this occasion, though, the baritone who was singing Rigoletto and the other operas in which I had no part refused to perform except in English. The compromise we reached, that Alfred and I should sing in Italian, and my Rigoletto in English, was such a guarantee of total shambles that it never came about. Instead we performed scenes from operas whenever O'Shea was to be the tenor star. He was a really fine singer, though no longer young, and his voice was in good condition.

I loved appearing with him, though several of our duets required an ardent lover, and he made it clear from the start that he would act only through the voice. "You'd not be wanting me to fall flat on my face, now would you?"

I knew what he meant. Booze was still a problem, and not one he intended to surmount. He remained firmly planted on the stage, singing with effortless passion, but without a trace of movement. Rodolpho, Pinkerton, Duke of Mantua, Romeo - on came a solid, handsome tenor, sang, and departed. From the vocal point of view he was perfect, though he presented one organisational difficulty. He was held in such esteem that he never finished an aria without the theatre erupting in applause. Then he would reward them with an encore, much to the fury of Arthur Hammond, our conductor, a purist who regarded such pandering as 'showing off'. But Alfred always won his point, and I have to admit that for each encore he made some vocal adjustments, much as Richard Tauber did when he sang 'You are my Heart's Delight' from 'Land of Smiles'. One could only admire his talent.

He and Mama set each other off perfectly, so when the time came for us to take our leave there was a sadness in the air - but not for long, in her case. Back in London we took up the threads of our lives. It was a difficult period for me. I hated the fact that I could never discuss my other work with her. Quite apart from the legal requirement, I knew that disclosure would only upset her, and leave her troubled and anxious whenever I was absent, even if only on a singing engagement. In the event, I only told her what I had been doing in 1965, after we had returned to France.

I had expected her to show amazement, but her comment showed just how shrewd she was. "I always felt, darling, that there was more to your travels than you admitted, you were in such strange places - most of them so very uncomfortable. Still, I knew you would tell me when you could."

Chapter Six

Wartime

Life in wartime London has been described many times, but everyone agrees that it had an intensity such as had never been seen before, and certainly vanished with the peace. Rations could be short, but they were fair. Dangers and discomforts attended everyone. People had their lives suddenly ended or at the very least totally disrupted by the bombings, but though they slept (if they could) in tube stations and shelters, the atmosphere of comradeship transcended all difficulties, so that I don't think the thought of defeat ever entered anyone's mind.

Nothing could have induced me to base myself anywhere but London, though I could easily have done so in Dublin, for instance. I turned that option down, though I had distant relatives in Cork, and many close Irish friends, and I'm only glad my controllers never ordered me out of the capital. Rabid Francophile that I was, I decided in 1940 that London was my spiritual home, and I've never lost the feeling.

It is impossible to over-praise the bravery of the Civil Defence Units, the despatch riders, nurses, and fire services; nor the resilience of those who lost their homes, or did volunteer work day and night to make things better for others. They were the unsung heroes and heroines of wartime England.

The gruesome sights they had to deal with, picking up charred bodies or worse still mortally injured people, were enough to unnerve the most hardened. I remember in particular one man who came into the Report Centre quite literally ill. He had seen a hand sticking out of the rubble and had been very gingerly digging round it. But there was no body attached to the arm.

My family was fortunate. We suffered blasted windows, shortages, and occasional cut-offs of gas, water or electricity, but these were minor. We had enough to eat, a comfortable home and with the debt mountain under moratorium, enough money coming in to maintain ourselves.

Mama joined the WVS and served meals in canteens in St. John's Wood and Finchley Road, but she was in a constant whirl of social activity. There were tea dances, theatres, entertainments for servicemen on leave, and all kinds of clubs. Some of these were to my mind rather seedy, and full of disreputable characters, but to Mama they were only underprivileged, and she enjoyed mixing with all of them - prostitutes (full- and part-time), pimps (black and white), small-time crooks, wrestlers, club-owners - she treated all the London riff-raff the same.

She had always had friends associated with the theatre, and the White Room Club became her second home. The pianist Marc Anthony, a little bird-like man from Penang, was one of her closest friends, and they gossipped daily. His circle included Anton Dolin, the dancer, who was quite delightful, and Robert Helpman, who was always witty and amusing, though his tongue could raise blisters if he chose.

Richard Carey the actor, (whom Mama always called 'Glorious Richard') visited us on his infrequent leaves from the Army (which he hated). He was longing for release, but he was a traditional English gentleman, and endured it with the appropriate stiff upper lip.

We saw Peter Coke quite often until he was posted overseas. On his last leave we had a farewell luncheon at the Café Royal, and coming away Mama distinguished herself by losing her French knickers in a festoon of satin and lace as we crossed Regent Street. Peter nobly bent to pick them up and stuffed them in his pocket, for discreet return in a less public place. Thenceforth she used a huge nappy pin to secure her pantalon, and was known to all as 'Madame Pin Pants'.

Another of her favourites was Philip Ashley, a would-be actor, in uniform for the duration. He, the painter Anthony Mendelsohn (who did my portrait, reproduced later on), and a wild Greco-Russian artist, Orestes Orloff, were frequent visitors to the White Room Club, also the Milroy, Johnny Mills's first club, Les Ambassadeurs and our home. Anthony and Orestes were lovers, and shared a studio near Chelsea Football Ground. Their relationship was exceptionally stormy, recalling Verlaine and Rimbaud. Orestes, who drank enormously and had a foul temper, thought nothing of picking up whatever was to hand and hurling it through the nearest window if Anthony said or did anything to arouse his pathological jealousy. Even his affection for Jane, his sister, could bring this on, yet they remained together until Orestes died. I was glad that Mama was happy and enjoying life, as it made my own absences less fraught. Certainly she showed no anxiety when I packed my bags.

The only man I took an instant dislike to was Pravoslav, a major in the Czech Tank Corps. He was arrogant, extremely good-looking, and utterly insensitive. In 1940 he arrived from France, and because he had received some of his pre-war training in Germany, he was asked to give lectures on the Panzer Divisions that had so devastated Europe. I disliked him from the beginning, as his demonstrations of how battles develop were always arranged to show the British losing, from a combination of cowardice, gullibility and failure to seize the advantage.

"Whose side are you on?" Mama would ask.

The answer was always a sneer. "I have to show you how incompetent you are."

His English was not very good or fluent, so Mama would hear his prepared talks and help him with the pronunciation. He was some ten years younger than she, but to my horror she fell for him completely. It made me dislike him all the more, as he would often complain to Mama that I was rude to him, and jealous of the attentions he gave her.

Far from it! I never disclosed to her how this paragon of manly virtues had suggested, in the most practical and really quite threatening terms, that it was time I yielded up my virginity. He, inevitably, was the man most perfectly suited by nature and training to cure my 'unnatural frigidity'. Only once did he enter my bedroom for this purpose (though on the pretext of checking that the blackout boards were in place) and he left it a bloody sight faster. He found me sitting up in bed, with my silver and nacre Micros revolver aimed at that part of his anatomy in which he took most pride, and which he had been so keen to deploy.

I had a licence for the gun, something of which this would-be Casanova was unaware. Within a few days of his return to his unit, I had a visit from the Special Branch. Two men called late one evening, and I had to endure a barrage of questions about my documents, my travels and my reason for having a firearm. In fact I had several revolvers at that time, presents from Army friends, but I kept these, and my Micros, very safely concealed as long as I retained them. Because the 'tap on the door' was unexpected I was in some difficulty. Should I disclose my work, identify my Master, or brazen it out and act the innocent? I chose the second course. My papers were in order, and I explained that I had only threatened to shoot the man if he continued to pester me. I asked who their informant was.

"We are not at liberty to disclose our sources of information."

I had not obtained clearance from my Master, so I still denied having a revolver, and repeated that I had been defending my honour with pure bluff against a loud-mouthed bully. Finally I suggested that they search the flat. "I've nothing to hide, you are welcome to look anywhere you please. Meanwhile, I'll make some tea."

We spent a chummy half hour over a brew. The sirens had gone and I think they were quite glad to be inside during the alert. We parted on good terms.

I was to have other encounters with Special Branch later on, but fortunately with no unpleasant results. In fact, I have met very few people who had any real idea of its function, and they have all been very reticent about sharing this knowledge. I know it worked very closely with MI5, and had a better relationship with it than with MI6.

I gleaned that those interned under Section 18(B) had first been under the surveillance of Scotland Yard and MI5, and that Special Branch had been responsible for breaking up Sir Oswald Moseley's British Union of Fascists and the detention of certain other key figures. At one time I know there were many thousands of Nazi sympathisers in England, and the general public would have been shocked had they known how many prominent men and women were pro-Hitler.

One whose name was no secret was the founder of the Right Club, Captain Archibald Ramsey. He was detained for a while at the outbreak, because his club was very pro-German and anti-Semitic, not unlike Admiral Basil Domville's rightwing organisation, the Link.

But enthusiasm for Hitler was by no means confined to the Right. The Astors and Moseleys are well enough known, and Bernard Shaw's fellow-feeling for another non-smoking, non-fornicating, vegetarian teetotaller may have blinded him to their many points of divergence. But what can one make of the remark of Lloyd George that for Germany 'Hitler was the Resurrection and the Life'?

Foreign nationals had been interned from the Declaration (many quite inappropriately) and few were released without exceptional circumstances. This led to some bitterness, especially among the Italians, many of whom had spent years in England, and considered themselves loyal subjects of the Crown who just happened, like my father in France, never to have taken up citizenship.

As for me, I became a Spaniard by marriage! This requires some explanation. False papers never presented any problem; passports, work permits and so forth were forged by masterly hands, but it was deemed more sensible for me, a young singer trotting off to neutral countries in search of engagements, to have a bona fide legal status which would withstand any scrutiny. A Swede or a Swiss would have been acceptable, but a stroke of luck brought me a Spaniard, the very best.

It was through my future brother-in-law, James Mason, that I met my husband of convenience. He had been standing in during a duelling scene in a film where James was working, but neither James nor Pam had any inkling of what was afoot. During a break he told James that he was desperate to find the means of staying in England.

James felt sorry for him, and invited him to a buffet party where I was present. We talked about the war and politics, and I realised that I had found the ideal man, whom my Master was still seeking. I asked him some pertinent questions, and we struck a deal.

James and Pam thought I was mad to contemplate a marriage of convenience, but they were wrapped up in their own lives, and had always thought I was 'peculiar'. If I wished to offer this fellow English asylum, so be it. They had no idea I wanted a Spanish passport, let alone why. They felt I could cope.

The Spaniard had no more idea of my motives than Pam. I fed both the same story - that I could travel more easily on neutral papers than if I was subject to the more stringent rules affecting a British citizen. For him, marriage to the holder of a British passport offered the right he sought - to remain in England, near to his married girlfriend, to whom he was devoted. Unfortunately his permit to stay in Britain was not being renewed, and he was due to return to Spain very soon. He was no admirer of Franco, and had good reason to fear being slung into the infamous Miranda jail once he got there.

We memorised each other's names, repaired to a registry office, and the deed was done. Whether he remembers mine I have no idea; his went on a long time, and all I recall of it are the elements 'Rodriguez' and 'Lopez'. We 'celebrated' with a quick drink in a nearby pub, and parted with a chaste handshake and 'good luck'. I learned later that the poor man was almost immediately arrested on some charge or other, and put away for the duration as an undesirable. For the rest of the war he was incarcerated, first in Lewes Prison and later in internment camps; a bit of a rough deal, and something less than cricket by the British, but better than winding up in Miranda.

There was nothing I could do. I was under orders to keep my nose clean, do what I was told and keep quiet. It was pointed out that my best interests were being served, because not only was I protected with genuine papers, I could claim that my beloved husband had been stolen from me practically on our wedding night - a victim of British injustice, interned for his political leanings. That these were hostile to Franco and Fascism was disregarded.

I let the whole episode recede from my mind. I was not personally involved, I had gained a secure cover, and the Devil could take the hindmost. Not a very creditable attitude, but one that fitted my new persona as a force to be reckoned with in the Intelligence world. In fact I was one of countless small fry running errands on behalf of genuinely important people.

My true status was brought home to me soon enough, but even on a reduced ego, life was exciting and comfortable in the Palacio Hotel, Lisbon, and the Ritz, Madrid. Nor did I turn up my nose at the best that Stockholm and Berne could offer. It was always my delight to see the cities lit up, so welcoming and cheering, and to be able to bring back presents for friends and Mama.

I went to Ireland frequently, to broadcast recitals and concerts. Joan Hammond's usual accompanist, Jenny Reddin (Christy's sister), played for me occasionally, but my regular pianist was a lovely lady called Kitty O'Callaghan, who greatly improved my 'artistic' capacity with her very delicate touch. The criticism was wrapped in Irish charm, and I remember her with great affection.

It was very easy for someone in my position to make contact with all sorts of people, especially at embassy parties. These were a surprise to me at first, because all nationalities, including those actually at war with each other, would be present. But I found that Intelligence gathering was not entirely confined to field officers, photography, deciphering or aerial reconnaissance. Gossip could supply some titbits, and so could the much-derided pillow-talk. Nor were inadvertent remarks to be discounted. Many people, momentarily off guard after a few drinks, could prove indiscreet. The shrewd spymaster is the one who can piece together many unimportant-seeming items to solve a puzzle.

This was the thinking behind Claude Dansey's decision to set up his Z Organisation, for which he secured the cooperation of Alexander Korda, later of London Films. There's a persistent rumour that it was through Dansey's influence that Korda obtained the finance for his company. Certainly filming offered locations all over the world, and contacts with foreign politicians and civil servants. A great deal can be gleaned from such sources, showing how very shrewd was Dansey's choice of friends.

Korda was also able to offer Dansey his office in the Empire State Building as a wartime base in New York, and from there he persuaded several people to undertake duties above and beyond their ostensible film work. One of these was the luckless Leslie Howard, the 'perfect English gentleman' (though I think he was German by origin - his original name was Stainer), whose KLM flight from Lisbon was shot down with no survivors in 1943, allegedly because it was believed Churchill was on board.

Dansey believed in disclosing as little as possible to as few as he could. His part-timers had no access to diplomatic bags, no radios, and no direct links to British embassies, military missions or officials. They were passed verbal orders, which they were expected to carry out to the letter. These instructions were very simple for me. I would collect or pass to those who approached me through many venues - shops, hotels, concert halls, press offices etc. Dusko, for instance, was always easily approached. He gambled and flirted in the casino, and was known to enjoy the company of a pretty woman. There were many like him.

They had no 'need to know' about each other, so I am still uncertain who else belonged to Dansey's 'private collection'. Many household names have been bandied about: Graham Greene, Dennis Wheatley, Malcolm Muggeridge are a few that spring to mind, but I know little about their activities. Wheatley certainly was not one of Dansey's, but Intelligence covers a wide area, and duplicity was as much part of Dansey's character as the charm that he exuded when he wanted to.

The most necessary activities in any branch of espionage are assessment and analysis. The gung-ho exploits of field agents are not to be denigrated, but success or failure lies with the assessors. Both Colonel Passy and Claude Dansey could regard problems, no matter how difficult, with a ruthless detachment that was their greatest strength. There was no place for compassion, and individuals could be sacrificed, sometimes deliberately, when the end was held to justify such means.

Many people paid dearly for their parts in undercover work. One I remember in particular was the elder brother of a young Welsh singer with whom I was very friendly. Twm Stephen was involved in the SAS 'Operation Bulbasket', which ended in disaster. He was caught wearing civilian clothes and met his end at the hands of Second SS Panzer Division *Das Reich*, beaten to death. They were notorious for their brutality, and their name will live forever in infamy for the massacre at Oradour sur Glâne. There a German officer was killed by partisans, and in reprisal the village was razed to the ground, and the entire population shot or burned to death in the church.

There were many others, and every imprisonment or death under interrogation had to be regarded as an instalment in the price of ultimate victory by the faceless men who sat behind desks and gave the orders. Were they ever troubled by conscience? I have no answer. Spymasters, like generals, stay in the background, and their innermost thoughts are never recorded.

Wartime Lisbon, like postwar Vienna, was a hive of Intelligence networks, and providing PIDE (Fernando da Silva Pais's Portuguese Secret Political Police) was not upset, life could be very agreeable. There was all the glamour of pre-war London, with an endless round of parties, especially in the embassies of neutral countries. Add to that the casino, the riding and swimming, and the street markets, which were similar to my memories of the Côte, and as full of marvellous flowers, fresh-caught fish and the produce of the only great colonial empire not at war. Such atmosphere, climate and entertainment sometimes made it seem quite impossible that torture, persecution and sudden death were rampant such a short distance away.

Dusko Popov was treading a very delicate line at this point, with his *Abwehr* control in Lisbon and John Masterman in London both awaiting his reports. London had to feed him the sort of information that would protect his position and satisfy his German masters, one of whom I met. He was a policeman called Kramer, and I knew he was a very clever man. I found him disconcerting - watchful, mild, very urbane and courteous. I was nervous of him, and felt that he missed very little, but of course I had been warned against him.

Dusko was certainly among the bravest of men, and one of the most delightful of characters. He loved life, but took the most frightful risks. Essentially he was a playboy, who expected life to provide him with good food and drink, pretty girls, and the opportunity to gamble, but he had had a brush with the German authorities before the war, having made some anti-Hitler jokes which they failed to find amusing. Now he intended to get his own back on the corroding evil of Nazi ideology.

I knew him through an official source, but Leos Milec introduced me to his close friend from childhood, Marko Pavicic, who had arrived in London from Marseilles to continue his diplomatic career in the service of King Peter's government-in-exile. They were both very well educated and excellent linguists, the pampered sons of moderately wealthy parents. They had spent school holidays together on the Adriatic coast, and Marko was as thoroughgoing a playboy as Dusko, and even better looking, though either could have charmed the Devil himself. As *bons viveurs*, their interest in women was avid, and their mistresses numerous. They rarely had fewer than two on the go at one time, and I used to tease them about what it must be costing them in lost sleep.

"Watch it! One of these days your ladies will catch up with you."

"You will protect me," was their reply, and in fact I did. Marko in particular would sometimes ask me to take a phone call and pose as his wife, if some poor girl was getting too possessive. He was not the faithful type.

One incident in Lisbon was very amusing to Dusko and myself, though less so for Marko. As the possessor of a large and very powerful wireless set, capable of picking up virtually any station in Europe, he was denounced and arrested as a spy. It soon blew over and he was released, but the Portuguese police could be very tough, and he was less than pleased with the episode. Sadly, he was to face far, far worse from his own countrymen when he returned to Yugoslavia after the war.

Dusko had infiltrated the *Abwehr* through the efforts of a German friend, Johann Jebson. Their friendship was very close, and when Jebson was finally arrested and unmasked by the Gestapo, I know what torment it must have been for him. It set alarm bells ringing in London as well. If Jebson cracked under interrogation, how many agents would find their necks on the block? I know for a fact that he didn't expose anyone, but not whether he was executed, though I think he must have been.

Dusko's path and mine separated, and I lost touch with him before the end of the war. He took up residence in the South of France, married, and finally died in 1981. I kept in close touch with Marko when he was transferred to Cairo from Lisbon, and today he and his wife are my dearest friends in Zagreb.

After Lisbon, Madrid and Algiers were the principal hotbeds of intrigue. At that time the *Abwehr* agents in Spain were being run by Gustave Lenz, a very shrewd operator, but the British also had excellent men in charge of the Iberian and African Sections. They were Dick Brooman White and Felix Cowgill. Cowgill was an ex-Indian Police officer, as was Claude Dansey's *bête noire*, Colonel Valentine Vivian.

Cowgill acted as sponsor for Kim Philby, who repaid him by ousting him from his job. This was typical of Philby, who was not only a remarkably likeable man, but a very mischievous one. There are many stories about him which show this propensity, but oddly enough I never heard anyone speak ill of him until his actual departure for Russia, and even then most of his colleagues felt a kind of regret at losing him.

From my own limited experience, I'm satisfied that Philby's motives were not mercenary. He was an ideologue, and I should have thought that his first marriage to Lizzy Friedman, a known and active Communist, would have been sufficient warning to those who recruited and advanced him throughout the war and beyond. Through Felix Cowgill he had access to secret information from Bletchley Park, and was in undisputed control of Section V when Cowgill was absent. The pickings must have been very rich.

Many secrets were supposed to be kept from the Russians, who even though fighting for the same cause (and their own survival) were not entrusted with all the deciphered information that poured out of ULTRA. To Philby, committed to the Soviet system as he was, it must have seemed a betrayal of a hard-pressed ally.

The most fascinating country for neutral embassies, legations etc. was Switzerland. The Swiss Intelligence Service under Roger Masson was small but efficient, quick to make use of all the sources at its disposal.

Masson made a point of allowing all the most notorious rings, including 'DORA' (headed by Sándo Rádo), Leopold Trepper's *Rota Kapelle* (Red Orchestra) and Rudolf Rössler's 'LUCY' group to operate without hindrance, as long as they observed the niceties of the host nation.

Rudolf Rössler was the most interesting, and certainly the most mysterious of these *grands chefs*. 'LUCY' provided information of the highest quality, unique in its accuracy, detail and reliability, which could only have come from someone in the highest echelon of the Nazi Party. It may have been Admiral Canaris, with his desire to seek a separate peace with the West. He, or other members of *Die schwarze Kapelle* (the Black Orchestra, a rightwing underground movement that wished to overthrow Hitler) may have been supplying Rössler with a steady flow of important information which he in turn passed to his Soviet clients. Regrettably, the truth is unlikely ever to emerge. Rössler took his secrets to the grave in 1958.

Rössler may have been a Communist. It's another area about which he was secretive. Rádo and Trepper (a Polish Jew) certainly were. Trepper's Red Orchestra was highly successful, and reputed to number three hundred or more spies and radio operators, known as pianists, arranged in cells. Then, at the height of its powers, it was infiltrated in 1942. Every member of the German cell was captured, and both sexes were fearfully tortured before suffering death by hanging or the guillotine. This was a favourite method of the Gestapo, who continued their mental torture to the last by making their victims face the blade as it descended.

A few months later Trepper himself was caught by the Gestapo, with whom he collaborated fully, and apparently of his own volition. It was a heavy blow for the Soviets, who on his return to Moscow confronted him with a treason charge, for which he received a fifteen-year prison sentence. He fought, successfully, to clear his name and was freed in 1954, dying in Israel in the 1980s. Meanwhile the Soviets still had the Hungarian Sándo Rádo.

He was a quiet, small, ordinary-looking man, but a gifted agent, able to inspire confidence and loyalty. He and his wife had become Swiss citizens before war broke out, and they ran a small cartographic business, which brought him into contact with, among others, representatives and officials of the League of Nations. For years he used it as a cover for 'DORA' under the eyes of the Swiss authorities, only being infiltrated by the Germans in 1943. Then the Swiss Military Intelligence rounded up his network.

Rádo and his family were not arrested, being hidden by friends, and eventually reached liberated Paris. Why he returned to Moscow is uncertain, but the gratitude of his masters took the form of ten years' imprisonment, from which he was not released until 1955. His crime was 'causing embarrassment between Moscow and Switzerland' (where the Soviets had no representation after 'DORA' was blown). Worse still, he had taken refuge for a while in a British diplomatic mission!

It would be interesting to know if Trepper and Rádo remained Communists to the last. They served the cause with zeal and determination, and deserved of it far better than they got from that ungrateful regime. At least one of Rádo's men in Switzerland learned the truth about the Soviets.

Alexander Foote, an Englishman who had fought in Spain against Franco had settled at Lausanne. He was a clever, pleasant man who spoke good German and excellent French. He had private means, but was recruited by Soviet Intelligence in 1938-9. Ursula Hamburger ran him, and he was among the last of 'DORA' to be arrested and imprisoned by the Swiss. I have always doubted that Foote was solely a Soviet agent, though as so often it is difficult to be certain of motives, loyalties, etc. He had the reputation of a playboy who entered the game for the excitement of the risk, but he proved to be a skilful and serious worker.

When the Swiss released him there was conjecture that he might have been a double agent, but these doubts were cleared up when he went to Moscow. No double agent would willingly walk into the lions' den, knowing the fates of Trepper and Rádo ... would he?

Foote was thoroughly interrogated, but well treated by the Soviets. Nevertheless, when they gave him a new territory he was so disillusioned by the system that as soon as he left Moscow to take it up he returned to the British. He died in the service of his own country, a double double agent, I presume. Someone, somewhere may know for sure, but not I.

Allied missions were under the same constraints as the Axis Powers. Claude Dansey had active agents there operating through the SIS Chief of Station, Vanden Heuvel. It would have been very easy for him to establish contact with Rössler, though I think Allen Dulles, brother of John Foster Dulles, who represented the Americans, had most influence of all. He was powerful, and I know from personal experience, very devious. He was so anti-Communist that he pressed for a 'soft' peace with the Nazis, who could then continue their aggression against the Soviet Union without the distraction of a western front.

The accepted opinion is that Dulles and Admiral Canaris were no strangers to each other's ideas, and their Zurich go-between was a Vice-Consul called Hans Bernard Gisevius. This flow of information was surely of benefit to the Americans, who may have shared some of it with their allies. But there was always a certain reticence between services: they liked to operate as single entities, and guard their own secrets from each other no less than the enemy.

Rumour held that Dansey disliked Dulles, but I disbelieve this. Their attitudes were very similar, though they may not always have used the same sort of approach; Dansey could and did ride roughshod over anyone he despised, as was most dramatically demonstrated in his dealings with Colonel Vivian, whom he treated as a bitter adversary rather than a colleague. Dulles, on the other hand, was always able to curb his antagonism if he admired the other man's qualities, and contrary to many of Dansey's critics, I believe they held each other in mutual respect.

In fact, at the higher levels, many of the international spy rings knew each other's operatives perfectly well. A known agent was preferable to an unknown replacement, and though direct fraternisation could hardly be practised, I would have been more surprised if contact had not been made, or if personal 'lines' had not been kept open.

I have sometimes been asked how I passed information on. In fact there was very little cloak and dagger about it. I was a courier to neutral countries only, where I was never required to develop the skills so necessary for the protection of field workers in enemy country, or later in the postwar world. I very rarely had 'need to know', and on the few occasions when I did music provided the perfect cover. My greatest asset was a good memory, as the information might be coded and must be relayed exactly.

My contacts were not seedy strangers in slept-in clothes, to be met in grubby bars or on railway platforms in the drizzle. Far from the dirty mac brigade, they were mainly pillars of society, upright citizens with an interest in the arts, such as might enjoy a passing flirtation with a visiting singer. Of course, it was possible for the wires to get crossed.

Such an event occurred in Lisbon, where I was meeting Dusko. A young, rather handsome German called Ernst Kampe began courting me. He was, he told me, a secretary at the embassy, but when I told Dusko of his interest he teased me unmercifully.

"You're an idiot, Diana. He's a well-known SS officer - very bright. He's probably been told to keep an eye on you."

Flustered, and not a little put out, I replied testily, "Then tell me what to do. He's invited me to lunch - should I refuse?"

"Good God no! Certainly not. Let him pay for your company. Enjoy yourself, and keep your ears open. Men like him get bored in Lotus Land, with no action. The atmosphere soon palls, and I don't imagine he'll be here for long. Do a little gentle probing."

It came to nothing. He was mad on opera and very correct in his approach, if a little heavy-handed in his flattery. Nor was he inclined to discuss the war. All I learned was that he had put in for a transfer to France where, as he put it, "I can serve my country to better effect." In what atrocities, I wonder, did this pleasant if rather stiff young music-lover take part?

It was very different for those couriers who worked in occupied territory. They took enormous risks, and were in constant danger of being apprehended or betrayed. This could imply weeks of interrogation, living in filthy conditions, humiliation, and the vilest tortures that the most depraved imagination could devise.

Yet knowing this, brave men and women chose such duties. There can be no higher expression of courage and integrity. I would never have had the bottle to volunteer for such a role, and I am thankful that my Masters recognised my limitations, and selected me for minor duties only. One man typifies them all, of whatever nationality, to my mind.

'Klara' was a Polish member of a section code-named 666. He was organised by the *Armia Krajowa* (Home Army) in Warsaw, and his job was to establish a transit route for couriers between Poland and England. The routes were to run through German-controlled territory, and to serve the secondary purpose of guiding shot-down Allied airmen and escaped POWs through police and military cordons.

'Klara' was one of four men in his group, and he travelled to Paris with forged papers describing him as a German engineer. Twice arrested, and twice escaping, he was rescued and brought back to London and General Sikorski. After convalescing from an operation on a broken knee he was parachuted back into Poland to form the Partisans of the Second *Armia Krajowa* Division in Krakow. Betrayed by an informer, he was arrested by the Gestapo, who subjected him to appalling torture but failed to break him. He was imprisoned first in Gross Rosen Concentration Camp, then sent to DORA in the Harz Mountains, then to slave labour in the SS Baubrigade Neusollsted, finally to the Death Camp at Mauthausen, from which he was ultimately liberated by the Americans.

In 1946, exactly two years after his arrest near Kielce, 'Klara' was reunited with his wife. They both received many military honours for their war work, and no one has ever deserved them more than this incredibly brave man.

Information, however collected, must be weighed, sifted and analysed before it can be accepted or rejected, regardless of source. Some spies and informers were of dubious value, double agents could spring surprises, and 'turned' agents might well be turned twice. I never envied the responsibilities of those who had to make such judgements. The smallest error could have the direst consequences.

An unfortunate misjudgement by the British in 1943 lost them the services of the spy Fritz Kolbe. A dedicated anti-Nazi, he believed that no internal plot would ever rid Germany of Hitler, and that his duty as a German patriot was to ensure an Allied victory. Kolbe worked in a Foreign Ministry department that liaised directly with the High Command, and was delegated to act as courier to Switzerland. When he approached the British Legation he was perfectly placed, yet they rejected him out of hand.

Shocked and dismayed, he tentatively approached the Americans, and the wily Dulles, having carefully and thoroughly checked him, made the fullest use of the 'treasure trove' of material he provided. Kolbe had impressed Dulles, not only because of the sort of information he could provide, but for his selfless devotion to his country. He wanted no financial reward, but took the terrible risk of being discovered for the disinterested and abstract ideal of restoring the integrity of German culture.

Kolbe helped unmask 'Cicero' (real name, Elyesa Bazna) who was sending very damaging information to the Germans in Ankara about British military plans. There had already been a lot of gossip about the nature of his relationship with the British ambassador, and it is certain that Cicero was able to use his position to some advantage. He passed documents of the highest classification directly to the High Command, and Kolbe was able, by analysis of its character and quality, to point the Allies in the right direction, even though he was himself unaware of that informant's name or position.

Kolbe did not fall silent until the failure of the 1944 plot against Hitler. The arrests, torture, and murders that followed that momentous incident were sufficient to send even the most courageous agent underground, and Kolbe was no exception. In that way he survived into postwar Germany, taking up the quiet, inconspicuous existence he had enjoyed before - one of the most fortunate of the Germans who dared oppose Hitler.

We should never forget that the first concentration camps, such as Dachau and Orianenberg, were initially filled with Germans; priests, lawyers, doctors, trade union officials, Communists, theologians, academics, homosexuals, Gipsies - the list is endless, and covered anyone who could appear as an enemy in the paranoid eyes of the National Socialist state. Those who were not for Hitler must be against him, and pay the price.

This is not to deny the heroism of the genuine German Resistance groups and individuals. I recall the names of Heinz Dirmeyer, a Catholic Social Democrat who stood out for decent values in wartime Vienna, Herbert Baum, who organised acts of sabotage at his factory in Berlin, the brother and sister team of Hans and Sophie Scholl, who as students began the White Rose Movement, Anton Schmidt, a Wehrmacht Lieutenant, tortured to death in Bialystock by Gustav Friedl for daring to oppose Hitler's New Order, and one of few survivors from all these, Victor Berger, an officer in the *Politische Abteilung*, who risked his life as an undercover agent for the *Bureau de Renseignement d'Actions*.

The Swiss authorities, in their determination to show how tough they could be, arrested and tried over a thousand people for betraying military or economic secrets during the war. The sentences handed down, including those on Swiss nationals, were long terms in jail, severe enough to dissuade anyone of faint heart or doubtful ideology. The networks operating there had to be very circumspect in their behaviour, especially the Germans, with their consulates in every Swiss city. So did the Spanish, who were openly sympathetic to Hitler, but guarded their neutrality jealously. Even the Free Poles were careful not to infringe the code with their mission in Berne.

Surprisingly, the jokers in this pack were the Chinese. Already at war with Japan, they passed (unofficially of course) some very useful information to the Allies, through the 'arm's length' link of a reliable informant acceptable to both parties. Even so every morsel of information, no matter what the source, had to be checked and re-checked. Nothing could be taken on trust.

I cannot close a chapter on espionage and its machinations without referring to Ede Fraser Smith, a most remarkable woman who was to become my greatest friend after the war. I was unaware of her identity while it was going on, though I knew that an Englishwoman was involved with the 'Swiss corridor', helping to organise an escape route for POWs. She provided guides, safe houses etc. and occasionally a chance to convalesce before going back 'down the line', and she ran considerable risks in the process. Most unusually, her brother was also engaged in secret work in London, without her or anyone else in his family circle knowing of it.

He was only able to tell his fascinating story in 1981, when Michael Joseph published 'The Secret War of Charles Fraser Smith'. He ran CT6, which provided all the gadgetry and special equipment, such as saws disguised as bootlaces, collar stud and button compasses, shaving brushes made to enemy specification, perfect replicas of German uniforms etc. Brother and sister kept their secrets from each other and everyone else for over thirty years, in her case, until after her death.

My Grandmama

The organ at
Tegynffyn
Llanfeltis,
home of the
Morgan.

Mama

My father (left), as he captivated Mama, with Uncle Bastitien

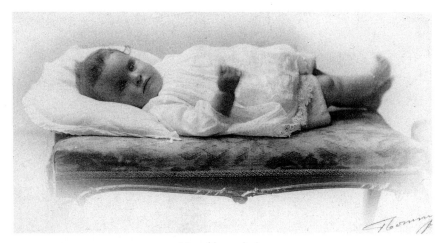

Myself as a baby

Myself at Sipton Park

The Castle of the Prince in Monaco

The old Casino – Le Palais de l'Europe – at Menton in the Jardin Bioves

Le Casino de Monte-Carlo on the Riviera Côte d'Azur

With Taffy at Menton

With Pam and Amos at Monte Carlo Sporting Club

*Riding Donna (above)
and Fleurette on the
Promenade, Menton*

Onyx – the mare that took Walter Sickert's eye

Tony the bear, Mama, Sheila and me at Wengen

*Mama and Anthony
tobogganing at Wengen*

*My brother Anthony,
skating on the lake at
Wengen*

Chapter Seven

Comings and Goings

Double agents are generally treated with some degree of suspicion. Their controllers never know when they may be exposed and 'turned', changing from priceless assets to calamitous liabilities overnight. One who suffered more than most from this was the much maligned and incredibly courageous Erick Erickson.

He was born in the United States and went into the oil business, starting his own consultancy in Sweden in 1924. He took up Swedish citizenship in the mid-thirties, and built up extensive contacts in several countries, Germany in particular. When war was declared he offered his services as a spy for the Americans.

Posing as an ardent supporter of the Nazis, Erickson was taken up by Göring and Himmler, who were so impressed by his Aryan fervour that they gave him *carte blanche* to travel the length and breadth of Germany to study and advise on the production of synthetic fuel oil and gases. In all he made over twenty-five visits there during the war, and his reports to the United States on what was going on and where were of inestimable value.

He played his part so well that he was blacklisted by the Allies, and most of his friends dropped him. I met him once in Stockholm, and heard his perfidy described in the bitterest and most contemptuous terms. 'Swedish traitor' was the least he had to put up with, and only after hostilities ended and his real work could be disclosed was his reputation restored. I myself only learned the truth when I met him again in the sixties, in very different circumstances.

A friend of Mama's, Captain Bertram Ratcliffe, had been a liaison officer on the staff of the British military mission to General de Gaulle, and after the war he returned with his delightful Danish wife Dagne to take up residence at the Villa Mignonette in Menton. We enjoyed champagne parties with many old wartime colleagues, including Erick.

It seemed that the Côte d'Azur was a magnet for retired agents - Graham Greene, Dusko Popov, Erick Erickson, Andre Dewavrin, to name but a few.

Another double agent, Roman Czerniawski, came under the suspicion of his Polish countrymen when he arrived in England.

In 1940, after the fall of France, he organised a network of agents in Paris, but was betrayed by one of his group, Mathilde Carré (code-named La Chatte). She had fallen in love with a German, Sergeant Hugo Bleicher, who worked for the *Abwehr* on the staff of Colonel Oskar Reile. Fortunately for himself, Czerniawski fell into Reile's hands rather than those of the Gestapo. After a stay in Fresnes Prison, he was offered a deal: 'Work for us, and we'll aid your escape to England.'

After a lot of heart-searching Czerniawski agreed. His main reason for accepting the offer was concern for the rest of his network. They had all been arrested, and Reile promised imprisonment rather than execution if he collaborated. I may say that German agents caught in Britain were often offered the same sort of option. Thus, equipped with a set of codes and ciphers and the code-name 'Hubert', Czerniawski was duly despatched to England via Madrid and Gibraltar.

There the Poles grilled him, then passed him to the British. After a prolonged de-briefing, it was decided that he should be set up under the 'Double X' system, feeding misleading information to the *Abwehr*. 'Hubert' became 'Brutus' as well, and was so convincing to his German 'masters' that he eventually tricked them into paying for false information about the D-Day landing areas.

Like many unsung and unknown wartime agents, Czerniawski received little reward for his efforts other than the OBE, but when I last met him, in Wheelers in Old Compton Street, he told me that the success of 'Brutus' was all the reward he could ever have wished for.

I met another most interesting Pole, Marian Rejewski, through Pierre Jounet, a newly-escaped Frenchman. At that time I knew nothing of the work that he had been engaged in, and only heard about it from a Swede.

The Swedes had always regarded themselves as the experts in the breaking of codes and ciphers, and took great pride in their Hagelin machine, which they used to great effect (as did the Japanese). Even so, the arrival of Enigma opened up a new dimension: Rejewski and the French General Gustave Bertrand, head of Section D of French Intelligence, had both played a very important part in its development, as the Swedes were quick to realise.

The story of Enigma has been told and re-told many times by historians and scientists. The best readily-available books are 'Most Secret War', by R.V. Jones, 'The Full Story of ULTRA', by Peter Calvocoressi and 'The Enigma War', by Josef Garlinski, but the more I have learned, the more I lean to the view that the Poles have received too little credit for the sterling work they did in the early stages of breaking German codes. Marian Rejewski and his colleagues Jerzy Rozycki and Henryk Zygalski were deciphering *Reichwehr* signals as early as 1932, and Marian, the best mathematician of the three, played a crucial role in the construction of the first Polish Enigma machines, examples of which were handed to the British and the French before 1939.

Dillwyn Knox, younger brother of Mgr Ronald Knox, was one of the group that took delivery of Enigma and had it installed in Bletchley Park, the British Codes and Ciphers HQ - at that time a very secret establishment, subsequently credited with remarkable achievements, without which, some say, the war might well have been lost.

It was based on a fine old house in Buckinghamshire, but numerous huts had been built in the grounds. Hundreds, and ultimately nearly three thousand, people were employed there, as the vital importance of Enigma and Ultra was recognised more and more.

It was strictly out of bounds except to those engaged in deciphering, cryptology, translating etc., their support staff, and the messengers who served them. Every conceivable nationality was monitoring round the clock, and once in, no one was allowed to leave. This was extremely irksome to the many intellectuals who were employed there, and who had had to pass the most rigorous security clearance to get in, likewise to the Wrens and WAAFs who operated the equipment and found themselves in what was effectively a prison, vital though they knew their work to be.

My meetings with General Bertrand and Marian Rejewski highlighted the contrast between the two men. Marian, quiet and modest, showed no rancour over the cavalier treatment and lack of acknowledgement that he received, while Bertrand showed open bitterness. He had been barred from Bletchley Park because of his earlier imprisonment by the Germans. He felt, understandably, that this cast a slur on his honour and reputation as the soldier who had been the prime force behind the escape of the Polish team EKIPA Z from Hungary to France, where he had installed them alongside French and Spanish cryptologists at Vignolles, near Paris.

Bertrand was fully aware of Enigma's potential, and had gone to great lengths to ensure the safety of his seven Poles. They were: their commander, Lieutenant Colonel Gwido (Karol) Langer, Major Maksymilian Cieski, Antoni Palluth, Edward Fokczynski, Marian, Jerzy and

Henryk. Once he had them safe at Vignolles he established liaison with Bletchley Park, which continued until France fell. Then the various groups were moved, first to Oran, subsequently to Algiers, finally back to France where he set them up in the Château des Fouzes near Uzès in Provence.

Under the code name CADIX they continued their work until in 1942 the order came for them to evacuate and try to reach safety. This was the end of the Polish involvement with Enigma, and within three days of their leaving Uzès the Germans had crossed into the French Free Zone, hunting for the cryptologist groups.

After their escape from Uzès, of which I don't believe any account has yet been published in English, though it is described in Wladislaw Kozaczuk's book, Marian and Henryk spent a short time in Nice, now occupied by OVRA, the Italian Security Police. From there they travelled to Cannes, playing a game of cat and mouse with the growing numbers of Gestapo men. Finally, on 21 January 1943, they departed from Narbonne, thence to Perpignan in the Pyrenées Orientales. Another train ride to Aix-les-Theimes on 27 January took them into the waiting arms of two young women detailed by the Frence Resistance to greet them like long-lost lovers, so as to draw suspicion from them should any German guards show too much interest. Hanging round their necks, the two girls took them to a nearby hotel where they worked as waitresses.

But now came the really tricky bit. Their mountain guide, arriving late and in a surly mood, decided that they must leave Aix for the Spanish border on the night of 29 January. Evading German and Vichy patrols, they trekked over the uninhabited mountain country, destroying all their bogus documents and evidence of having been in France. If the Spanish authorities caught them, they must not be handed back to the Vichy authorities as French citizens.

Shortly before they were to reach the border, the guide began muttering angrily that he had not been paid enough for the risks he was taking, and began threatening them with a revolver. The Poles knew they were within a few kilometres of Spain, but it was dark, and they had no idea of the direction. They could gain nothing by quarrelling with the man. They had simply to cough up all their remaining cash, after which he escorted them to Puigceida.

There they were apprehended by the local police, who were by this time used to a flow of doubtful characters fleeing across the mountains. A few days later the Guardia Civil took them to a district prison at Séo de Uigel, where they remained until 24 March. From there they were transferred yet again, not to the notorious Miranda prison, but to the marginally less unpleasant Lerida, 80 miles north of Barcelona. There they remained until July, before being released through the intervention of the Red Cross. Once again they prepared for an illegal crossing, this time into Portugal, whence their escape to England via Gibraltar had been arranged.

They were lucky at that. Some guides not only shook down their charges, but got paid at both ends by doubling back and selling them to the Vichy authorities after re-crossing the border in the wrong direction. The Maquisades soon got to hear of this, and published their names and faces for reprisal after the war, which was often carried out with the full brutality of the times. Those who had practised extortion without treachery were spared, however; neutrals always reap the best fortunes of war.

Their colleagues were not so lucky, Jerzy Rozycki was drowned when the ship bringing him to England was torpedoed; Gwido Langer and Maksymilian Cieski were betrayed to the Gestapo, but survived their interrogation and imprisonment in the SS concentration camp Schloss Eisenberg, from which the Americans liberated them in 1945; the other two were sent to Sachsenhausen Orianenberg and died before the war ended.

When I first met Marian he held the rank of sergeant, and I gathered from his very discreet remarks that he had undergone lengthy interrogation after arriving in England, and that he and Zygalski had finally been assigned to a Polish unit at Boxmoor under Kazimierz Zielinski and Tadeusz Lisicki.

It was only after the war that I understood why he and Bertrand had not been put to work on Enigma. Both had been captured, and both escaped, which suggested that they might have made, and decided to keep, the sort of double bargain that both sides sometimes offered enemy agents. It was the policy of the time, to which the ill-starred genius Alan Turing had often indicated his disagreement, that no one who had been in enemy hands should work at Bletchley Park, hence Bertrand's ill feeling.

The brilliant, modest Marian took it more calmly. He got on with the job he was given, breaking the latest versions of the SS codes and ciphers. It was important work, for at this stage in the war the powers of the SS were increasing. Their codes contained life-and-death information for soldiers, partisans, and resistance groups, relating to SS battle plans, arrests and round-ups. Unfortunately the Poles were not allowed to know how much their code-breaking had achieved. That secret has never been divulged, and I expect the archives to remain inaccessible for the foreseeable future.

After the war Marian Rejewski returned to his wife and family in Bydgoscze, having been honoured by neither the Allies, the Polish government-in-exile, nor the Communist government imposed by Stalin. All he got until his retirement in 1967 was clerical work in various state-owned firms. After retirement, and until his death in 1980, he achieved some recognition as the selfless son of Poland he was. To make up for their total disregard of his service to his country, the Government encouraged writers, scholars and scientists to seek him out and learn the real beginnings of Enigma.

I re-visited Warsaw after his death. Martial law had been declared, and I was anxious to see my friends again. Accompanied by Dr Wladislaw Kozaczuk, probably the greatest authority on Marian's life and work, I was able to enjoy a quiet visit to his widow, Irena, and their daughter. They were able to show me many letters from cryptologists all over the world, paying tribute to this self-effacing pure mathematician.

Apart from my trips to Europe, I found life in London much the same, and was happy to be there, sleepless nights, queues, and shortages notwithstanding. After one night of heavy bombing I made a tour of the local streets, a rough square bounded by Paddington Street, Marylebone High Street, George Street and Baker Street. I saw that the pub at the end of our road had been virtually demolished - certainly the front was caved in. A couple of Civil Defence workers and ARP wardens were moving gingerly in and out of the building, and as I approached one whom I knew well by sight called me over.

"Come and see this - you won't believe your eyes."

Inquisitive as always I accompanied them over the rubble, to see that the steps leading down to the cellar were quite undamaged, despite the destruction above.

"You've seen nothing yet - it's down there - don't faint on me, will you?"

This was fair warning of some sort of gruesome revelation, but I wasn't especially squeamish. I had seen some fairly ugly sights by then, and could conquer a heaving stomach, but what I saw was indeed a shock. The publican, his wife and their teenage son were lined up like sentinels against an inner wall, unmarked except for falling dust and dirt, and all three stone dead.

"Yes, love, you've guessed it. They're done for. Bomb blast, shock wave, but not a bloody mark. I tell you, it gave me the willies."

It gave me the willies as well. The bomb had accidentally achieved the old pioneering trick of killing a squirrel by shooting the branch under its feet. I had heard of such things, but the sight was chilling, and I was glad to clamber out over the bricks and make for home. I hadn't known the people, but could only feel pity for the waste of it all. If only they hadn't been in contact with the wall ...

Later I was to see for myself, and weigh London's experiences against those of Rotterdam, Warsaw, Belgrade and Berlin, among others and concluded that we had been very lucky.

Only once were we forced to leave our flat and visit a nearby shelter. A landmine had fallen opposite and failed to explode, so several blocks were evacuated just in case.

"Mama," I said, taking charge as usual. "You carry my records and I'll bring the cat."

What a joke! Poor Mama weighed down with three boxes of highly inflammable wax records staggered towards the shelter, with me in hot pursuit carrying my adored midget ginger cat 'The Brigadier' in his basket, yowling his head off.

"You can't bring animals in here, Miss," the harassed-looking ARP warden said gravely, barring my way into what looked like an overcrowded prison cell. Young and old were herded together, including one or two children from our block, and in the dim light they all looked pale and ill at ease.

It was my first glimpse of life in the shelters, though I'd seen newsreel pictures of the tube stations. The thought of spending night after night cheek-by-jowl with this mass of people filled me with horror. Far preferable to take your chance in your own bed, or someone else's if that was your inclination.

"Sorry, Miss, no animals," the warden repeated adamantly.

"Fair enough, I'll go home," I replied. "Mama, you stay here, I'll see you later."

No way. Mama, carting the records, was out of the place in a flash. "If we get blown up, let's go together." We crept back to our beds. Next morning we were told everyone must leave the two blocks nearest the landmine while it was defused.

This time, with a few clothes hastily packed, Mama, 'The Brigadier' in his basket and I set off for Bickenhall Mansions on the opposite side of Baker Street, where Roy Kellino was living. By now he and Pam had split up and Roy, always the gentleman, had moved into a flat of his own, and allowed James Mason, by now formally engaged to Pam, to move into the marital home in Dorset House, though once war was declared they decided to move to Beaconsfield.

Roy made us welcome, Mama had always had a soft spot for him, and he was more a member of the family, far closer than James or Sheila's husband, Bill. She believed he was rather selfish, and took Sheila for granted, and she may have been right. He was not my favourite brother-in-law, but I guess he made Sheila happy; their marriage certainly lasted well.

Roy and I had an excellent understanding. When he was busy pursuing a new romance I hardly saw him, but once it was over and he wanted a companion to visit the Embassy or the 400 Club, then I would be his partner for the evening. He was great fun, a very kind and gentle person, and had been hard-hit when Pam decided that she wanted a divorce. Fortunately he and James were able to remain friends, though until he married his third wife I think Roy remained a little in love with Pam.

Weekends at home were generally hectic, as many of our friends got 48-hour passes, or were on embarkation leave. Dennis Edwards, our actor friend from Margate, had joined the Medical Corps and gone to South Africa. Others went off on ill-fated flights over Germany or elsewhere. Looking back, I can see how we were becoming hardened to grief and regrets. Everything was transient, leaving no time for mourning, or self-pity either. There were too many deaths and maimings to think of, among servicemen, bomb victims, and those in Resistance groups overseas. Betrayal, torture and death were everyday occurrences, and it still amazes me how we coped with the knowledge and the losses.

Like all young women of reasonable looks, I had many admirers, but until halfway through the war I remained a virgin. My women friends teased me over this, my boyfriends tried sundry ingenious means to persuade me to 'live for the moment', but stubbornly, and for no good reason, I refused them all. Only Colonel Dansey would have approved of my virginal state. According to Colonel Passy, he once expressed the opinion that 'sex and romance are best left alone in time of war, as they only caused problems and interfered with the job in hand.'

I never asked if Passy was following that advice, though I suspect not. He was a very attractive man.

One of my most ardent admirers, and would-be awakeners into a life of love, was a French restaurateur, Jean Pagès. He had come to England to work with Mme Prunier, and when I first met him he had just opened his own restaurant, 'La Coquille', in St Martin's Lane.

He was appointed to cater for the Free French canteen, which entitled him to charm his civilian clientéle in a smart military uniform. He cut a broad swathe, though I only learned later that he was not only married with two children but had a long-term mistress as well. He certainly let none of them inhibit his wooing of myself.

I was not to be won, but never have I received so many gifts of flowers, perfume, chocolates etc. from any man. He was unable to understand that I was immune to him, so he continued the barrage of cajolery, flattery, and daily deliveries to my door, each accompanied by appropriate protestations of love. He doubtless felt that I was leading him on, for I accepted them all - except one. For Christmas he gave me an enormous case of *maron glâcés*, an expensive delicacy which I loathe, and told him so, ungrateful little beast that I was.

Jean was certainly a rogue, but he came to a sadder end than he deserved. He opened a second, and highly successful restaurant, 'La Cigale', but was indicted with tax evasion and black marketeering, and ultimately imprisoned. The jail sentence he received was very severe for such minor crimes, especially as much of the testimony against him came from very dubious sources, but I suppose he was guilty.

On his release he returned to Paris, where he opened 'A la Fourchette', the first fast-food bar in the Huitiéme Arrondissement. I often met him when I stopped over, but though I, and many others, showed him that we were true friends who didn't hold his past against him, prison seemed to have taken his joy in life. He had become moody and withdrawn, and there was an underlying bitterness when he would laughingly point to his record and say, "I am a criminal."

I was on my travels when I heard of his death by suicide.

In time I formed my first serious attachment. Major Mohammed 'Tara' Khan was an Indian Army officer engaged in Military Intelligence (though I didn't know that at the time) when I met him at the Grosvenor House Officers' Club. He was tall, rather pale, and came from near Srinagar. He was also extremely handsome, danced exceptionally well and wore his uniform with the utmost panache. We were together whenever possible, but as an affair it had a doomed look to it from the start; we were both living lies, which mix badly with love. He only gave me a truthful account of his army service just before he left for Burma, and that was under duress. Still, we had many happy months together, which is more than was granted to many couples before they were separated, first by distance, then by death. I'm happy to be able to say Tara survived the war and returned to Kashmir.

I've never forgotten my first meal with Tara. He asked me if I would like to eat curry, and rather than admit I didn't know what it was, I airily said, "Oh yes, delicious." We duly repaired to Shaafi's in Gerrard Street, where I found myself the only female in a room full of turbaned Indian military men.

Lal, the waiter and the owner, whom everyone called 'Uncle', went to great pains to advise me what to eat, but when Tara asked me if I would prefer mild or hot, I nonchalantly replied, "I'll eat whatever you eat."

Oh God! I coughed and spluttered, my eyes ran, my nose bunged up, never have I been so ashamed and embarrassed. All the other clients tried not to be seen looking at our table, their politeness was unbearable, though I caught one or two smiles sneaking between Tara and a simply gorgeous-looking Sikh. Poor Tara was very solicitous, and felt he should take the blame, which was nonsense. It was my stubborn determination to look as though I knew everything. Later I came to love Indian food, and for many years during and after the war Shaafi's was a favourite haunt of mine.

A woman 'friend' of mine had taken a real dislike to Tara, and reported him to Special Branch, stating that he was wearing a major's crown and the ribbon of the Military Cross, to which she was sure he had no entitlement. This was a serious charge, and looked more so when the War Office and the Indian Office both denied having an officer of that name and rank. Consequently two men appeared at my home to question me about him.

I was unable to satisfy them, and they obviously suspected me as well. After they had gone, I took advice from my Master (not Claude Dansey, who didn't often deal with part-timers, but an intermediary whose name remains secret) and tackled Tara myself. He was only prepared to give me a telephone number, which I could ring if they called again. Two days after he left England, two more senior officers arrived on my doorstep, in an obviously unfriendly state of mind. They were patronising and threatening at the same time, which riled me to the extent that I became as awkward as I knew how. I knew that I must ultimately hand over the number, but while they patronised, I condescended right back.

I was most incensed by the sneering and smirking way they denigrated me as a woman, and Tara as an Indian, and after they had gone, I made direct contact with Tara's control. From him I got the most courteous reception, a very sketchy explanation, and grateful thanks for being so discreet.

A few weeks later the officer in charge of the investigation came to see me, and we finally established a friendly relationship of which I was glad later on. It more than compensated for the sudden loss of my friendship with the lady who had reported Tara. Whether her suspicions had been aroused by jealousy or racism I don't know, but I suspect the latter. To my surprise I found a great deal of prejudice against the Indian people, all the more inexcusable considering the service they gave the British Army. Theirs was the greatest volunteer force ever raised on behalf of the Empire, and the medals they earned, including several VCs, were hard-won.

Tara was quite typical. He came from a famous military family, and entered the Indian Army as a matter of course. He was expected to serve until the time came for him to take over from his father on the political scene. I was very interested to hear him talk about Indian politics, and the divisions that existed between Hindus and Moslems. After attending several 'Free India' meetings, I reached the sad conclusion that blood would most certainly be shed unless Jinnah, Ghandi and his son-in-law Pandit Nehru could come to terms. Krishna Menon was a fine orator, but Jinnah was a real firebrand and an uncompromising fanatic.

It was during this period of the war that we moved house yet again. Our flat was too small, Anthony had decided to quit farming to try for a commission in the RAF as an interpreter. He was under age, and had been told to re-apply when he was eighteen, so meanwhile he got himself a job as assistant stage manager with Tom Arnold, the impresario.

Mama had always longed for a son of hers to emulate the love of her life, Jack Buchanan, and on one occasion she had taken Anthony to the Palladium, where she enthused over the joys of treading the boards.

"I'll do it, Mummy," he replied. "I'll go for the theatre if that's what you want."

"But darling," Mama said gently, "You need talent for that."

"Really?" Anthony asked, "Where do I buy it?"

Oddly enough, he proved he could manage a touring company, do a song and dance, and generally compete as well as most entertainers in ENSA. But his staying power was limited, and after several months and innumerable liaisons with pretty but unsuitable girls, he left to join the Free French Press Office.

It meant that he was back living at home, so we needed more space. We offered the flat to some friends who had been bombed out, and moved to a house in Trevor Place, Knightsbridge. It had two or three rooms on every floor, stairs, stairs and more stairs, but at least there was space for everyone.

In the basement there was a boiler room, a kitchen that crawled with cockroaches (which terrified me by night), and a couple of empty rooms and a washroom, which we gave over to an elderly woman who had been bombed out. In return for a roof over her head, she kept the yard and the front entrance clean. She was very partial to drink, and any food we didn't use found its way downstairs very quickly indeed.

On the ground floor there was a study and a huge dining-room, ideal for open-house entertaining. We had the Dutch, the Yugoslav and the Polish contingents virtually on our doorstep, so what with the British and French groups, Tara and some of his Indian colleagues, it could be a truly cosmopolitan table. How we managed for food and drink seems miraculous, but each fellow brought something for the pot or the larder shelf and a bottle. 'Make do and mend' has many connotations, and what went into the soups was nobody's business.

On the ground floor we also had a large hall, a cloakroom and loo, and a tiny little strip of garden, very necessary for us, as we took in any animal needing a home. By 1943 we had Toti, a standard poodle, Otto, a German shepherd, Malcolm, a miniature poodle, two Chows and several cats. They all seemed somehow to understand that they must get along together, and amazingly, they did. Cats and dogs shared beds, bowls and us, in that order.

On the first floor there was my music studio, a lovely room where I could study and prepare my work without interruption, and opposite two rooms and a bathroom, which we made over to Anthony. This gave him some privacy, and we were spared some of his girlfriends' twitters. On the second Mama and I had our bedrooms and shared dressing room and bathroom. The top floor had three rooms, kitchenette and bath, which we kept empty until we could find an ideal housekeeper.

I was hankering after a horse; mad as it seems in the context of the time, I wanted to ride, even if only on Rotten Row, so I started looking for stables, of which there were a number in mews in the Knightsbridge area. But before I could consider keeping a horse or two for when I was at home, I needed to find a suitable person to exercise it, look after the other beasts, and be helpful to Mama. Trevor Place was a big house to run, the dogs needed regular walks, shopping and ironing must be done, and this all needed a safer pair of hands than those of our daily, a dear little woman called Mary, who came in for a few hours, and whose chief mania was cleaning the parquet floor of my music room.

"There's nothing like a good polishing to keep your mind off the miseries," was Mary's line, and she believed it. Every floor, every stick of furniture shone like a jewel, but her time was spoken for by a husband and two teenage sons who, as far as I could judge, never lifted a finger to help.

I was still looking for a stable and helper and had a stroke of luck. I found stabling at Montpelier Mews, very close to Trevor Place, and as I was looking it over, I overheard a woman enquiring about work from the mews proprietor. He had nothing for her, and she walked away with a disconsolate air. I noticed she had a small wire-haired terrier with her, and both looked utterly dejected.

I hurried after them to offer my proposition of a rent-free home, a very small salary, no set hours, and a lot to do when I was absent. Could she drive, ride etc?

She could, and would.

Gwen, or 'Knoxie' as I called her, and I have remained friends to this day, and I later spent a lot of happy time with her in California, where she settled after the war.

When she came to London she was going through a very unhappy period. A 'gentlewoman', inexperienced in life, she had spent her youth caring for her parents in Sevenoaks, unmarried and without serious suitors. Her neighbour, Collie Knox, one of the most handsome men imaginable, became a close friend, and when war was declared they decided to pool their resources. Gwen, now on her own, was to sell her house and move in with Collie, but when I met her they were living in a London flat.

What Gwen, in her innocence, had never realised was that Collie had a boyfriend, a young German actor called Wolfe, who had been interned and could only be released into the guaranteed care of a married couple of solid background. Once the plot had worked, and the young man arrived from his sojourn on the Isle of Man, he made himself quite plain in a single sentence.

"There is no place for you here: Collie no longer needs a wife."

It was a terrible shock, and for a while Gwen refused to accept the situation. She had loved Collie for years, and could not believe the ugly truth that lay behind his actions until she had been subjected to sufficient abuse and humiliation for the lesson to sink in.

Another young German was released at the same time as Wolfe, and became aware of the tension. He was not so unworldly as Gwen, and advised her to leave and apply for a divorce on grounds of non-consummation, as being less scandalous than the truth. When we met she had taken the first step, and divorce followed shortly. She set up home on the top floor of Trevor Place, and was a great help, though not as good a horsewoman as I had hoped.

On the impulse of the moment I had bought a bright chestnut mare called Jezebel. She was not an easy ride, but Knoxie showed no disinclination to try her out. "I've ridden for years," she said, "I had my own horse and rode daily."

Fair enough, but the moment I saw her mount I had misgivings. I foresaw trouble when Jezebel put in a couple of quick bucks as she reached the tan of Rotten Row. Before I could call a warning Knoxie was taken for a ride, or bolt, the full length of Rotten Row from Hyde Park Corner to the far side of the Serpentine. I offered a silent prayer (more for Jezebel than for poor Knoxie), and have never felt more relieved than when horse and rider reappeared, at a sedate walk. Knoxie was grey-faced and trembling, but in one piece, while Jezebel was looking cocky and pleased with herself.

Knoxie made life much easier all round. I was away about one week in three, and sometimes longer than should have been necessary because arranging flights was a problem. KLM flew from Lisbon regularly, but tickets were scarce, and this applied to all journeys. Ireland was the easiest place for me, but even so I wasn't always able to arrange my dates of departure and return. It took a load off my mind knowing that Mama was not having to cope alone with the household and her private life - for one thing, I knew which would be placed second.

Mama was making use of a friend's flat in Leamington, and I spent a few days there from time to time, generally to extricate her from some 'wonderful man' who now proved to be no such thing.

I had cause to bless Leamington, because on the night that Coventry was shattered by bombs I had been intending to go there on business. But as Mama was somewhat entangled, I decided to make a flying visit to the flat and give her a good talking-to, a decision that may well have saved my life. I shall never forget the horror of that night, with the reflection of the fires lighting up the skyline.

There were two schools of thought after the Coventry raid. The first was that the city should have been warned, to minimise the appalling consequences of the bombing. But according to the highly-placed minority, whose decision it was, this would have told the Germans that we were reading the ULTRA codes, which must not be divulged. This is one of the great disadvantages of Intelligence. The most valuable information is the most likely to compromise the agent once it is put to use.

The main Czech army camp was in easy reach of Leamington, and on one or two of my short stays I was able to observe them at close quarters, disporting themselves in the Pump Room and various clubs and coffee houses. They were certainly well-mannered for the most part, good-looking, well turned-out and proud of it. Their impact on the local women was considerable, which their British counterparts failed to relish, calling them 'handsome charlies'.

Most people joked about the Italians, and in fact I was reported by a Czech Lieutenant called Smetek who had overheard me defending the Italian soldiers. The gist of my remarks was that they had shown their good sense by being taken prisoner by the Allies instead of fighting for the Germans. This indiscretion was reported to Czech Intelligence, and my old friend Major Pollak warned me to expect yet another visit from Special Branch.

The expected visit duly took place, but this time there were no problems. I explained that my remarks were overheard out of context, and that the report stemmed from an officer with whom I had clashed on several occasions, as I found him very anti-British. He was, in fact, though certainly not disloyal. He was full of military gripes and diatribes about how inefficient and snobbish our army was, how we'd failed to back up the Czechs or the Poles in 1938-9, how we drafted foreign contingents for the dirty work, how we should have opened up a second front to take pressure off the Russians and so forth. I would never have reported such talk normally, but this is what happens if the pot insists on calling the cream jug black!

This incident reinforced my marked preference for the Poles. Compared to them I found the Czechs tough, hard-working and very capable, but very narrow and, unlike the Poles, without much sense of humour. Again, unlike the Poles and Yugoslavs they were fortunate in their losses. True, they were occupied, and Lidice stands out as a monument to their country's suffering, but their actual casualties amounted to no more than 100,000, against the several millions lost by the Poles, and the monstrous devastation suffered by the Yugoslavs.

Our family had scattered. Vivian and Judy were now living with their two sons near Braintree, running a chain of lorry drivers' cafes. Sheila had gone to Canada when Bill was transferred to the Empire Training Scheme, and was starting a family, Pam and James were in Beaconsfield with cats galore and a retinue of ducks, chickens and a goose that adored James and followed him around, Aunt Ethel and Uncle Mac had decided to return to London and taken a flat in Clarence Gate Gardens, Aunt Elsie of the pure and lovely voice was working in the Admiralty Library, Aunt Christine was digging for victory at Buntingford, and Mama's cousin Captain Neville Harvey was on the Admiralty staff where he was chased incessantly by various ladies, though none managed to catch him. He was a wily Welsh widower with two little girls and a special love of Italy, which endeared him to me.

Like all male Morgans he enjoyed a drink, and deeply resented the Welsh Sunday drinking laws, which were widespread in his time, though now confined to a single pocket of Sabbatarian illiberalism. When he and my mother last stayed in Saundersfoot after the war, he was unable to order the lunchtime drinks in the hotel as he and his family were not residents. He blew his top at this, declaring that he had served his country in two World Wars, only to find that on the word of a member of a reserved occupation he was to be denied a dry sherry in the Land of his Fathers.

The waiter suggested that Mama order herself as many sherries as the party needed, and they were solemnly lined up in front of her, to dispense as she chose. It was a flagrant breach of the spirit of the law, and a doubtful observance of the letter, but it saved everyone's face, and the waiter from the verbal asperity and physical danger of Neville's low esteem.

Chapter Eight

Ill-omened Loves

We were frequent visitors to a restaurant in Baker Street called The Dutch Oven. It was owned by a tall, elegant North Country lady called Florence Hunt, who rapidly became a friend of ours, and of all her clients, whom she seemed to know by name. 'Florence' seemed a most unsuitable name for anyone so attractive, and by common consent we renamed her Renza. It was a most delightful eating house, and the food served was beautifully cooked, inexpensive, and copious. My poodle, Malcolm, was a great favourite with Renza, and we nearly always carried home a huge cooked lamb bone from which I cut his dinners. I then boiled the bone down to make soup for ourselves; a sequence of events which could hardly take place anywhere except in England, come war or peace.

It was at The Dutch Oven that Mama fell in love again. She was still full of life, and although no longer slim, very lovely. With her blonde hair, blue eyes, perfect features and teeth she embodied a femininity and vitality which few could resist. In the immediate aftermath of short flings with Leslie Hutchinson (Hutch) Frisco, the owner of a drinking club and 'Butcher' Johnson, the all-in wrestler, she observed a solitary figure.

"Looking so sad, Diana, so very sad." With these ominous words she gathered him up for what was certainly the interlude of his life.

The Canadian Philip Granville was a champion long-distance walker. His mother was a full-blooded Blackfoot Indian, his father was a trapper. Between them they provided him with very little education, but he discovered an inherent and almost miraculous capacity to relieve the pain of the sort of injuries which athletes sustain. He began his walking career purely by chance, but once started he won everything on offer. His ambition was to take an Olympic Gold, but a freak accident prevented him from participating. He had been competing in a marathon when an opponent spiked his heel at an early stage. Philip kept on regardless, and permanently damaged his achilles tendon in the process.

With his career as an athlete ended he came to England, where he established himself as a masseur and physiotherapist in London, and built up a clientéle among sportsmen and women and what would subsequently be called 'beautiful people' - stars like Margot Graham, Michael Rennie, Peggy Cummings, Raymond Lovell and Naughton Wayne. He also looked after many members of the House of Lords, mercilessly condemning their eating habits. He didn't go a bundle on drinking and smoking either, and favoured us with many tirades against the frailties of his patients.

"I told Margot that her body was a gift from God. She has no business abusing it."

I would not have liked to come under his huge hands when he was in an unforgiving mood, though he was by nature the gentlest and kindest of men. Certainly, he was among the nicest of Mama's great horde of swains and lovers - simple, honest and quite incapable of guile. A sophisticated socialite, used to the company of very worldly men, she found in this tall, grave man all the sincerity that is so often missing from the games played between woman and man. He had little to offer her financially. He earned well, but he gave his services free to those who were unable to pay. He had no interest in money, but a natural piety based on the belief that people ought to be good to one another.

Their relationship lasted two years until, like so many very healthy and abstemious people, Philip was diagnosed with cancer of the kidney. He died soon after being admitted to hospital. Mama wept many tears over him. He was a man unlike anyone she had ever known.

Her next full-scale love affair could not have been more different. Oliver Rigold was a very complex, not to say crazy man. He remained a constant factor from 1944 until Mama's death in 1974 and beyond, when he became like an orphaned child to Anthony and me until his own death in the early eighties.

He was an engineer, last of seven children of a Sussex woman and an Austrian Jew, and first met Mama while on leave from the Gold Coast, where he was in charge of an oil-drilling unit. When sober he was one of the most amusing people imaginable, with a zany sense of humour, but he was given to savage drinking bouts which came close to destroying him. Then he was like a man possessed - violent, spiteful and unbalanced. Afterwards he would be abjectly contrite, weeping and begging forgiveness. "Don't be angry with Ollie. You know I don't mean the things I say or do!"

I was disinclined to forgive. He would use the most vile and abusive language, try to smash the furniture, and threaten Mama with a knife. I soon grew to hate him, and told Mama that if he went on spending his leaves with her, I would move out. I wanted her to be happy, but I couldn't take the hysteria that followed his drunken rages; moreover, I feared for her safety.

Oliver suffered from the gruesome combination of religious mania, a mother fixation, and very low sex-drive. Together they created tensions in him that drink alone could release. More than once I threw him out of the house at gunpoint, and had he harmed my mother I would have shot him. But within days he would come crawling back like a whipped puppy, begging forgiveness and weeping like a child.

I was glad his work kept him away for such long periods, but his leaves were correspondingly long, if irregular.

Oliver's bursting into our lives coincided with the turning point of the war. The Russians had rallied and were advancing, the Poles were having to contend with the tragic end of the Warsaw uprising, and the Allied armies were on the move across Europe, slowed as much by shortage of petrol and disagreement in the High Command as the German resistance, desperate though it often was. There were no more air raids, no more V1 flying bombs, with their rackety engines whose cut-out meant they were about to crash on someone near you, no more V2s falling without warning faster than sound, and quite impossible to stop. Planning for peace was becoming a reality instead of a dream, though the price of victory had yet to be paid.

Like most young people, I had survived the war years relatively unscathed. Separation from family and friends had caused disruption and tears for everyone, but there had also been the fun. The war gave the perfect excuse to damn tomorrow and live for the moment.

In retrospect I have come to the conclusion that the war was far worse for the middle and older generations, because not only had they known it all before, they now had to see the flower of the country's youth lose their lives once again in the cause of justice and freedom, so soon after the appalling and unnecessary carnage of the First World War.

By 1944 my travels had virtually ceased, though I still made frequent visits to Dublin. Apart from music clubs, the odd concert and a few broadcasts, opportunities for an operatic singer were rare in England, though Mama and I had become great friends with Rudolph Dunbar, the negro conductor who had been so acclaimed on his Albert Hall début in 1942. He was a very handsome fellow, but he had an arrogant manner which could sometimes ruffle feathers. Mama felt that it masked a deeper insecurity. For a negro to make the grade in any branch of music other than jazz, especially as a conductor, required a great talent, but it also brought him into frequent contact with entrenched racism.

He was very keen for me to do a series of recitals with him, and as he was also an excellent pianist and first-class clarinettist, he had chosen Schubert's 'The Shepherd on the Rock' as our main piece, a lovely work for soprano, pianist and Rudolph.

Unfortunately our proposed concert series fell through and it was then that Walter Susskind and Arthur Hammond, the principal conductors of the Carl Rosa Opera, invited me to join the cast, and Mrs Phillips, who was in charge of the company, showed herself willing to have me either as guest singer or permanent member. Neither was possible, because my other work was still of paramount importance to me, if not to my chief. He was finding little for me to do now, but realised I was hooked on the profession, even though I was only at its perimeter.

For me the grey world of Intelligence had a fascination all its own. Many writers, even those who have been members of the firm, have made critical remarks about the lack of cooperation between services, the disloyalty, backbiting and everlasting rivalry between departments. I cannot deny that these elements existed, but for certain characters the profession offers a kind of haven. In my case it was a protective screen, away from the limelight, where I could enjoy a sense of belonging.

It had also opened my eyes to a political world, and the effect of this devious, complex and fascinating world on European affairs. I was transfixed with a desire to see the war-torn cities and countries of Europe, and my only hope of doing so lay in my remaining within at least the outer echelons of the Service.

Meanwhile I embarked on my second love affair - with a German! I met Baron Gunther von Kettler, only son of a Prussian general, through Gwen Knox. My choice was viewed with disfavour.

"Have you gone mad, Diana? A German, a general's son - have you not noticed? We've been fighting the bastards since 1939."

"Neither Gunther nor his father is a Nazi."

My reply was lame, because I had no idea if Gunther's father was or not. But I knew he came of the sort of family that would despise Hitler's social origins on general principles, and would most likely have Conservative Monarchist leanings.

"What was he doing in England in 1939? Spying?"

"Certainly not. He was visiting friends, and trying to get out of the army."

These words were greeted with disdainful disbelief. "Come off it! Get out of the army - we know he was in a crack regiment!"

"Yes, all you say is true, but remember, although he was interned he was cleared and freed after screening."

I was losing my temper, something I knew could be fatal. I'd only done so once before, and taken a drubbing. It happened right at the start of my duties. Because I was angry I left the room muttering some fairly rude words, under my breath as I thought but evidently not by far enough. The set of my shoulders must have been enough to tell my Master that I had formed an unflattering opinion.

"Come back here - if you have anything to say, say it to my face. Out with it!"

No escape, so I repeated the offending phrase and was dismissed, uncertain whether I was to be thrown out on my ear. Luckily my Master was an unusual man, harsh and tough, but with a sense of humour and a belief that those who worked for him should be free to voice their opinions, however at odds with his own. But I had learned not to overstep the mark. I was too ignorant, and too unimportant, to argue with the experts. Instead I became a 'watcher', and from this angle I found I was able to assess with detachment - the crucial requirement.

My relationship with Gunther was accepted, though without enthusiasm, and only after his background had been exhaustively checked. His experiences had left him very sensitive and vulnerable, which was hardly surprising. His upbringing read like a Grimm's fairy tale, designed to sadden and brutalise his kind and gentle nature. His parents had divorced while he was quite young, and he was only able to see his mother when his father saw fit, which was rarely.

Never allowed to speak unless first addressed by an adult, he spent many lonely years on his father's estate with only a tutor and the servants as companions. He must click his heels, bow to the room on entering or departing, and never turn his back on his father. These were the rules to be obeyed, or else! He told me that the very first time he attended a dinner party someone turned to him and actually asked a question, which so astonished him that he was unable to reply.

Forced by filial duty into a cavalry regiment, Gunther seized on the opportunity of a long convalescence away from home after a riding accident which broke both his knees. He loathed army life, so for him immediate internment in 1939 was a matter for celebration rather than despondency. His worst moment came when the first POWs arrived. High-ranking German officers fell upon him with delight, much to his horror. To find the scion of a famous Junker family imprisoned by the wicked British before he had had the chance to strike a blow for

Fatherland and Führer filled them with sympathy. Little did they know! Gunther kept his own counsel, or he might have been beaten up or even killed as a traitor.

It was difficult for either of us to establish a normal affair. He was recovering from some traumatic experiences: camp life, though not especially arduous, was not easy to adapt to, as any POW will tell you. Add his lack of Nazi enthusiasm or even much feeling for Germany and its ambitions, and Gunther was at a double disadvantage among diehards of the Wehrmacht Officer Corps, and worse still, fanatics for the Third Reich.

He was moody and demanding, whereas I, with my tendency towards remoteness and withdrawal, lacked the understanding he needed. We were both unable to start the sort of quarrel which might have cleared the air, while my refusal to discuss my absences made him suspicious and left me annoyed and aggravated by his insistence on questioning my actions. Yet we had a genuine affection, if not love, for each other, which we never lost. Circumstances forced us apart, but we remained lifelong friends, and might well have married but for the events of 1944-45.

My accident, described later, obviously put an end to our sex-life for a while, but we actually finished over a very silly quarrel. Three of our Chows got into a fight, and I shouted to Gunther to wade in and help me separate them. I was afraid that one or other might suffer injury, and they were powerful, heavy dogs, and not easy to part. We succeeded in the end, but I was angry that Gunther's efforts had been a bit half-hearted. He muttered that he didn't want to get bitten.

"And what about my dogs? If they get a torn ear or similar I can't show them - they're marked for life!"

It was not a reply to soothe wounded male pride. "I see, your dogs' ears are more important than my hands. Of course, scars don't matter on you, or on me either, but the dogs ..."

It made for a very cool atmosphere, which somehow never quite warmed up again.

By now I had two horses installed in the Montpelier Mews stable, which was run by Mrs Smythe, a very kind lady with two horses and a pony of her own. There were two girls to help out, one of whom, Fiona Fraser, was at that time sixteen years old and very pretty. She was also an excellent show rider, and joined forces with Esmée Smythe, who had run a small stud with her mother in Peterborough. Her animals were in first class condition, and I had no qualms about leaving my two mares with her.

Esmée was a sympathetic rider with a genuine love of horses, and looked superb on a side-saddle. She had competed and won many hack classes, and taught pupils under Horace Smith and his daughter Sybil at Cadogan Square and at Maidenhead. She had also doubled for several film stars when they were expected to show equestrian skill they didn't possess, including Ann Todd in 'South Riding'.

Our mutual interests made for friendship, and Mama and I were both pleased to note that Anthony was not averse to courting Fiona, who reciprocated quite openly. He had already been engaged on several occasions, but like Uncle Howard before him, he tended to lose interest and opt out of any serious relationships. We hoped Fiona would not be too badly hurt if he acted in this fashion, but as everyone has to learn from experience, we stood on the sidelines and said nothing.

Air Chief Marshall Sir Trafford Leigh-Mallory, an old friend of Mama's, had very kindly arranged for Anthony to take up duty as an Airforce interpreter, the job for which he was previously considered too young, and Mama and I were both delighted. It meant that he would have a position to maintain, and he would be out of London. His work at Carlton House Terrace with the Free French offered him too many opportunities to frequent sleazy bars, pool-rooms and clubs in Soho and elsewhere, but particularly the French Pub, where he could and did mix with pimps, tarts and black-marketeers.

Whether it was the thought of military discipline that decided him to turn down the opportunity, I don't know. I was away at the time, and returned to London to be greeted with the news that -

"Tony has joined the NAAFI!"

"Mama, you mean the RAF." I was sure she had got it wrong, but no - the ungrateful bugger had played us all false, and refused the King's Commission in time of war.

"Why?" I screeched.

"I want to go across to France, where I can be really useful," was his answer.

His reasoning was beyond me. He could have been overseas with a cushy, commissioned, useful RAF job, instead of which he was going to drive an inglorious NAAFI lorry, dispensing food and drink under conditions of various and extreme discomfort.

Mama was not best pleased either, having pulled strings to ensure preferential treatment for her baby boy. Furthermore, he would have been far more of a national asset in the RAF, since his schooling in France, Switzerland and England had made him fluent in German and

French. We argued to no avail. He had chosen his line of country.

February 1945 saw the accident that interrupted my life and very nearly ended it. A freak fall from my mare Althea left me pinned underneath, then rolled on and trampled. An emergency examination revealed a great deal of internal damage, and over the next six months I underwent much pain, many visits to the operating theatre, transfusions, and all the rest of what is now called 'life-support'.

For poor Mama all the anguish she had suffered watching me take my falls as a child and a teenager came to a head with this disaster. Anthony Charles, the surgeon, was non-communicative, and would only make such statements as "Your little girl is very ill. If penicillin doesn't work, I fear the worst."

When she heard this Mama was so flabbergasted she could only answer. "But who will do the housekeeping, see to the ration books?"

She told me afterward that Mr Charles turned a scornful eye on her, and departed without a word, but as summer progressed and the war ended, they formed a real friendship. What man could resist Mama?

Freddie Peel was my GP, a South African doctor practising in London, always kindly and gentle, and with a droll sense of humour. He would sit by me when I was at a low ebb, holding my hand and saying, "Fight hard, Diana, the worst is over." I think in retrospect that Freddie felt responsible for some of the medical mistakes that were made in my treatment; but the combination of injuries I had made diagnosis and effective treatment very difficult as they interfered with each other. How do you mend a pelvis, spine and crushed tissue simultaneously?

Anthony Charles was quite selfless, and would often appear still in black tie from some formal occasion or other, to stay up with me, willing me through the worst hours of the night. My nurses were truly angels, and I owe my survival just as much to the strength and courage they were able to impart. If anyone was ever kept alive by sheer will power I was, and the power came from those who cared for me through those long, dark weeks.

The experience I find hardest to describe is when I actually succumbed and briefly left the world. Death had stalked me on several occasions, but until this special moment I had clung to life. Now the curtain fell, and I found myself in a peace and tranquillity I have never known before or since. There was neither pain nor fear, just a drifting through space, slowly and serenely towards an arc of light which widened as I approached it. There was no sound, nor did I encounter the glowing figure that has sometimes been reported on these occasions, but I felt a sense of being supported by tender, invisible hands.

Then it was back to the pain, injections, drips and a priest standing by my bed. "You've come back to us, then."

Had I been able, I think I would have screamed. "Why didn't you let me go? I saw Heaven!"

Heaven was denied, and I had to start fighting again, but now it was different. The moment of passing from life into light had taken away all my fear, and now I knew that I owed my mother, and all those who had prayed and fought over me, to recover and take up whatever challenge came my way. One challenge that I would never have to face was motherhood. The internal injuries made that forever impossible. Yet once again, I had been lucky. This news would have devastated many women, but I was and am without maternal instinct. I had other and more pressing worries.

The uncertainty over whether I would be able to take up my singing career again made my convalescence particularly irksome. Two things had been made painfully clear: I could not ride again, and for the present I must leave my home and live in a bungalow or face imprisonment up the stairs of Trevor Place. This decision was an easy one. My dogs, cats and horses were more important than a house, and Mama was able to arrange a quick sale and find The Knowle, a property in Virginia Water that might have been built for us. It was a huge colonial-style bungalow, with wide doors and large rooms, built by an Australian to his own specification. It had seven acres, outbuildings, and at the end of the long drive, a gardener's cottage complete with handyman who came with the tenancy.

The bungalow was perfect for our purposes. It had a central hall, a huge drawing-room leading to the garden, and separate wings on each side of the living-rooms. Mama had a bedroom and bath leading to the garden, and a small spare room which we used as a puppy nursery. On my side I had a large bedroom, a smaller spare room and en suite bathroom, and finally two small staff rooms with bathroom self-contained. Add kitchen, scullery, walk-in larder and access to dairy, and we were complete.

The gardens were a delight, mainly flat, though from the front where the patio extended to the lawn the land fell away very gently towards a small orchard where squirrels raided the walnut tree, however hard we tried to protect the nuts. They were so amusing to watch, we could hardly begrudge them the fruits of their endeavours.

On leaving hospital I paid a sad farewell to Trevor Place, but the prospect of my own smallholding compensated for seeing the sale not only of our home but most of the furniture as well. My accident had cost me dear in pain, and crippled us financially as well. There was no NHS in those days, and I was an emergency, with private surgeons and their teams called in to attend. Still, I was alive, and with Mama was already planning a future which would be different, but not without hope.

We would breed Chows, and perhaps miniature poodles; send the mares to be covered and sell the foals when mature, keep chickens, goats etc. For someone barely able to crawl at this stage, it was a grandiose plan but it buoyed us up and kept depression at bay.

Operation Noah's Ark soon took shape. We joined the Rabbit Club, and went for Belgian Rex and Old English breeds; we joined the Goat Club, and were soon proud owners of several Sanaans, Toggenbergs and Nubians. We also had ducks, hens, cats, and soon eighteen dogs and bitches. What we didn't understand at the time was that foodstuffs for horses, goats, rabbits etc. were still rationed. The beasts must be breeding stock of good quality, and even then the quantity allotted was never sufficient. To get round this mares were allegedly sent to be covered every year, and their phantom progeny registered, so as to get sufficient feed for others to bear healthy foals.

It takes a tremendous amount of work to establish a smallholding. Dog-runs must be made, rabbit-hutches and goat-pens built, horse-boxes and dairy equipment bought. Last but not least, chicken-coops and grassy areas for our hens to scratch around in. We had a hundred White Wyandots - not good table birds, being small, but excellent layers, and delightful characters.

The one great enemy was our cock bird. He would attack anyone, but me in particular. I was slow to react to his sudden pounces, and he obviously knew when I was engrossed in egg-collection. I vowed he'd end in the pot, but he never did - too damned good at his job!

I still had a nurse in attendance, and for help we had a girl who came in daily to do the housework. The gardener/handyman seemed to spend nearly all his time shooting at Bisley, but at least he had the decency to provide for the pot as well. We never enquired where he went poaching, just grabbed whatever came from his bag and cooked it.

As our animal farm grew so fast we took on extra land just outside our boundaries, which qualified us for the help of two German POWs. They were due for repatriation, but because their homes were under Soviet control they had chosen to stay in Britain. They were worth their weight in gold - clean, hard-working, used to farm life and good with livestock. Without them we could never have managed the milking, feeding, cleaning and the mass of paperwork required by the Ministry of Agriculture before we could draw the basic food allowances. Add to that the entries to shows, pedigrees to fill in etc. and our days began at six and ended near midnight.

I had to learn how to milk the goats, and one in particular was a real sod. Mathilda had the greatest character, and was a real charmer - except when being milked. She would wait until literally the last drop had been squeezed from her udder, then whip up her leg and overturn the pail. It developed into a battle of wits and timing, and I was usually placed second.

Other occasional duties were whelping, foaling, and attending the births (usually twins) of the goats, but worst of all were 'killing days', when rabbits, kids and hens were despatched. Mama never appeared until the fell deeds were done, and I only in the beginning, to satisfy myself that the creatures were killed humanely.

Mama, for all her childbearing and experience of life, had never seen animals born, and her first taste of things to come left her shaking at the knees. Shortly after our arrival at the Knowle, Hebe, one of our chow bitches, gave birth late in the evening. I, still pinned in my bed, could do nothing to help, only offer advice. I shall never forget Mama's horrified wail as one pup arrived after the other.

"Diana, it's like pennies from Heaven. How many more?"

Six, by final count, and the joke was that though they looked like chow puppies for the first week or so, the ghastly truth soon emerged. They were not the offspring of our magnificent black chow dog, but of my wicked poodle, Malcolm. We had six unsaleable 'choodles', adorable, but an inauspicious start to our new venture.

For all that, the choodle pups were quite enchanting. Chowists will know that the unique blue tongue is not present at birth, but changes from pink to the lovely smokey colour in a few weeks. In the case of our wriggling, roly-poly black pups, this process began normally but ended with a motley mixture of spotted, striped and multicoloured tongues, together with ears that instead of being pricked upwards turned down like dark rose petals, soft and silky to the touch.

The financial loss of six saleable Chows was a serious blow in the context of the endless demands on our cash, but each of these unusual bastards found a welcoming home, and the only bitch in the litter went to a man confined to a wheelchair. His daughter was looking for a pet to keep her father company, and little Sally was her choice. We had numerous letters over the years, recounting the quite extraordinary relationship that developed between Sally and her crippled master. It was heartwarming, and quite sufficient to offset any disappointment we may have felt.

As a footnote, I must add that Hebe would never mate with another of her own breed - she had obviously lost her heart to Malcolm, who was devoted to her.

Many friends took to coming down for weekends and we encouraged them to fill baskets with home-grown vegetables and fruit. Eggs, goat-cheese etc. were also available, but when it actually came to having to pick their fruit or cut flowers, we found a lack of enthusiasm which left us open-mouthed and in my case, not a little angry. They wanted the produce, but not the effort of collecting it, which was maddening, as Mama and I were always at full stretch, and yet felt that hospitality required that we take on the additional work of doing their picking.

The only blot on the landscape was Oliver. Back from the Gold Coast, his health none too good, he was on a prolonged leave which he intended to spend with us. "Hélène, I need you, I'm not well," was his opening grizzle, and tears would fall at the drop of a hat.

'Gin tears', I called them when, after a couple of days spent in drinking clubs in London he would appear at The Knowle, sick, shaky and forswearing alcohol for evermore. We had many bumpy rides with him. Drunk he was impossible, dried-out he was pathetic, but Mama seemed unable to resist his pleas for understanding.

"I love your mother, Diana," he would tell me again and again.

"Pity you never show it!"

My replies were rarely this polite, but I maintained an armed truce with him as best I could.

Into this melting-pot came my father! He had spent a lonely and miserable war keeping a low profile in a small village high in the Maritime Alps. His deafness had got a lot worse, and he couldn't understand why Mama would not return to France. She gave as excuses my condition at the end of 1945, and our subsequent involvement in animal husbandry, but made no mention of her involvement with a drunken, self-pitying Englishman.

Louis arrived in England in the spring of 1947, with reunion in mind, poor man, but there was to be no rapprochement. Mama had put her roots down, or at least lifted them from Menton. Her horizons were no longer his. All her children were adults; married, divorced, with or without children, but settled in various ways. She had no desire to return to a small French town cut off from all her family, her friends and Oliver.

Louis's arrival created an uneasy atmosphere at The Knowle. My parents had not seen each other for seven years, and Louis had had the worst of it. His war had been uneventful, but full of various privations; Mama had known danger, but also adulation and gaiety. Now she found that there was a language barrier between them, and that Louis's deafness made conversation tiring and stilted. It loosened the ties of mutual interest that had once bound them together, as did his depression, made worse when he heard the verdict of the specialist: there was no operation that could free him from his silent world.

He had no place in our daily farm routines, and we could not vary them for him or anyone else, so he was left on his own. He became bitter and morose. He had expected Mama to pack up, return to France, and take up their old life together. She was determined not to leave England except for short visits. "Why don't you sell the business, and retire?" she suggested. "Come to England!"

It was disingenuous on her part. Louis enjoyed his Estate Agency. He had his *copains*, Brunetti, Gishewauer, and Pierrot and Bourgoint, his partner. He had the Casino, the restaurants where he was a valued customer, his nieces and the priests. He could never have uprooted himself, as Mama was fully aware. She had no wish to hurt him, but she could not imagine life in Menton without me and Oliver.

During Louis's stay we had to shift Oliver out of the guest-room and into a bedsit in London, where he spent his time visiting drinking clubs and making abusive phone calls - to me, as I would not have him hurling insults down the phone at Mama. On his drying-out days, the calls would become lachrymose, with him begging forgiveness and vowing undying love for Hélène, 'my angel of mercy'.

It was a hellish three weeks. Apart from the unspoken words of disappointment and reproach, Louis's appetite was a further irritant. Not that we were short, or begrudged him the food. Far from it; we had home-produced fruit, chickens, vegetables, rabbits etc., but we were always so busy that meals must be grabbed in passing at odd hours. The animals came first, and often we would all meet together - German boys, the daily, kennel girl and family at the same table - for a meal of soup, baked potatoes, vegetables, and a hunk of bread and cheese, washed down with numerous pots of tea, mid-afternoon.

This was anathema to my father. Lunch should be at 12.30, with adequate time to savour the menu, and dinner should be served at 7.30 for 8.00. During the war he had perforce endured several years of poor eating, but he was not prepared to join us in our uncivilised habits. The table must be set, wine served at the correct temperature, a meal of at least three courses consumed with due formality, with coffee and brandy to follow *dans le salon*.

Bloody boring, and we hadn't the time!

Louis left England, never to return.

Meanwhile Anthony sprung another surprise. This was not unusual in itself, except that it took the form of getting married. There was neither warning nor discussion - the first we knew was seeing a picture of him with his bride. Fiona? No - Esmée Smythe, a woman a good ten years his senior, and with a certain disquieting vagueness in her background. They telephoned us once the deed was done, but Mama could hardly be expected to show much enthusiasm for a marriage celebrated in secret, or invite the happy couple to visit.

Anthony was just twenty-one, with no formal or professional training, only a talent for turning his hand to what lay in its grasp, and Mama felt that he had fallen into a trap. Certainly, a few years later when he gave his reasons for marrying he mentioned that he was lonely when we left London, and felt 'abandoned'. It was no good reason to take on the responsibilities of a married man, though in fact Esmée took most of the decisions. Unfortunately for both of them, the first was that they should take up the insecure lives of cinema 'extras and stand-ins' rather than live in the country and run a stables.

This marriage caused a breach in the family which lasted several years. I was sorry about this, just as I was sorry about Louis, but my concern was always for Mama. No two people could be less alike in our habits of mind, but I can never remember an angry word passing between us. Not once did she question my decisions, or try to push me in my career.

She was supportive, but never demanding. Our only serious disagreements were over her lovers.

I thought her choices were often unsuitable, and she could see in all of them virtues that I could not. She kept her own counsel about the men in my life, but then there was much less to talk about. Until we came to Virginia Water I was so much on the move that my romances rarely flourished. Mama liked Tara Khan, though she and Gunther had reservations about each other. I think she found my flirtations amusing, though she took me to task for being 'cruelly off-hand'.

"You encourage them, then drop them flat - a Morgan to your fingertips. You must not be unkind."

Dear Mama! I have neither your patience nor your kind heart - never had. If I got bored, that was it. Open the door and walk off. Simple.

No sooner had Louis given up and gone back to France than Oliver was back, but luckily Mama's trip to New York to join Pam and James coincided with his return to an oil-rig in some ghastly part of the Middle East, where he could offset his bouts of drunkenness with bouts of religious mania.

I called it 'trying to buy his passport to Heaven', with a rudeness I don't regret. It was impossible to feel pity for him - at any rate I found it so. His habit of blaming everyone else for his lapses infuriated me, and I feared the effects his violent temper might someday have on my mother.

Little could I guess that in his old age he would become virtually a dependent on my brother and myself, not so much financially as spiritually. He was alone, sad and in poor health, and we could not turn him away. Perhaps I'd mellowed by that time, though I still had a name for travelling by broomstick.

Mama leaving for New York brought a lot of excitement, to which was added a visit from a Spanish baritone with whom I had sung in Lisbon early in the war. Raimondo Torres and I were strongly attracted to each other, but he had a wife and I had my principles (then). The San Carlo Opera Company had been invited to Covent Garden, Beniamino Gigli and his daughter, Rina, were to perform in 'La Boheme', and Raimondo was taking several roles. He had found out my address from a colleague in London, and came to see if I was fit enough to re-start my musical career.

I hadn't sung a note since my accident, and I dreaded the horrible sounds that might emerge when I dusted off my vocal chords, but there was no escape. Raimondo stuck himself to the piano and ordered me to sing the duet we had performed together, as Rosina and Figaro from 'The Barber of Seville'.

Apart from a few crickles and crackles in my top notes we cruised through it. My breathing had got slack, but my voice was supple and fluid, the runs and roulades came easily, and after a couple of try-outs I was told to come to London and audition for the company before it returned to Italy.

There I sang for Alberto Erede, a first-class musician who later became one of Italy's finest opera conductors. He advised me to travel to Milan and start a year of hard study, not only to get my vocal capacity back to its best, but also to learn that notes alone are not enough.

My capacity to learn and sing anything at all in the bel-canto repertoire was not lost on Erede, or indeed other conductors. A very extensive range, a naturally developed chest voice and extreme agility were apparent whenever I indulged my joy in singing. Anatole Fistulari once asked me who had taught me to trill so beautifully. I remembered looking at him blankly. "Nobody," I replied. "It's not difficult."

Nor was it. I loved cadenzas, I felt like a bird uncaged, abandoned to flight, untutored and truly ignorant of the vocal technicalities as I was. To Maestro Erede this was a dangerous path for a singer as young as I had been at the time of my début.

"You must learn, Diana, you must understand not only the words and phrasing but the demands. You must be in control of your technique."

All the coaches with whom I worked, and who gave me so much of their expertise, recognised that I had a natural talent. 'Born to sing', as they put it, with much truth if no great originality. I valued all they taught me, and recognised their kindness, but they could not wish upon me the one ingredient I lacked - ambition.

"Remember, Diana," Erede said (he was a gentle, kindly man), "you are a very pretty creature, and young, so many faults are forgiven; but five, ten years from now, you will be judged on your art, your use of voice, your musicianship." I knew his advice was good, but how could I leave the little farm and the creatures?

Once again, circumstances forced the issue. My two German lads were being sent home, my kennel girl got pregnant and decided she must marry the first man she could catch as she couldn't catch the father. (In fact she married an unsuspecting boyhood swain.) Then Mary the daily was needed at home to nurse her mother who had broken a leg. Faced with so many urgent decisions, I called on an old farmer friend for advice.

"Give up, Diana, you can't make it pay. I doubt that you can continue working all the hours you do unless you get good hands to help, and they cost too much. Get out now."

It was an unpalatable truth. Neither Mama nor I could bear to sell stock to people we didn't know or like. Our puppies had to go to well-vetted homes, and this took time and didn't always command the highest prices. Wages, feedstuffs, and general overheads were all too high, and our money was running out. Very sadly we set about the parting of the ways.

Horses, goats, rabbits and hens went for sale, the dogs dispersed. The Chows went to a well-known breeder from whom we had purchased our first stud dog. We gave the two poodle bitches to friends. Poised on the edge of a new adventure, we nonetheless took two Chows, one cat and a poodle back to our original flat in Luxborough Street. There we had a young Irish girl, Bridie, who had been invalided out of the army with TB and wanted a job as housekeeper where there were a few animals. Connie Collett of Barwick Kennels had recommended her, and as our flat was now back in our hands we left her in charge and departed for Milan.

It was not my only new beginning that year. In London I had fallen in love again, and begun an affair that was to last several years. He was entirely unsuitable, a married man with two children, a noted philanderer, but a famous and magnificent baritone. It was serious, but he was based in Rome and things would be difficult. Aside from that, I had my more creditable secret desire. I still wanted to explore the war-shattered countries of Poland, Yugoslavia and Germany.

Mama, 1941

Me in 1941

Myself on Onyx and Beckley on Astrid, with Rippy

A portrait of myself done by A Mendelsohn

*Me swimming in the sea at Menton
– my feet are touching the bottom!*

*With family and friends at the lunch party given after the marriage of Danielle
de Rosso in December 1967*

Mama and myself with chows Gintee and Boo

Mama with Lili and Boo in the pram after Lili's accident

*My final curtain call
on stage, in a concert
at the Wigmore Hall in
1962*

*Myself with friends at
St. Agnes on the Côte d'Azur*

Mama with Peter Coke and his mother Connie, in Monte Carlo

My father Louis, shortly before his death

*The village green
at East Dean –
the view from our
Restaurant
Grimaldi*

*A recent picture of
my brother Anthony*

*Me and my cats
up on the roof
garden of the
restaurant*

Chapter Nine

Milan

Milan is the centre of North Italian industry, and like the rest of the north, looks down on everything from Rome southwards as being 'not properly Italian'. Like Turin, it was in 1948 full of militant trade unionists. Wildcat twenty-four hour strikes affected everything, especially telephones, railways and taxis, or so it seemed to me, and all services, especially the lifts, were likely to sprout 'Out of order' notices.

La Scala was no exception, although for different reasons. Lack of funds delayed the opening, and it was common for leading singers to demand payment in cash before leaving their dressing rooms.

Mama and I installed ourselves in the Hotel Primo Scala, opposite the Opera House. We had a twin-bedded room with bath, and a tiny entrance lobby. Breakfast was served to us, but there were no other meals, and it was forbidden to cook for oneself. We were very short of money; rigid exchange controls were in force in England, and though Louis helped out as much as he could by sending occasional packets of cash, my earnings were still negligible. Victor de Sabata had arranged free study for me under Maestro Ruffo, but I still had my living expenses, principally rent on the room.

In our straitened circumstances Mama and I had to plan our daily expenditure very carefully, which she found a dreadful burden, but with which she coped extraordinarily well. Having bolted down our continental breakfast, she would go shopping for our supper. By gesticulating, pointing, and adding an 'o' to the end of every word, she always ended up with what she wanted. The shopkeepers beamed on her, and ensured that *la bella signora* was served with the best ham, cheese, bread, butter, tomatoes and fruit.

We cooked on a tiny camping stove which, together with two cups, cutlery for two and a can and bottle opener, we had smuggled into the hotel. There we concealed it in one of Mama's hatboxes in the wardrobe. Suppers were eaten with guilt and giggles.

A stroke of luck gave us excellent lunches. Victor de Sabata, who also lived in the Primo Scala, introduced me to Guido Cantelli, a young conductor who had graduated from being his protégé to the only real contender to replace him when he stood down. He was a brilliant musician, a most handsome man, and a genius with the orchestra. I met him again in one of La Scala's corridors, and he asked me how I was settling in. In the course of conversation he mentioned a small café restaurant that he could recommend highly if I wanted a good cheap meal. He had advised a number of young *cadetti* to make use of it, as it was hard by the Opera House, and meant they had no excuse for arriving late at classes.

"Tell Stephano I sent you," he said in parting, and this introduction saved our bacon on more than one occasion. Stephano was one of the owners, and acted as barman and waiter, while his brother, Cesare, worked in the kitchen. He took us to his heart, and whenever possible we took lunch there. We had pasta and salad, mineral water and coffee.

After a few visits Stephano suggested we eat an escalope Milanese or Osso bucco, and I had to come clean and explain that our finances could only run to the cheapest dishes. He was horrified, and bolted off to tell his brother, returning with a fistful of lire.

"You take what you need, you eat what you want - if Maestro Cantelli sent you here, he thinks you're a good singer. You must eat well to sing well - we'll look after you - how much money do you want?"

We were overwhelmed by this generous gesture. It was trust and faith, offered by two total strangers, themselves working all the hours God sent to make a living for themselves and their families.

"Stephano, listen." I told him how much we appreciated his kindness, but that we could manage providing we kept to our budget.

"No, no, signorina, it is not right. You eat what you wish, you pay only for pasta - you and your Mama. Holy Virgin! My brother and I wish for you to enjoy yourselves, eat well, keep healthy, and sing like an angel!"

It took a lot of gentle persuasion to make Stephano accept that we truly enjoyed pasta and salad, but every now and again we would eat an 'experimental' dish that he specially asked us to try. More than once I borrowed from him to pay our hotel bill, repaying him once I had earned a few fees or when money came from France. It was a giddy balancing act, which I feared would upset Mama, but not at all - I think she found it amusing, and a challenge.

"Darling," she would burble, "I've managed on less money today, and bought a few extras."

I would sometimes wonder if the delicatessen owner she used gave her a discount, he was always paying her compliments - *la bella Inglese*, her blue eyes, her blonde hair, her chic - quite obviously entranced him.

My lover, whom I do not intend to identify except as 'Franco', was based in Rome and wanted me to join him there, but this was impossible for several reasons. My coach was at La Scala and Alberto Erede, with typical generosity, had offered me the chance to study some modern works with him, again free of charge until I was earning some decent fees. They included Pizzetti's song-cycle, 'Tre Canzoni' and works by Malipiero and Ghedini, as well as Debussy and my best-loved song-cycle, Ravel's 'Scheherazade'.

These things aside, I wasn't keen on living very close to Franco's family. The world of opera is gossipy, and I had no intention of creating a scandal or hurting his wife beyond what his neglect must inevitably entail. In retrospect, my scruples were futile, because Franco spent two days a week at La Scala, and our names got linked, for all our discretion - well, mine, anyway. Franco was possessive, and let his jealousy fuel the tittle-tattle. If I came back half an hour late from a lesson, he would round on me with "Where have you been? What have you been doing?"

At first I would react with hurt pride; I did not regard it as a compliment to be distrusted. But after a while I saw the possibility of repaying him in his own coin. "I've been indulging in misconduct."

"Where? With whom? That bloody Spaniard, I suppose."

Franco was referring to the baritone, Raimondo Torres, with whom he was not the best of friends, but I was, truly, 'just a good friend' of his. I was certainly not prepared to stop seeing him.

I had other friends in Milan, including Vittoria Palombini, a mezzo soprano from La Scala who had a very handsome lawyer husband, and a girl a few years younger than myself, Carla Manzoni, whose father held an important position in the Fiat Group. The family lived in luxurious style and gave delightful parties. It was all very formal, with a white-gloved butler, and uniformed maids bobbing about in truly Victorian fashion; if you wanted a glass of sherry it would be served on a silver salver by an obsequious footman. It came as rather a shock to Mama and myself after our rough wartime standards. We had lost the art of gracious living, and it took a while to return to a pre-war frame of reference.

Time hung heavy on Mama's hands in Milan. My studies kept me away from her, as did my lover, but the Manzonis kindly took her into their circle, with the predictable but happy result that she very soon found herself being courted by a charming and distinguished lawyer, Enrico del Vecchio. He was elderly but still very attractive, widowed, and best of all, spoke perfect English. This was a boon, because Mama had barely three words of Italian. Carla was also fluent in English, her parents and many of her friends less so, but still competent. French was rarely heard, which surprised me so near the border, but Mama was much relieved, having spent nearly seven years without having to do battle with a foreign tongue. Now she found herself mixing with many Italians, and able to make herself understood.

Carla was going through a rather unhappy time when I first arrived in Milan. She was madly in love with a man whom her family regarded as unsuitable. "I don't care, Diana," she would tell me over coffee at Biffi's, in the wake of the latest row, "I will not give up seeing Giorgio to please my father, and he can rant and rave as much as he likes."

Carla was her father's pet. Her two brothers were expected to conform to his plans, but she was granted self-expression. She gave full vent to her naturally rebellious character, arguing the toss with her elders just like a certain girl from Menton. That girl had now grown older and a little wiser. I feared she was storing up heartache for herself, because I had heard on the grapevine that her beloved Giorgio was already married but had deserted his wife in Calabria a couple of years previously. Maybe the Manzonis knew about this, but hadn't wanted to hurt and alienate their daughter by telling her in case it was only a rumour. If so, it was not my intention that she would learn it from me.

Mama and I would sometimes lay bets with each other as to which of us would get the most muttered flattery as we walked down the Galleria. By mid-day all the cafés and sidewalks were full of men, with hardly a woman in sight as we trotted off for lunch. It was really quite funny. I came to the conclusion that unless you were positively ugly, every Italian male felt duty-bound to make a pass at you. I won more points for my big green eyes, but Mama won more with her golden hair. Not bad for a woman nearer sixty than fifty, and who had borne six children (not to mention miscarriages) besides.

Of course, such street pleasantries were never heard in the Manzoni circle, which was very correct.

There has never been anything to surpass a first night at La Scala. There were the most beautiful women, soignée, coiffed, in elegant gowns and wonderful jewellery. The Opera House was decorated in white, gold and scarlet, with valets in black coats, gold chains and knee-breeches showing the audience to their seats, flower garlands hanging from the boxes, a wonderful sight, and quite awe-inspiring from the stage.

It was a world of its own, with costumiers, set-builders, make-up artists,

Maestri, practice rooms, a vast orchestra pit, and a huge orchestra, who enjoyed teasing us by pretending they could see up our skirts when we were on stage. As I always wore a mass of frilly petticoats (though never any knickers) I felt anything belonging to me would be pretty well obscured from a worm's (or clarinettist's) eye view, but it was all good-humoured. Classes were less so; some of the singers being coached there, for all their glorious voices, were rather stupid, and cultivated the sort of egos that they imagined were suitable for the prima donnas (of both sexes) that they hoped to become.

I was fortunate in my teachers. Spencer Clay in London, Ruffo and Erede in Milan, all three quiet, gentle men who never raised their voices. With them my work could progress in the calm atmosphere I needed, for I hated the explosive tempers that so many of my fellow artists made their trademark. It was their nature, and they meant little malice and no harm, but I found it wearing. It proved my father right - I hadn't the Italian temperament.

Over the months it was my great good fortune to be able to cover for several sopranos, among them Mafalda Favero who with her husband Feruccio Tagliavini were favourites of mine. They were both fine singers, stylish and elegant, and I was able to understudy the role of Suzel in Mascagni's 'L'Amico Fritz', an opera they had made very much their own. Separately beautiful, their voices fitted and blended to perfection - there must be many who, like me, remember their exquisite singing of the 'Cherry Duet'.

Another remarkable soprano, Margharita Carosio, was nearing the end of her career, and again I was on standby in case she was unable to fulfil her contract in Trieste. The Teatro Verdi is a delightful house, and I had high hopes (and frantic stage fright) of performing there. As it happened Carosio sang both her Mimi and her Violetta with her customary skill, and my only appearance was in a concert hall, where I sang an aria from 'Il Piccolo Marat', another little-known gem of Mascagni's.

A pet singer of mine was the tenor, Giacomo Lauri Volpi, no longer young by then, and I have to admit, past his prime; but what a man! So handsome, and the best Manrico in 'Trovatore' I'd ever heard. Tito Schipa, the most elegant singer of his day, used to tease me, and say I only enjoyed beefcake tenors. I certainly loved big voices, and good looks were not to be sneered at either. It was the dark timbre of voices like Ramon Vinay's amazing Otello, and the baritone Gian Giacomo Guelfi that appealed to me - the Caruso quality, a rich, velvety sound foreboding tragedies to come. I loved murder, mayhem, and star-crossed or unrequited loves, so that I never quite appreciated the talents of those who sang the leads in 'Don Pasquale', 'Il Barbiere' or 'Gianni Schicci'.

Mariano Stabile took me very much to task for not enjoying 'Falstaff', regarded by most musicians as Verdi's greatest work. I admired it, but it didn't delight me. I make no apology for my taste now, nor did I then.

Eugene Conley, the American tenor who made his début at La Scala while I was in Milan, and John Lannigan, an Australian whom I'd met in London when he was singing at the Stoll Opera for Jay Pomeroy, both had light voices, and excellent singers though they were, I could never thrill to their sounds when set against a truly dramatic tenor singing 'Cielo e mar', or a baritone like Guelfi's rendering of the 'Credo'. They could send shivers down my back.

An amusing incident took place when Eugene Conley found himself facing the demands of the official claque. Ettore Parmigiani, who organised the claque, explained the tradition, and pointed out the many benefits to be derived from contributing to such a time-honoured institution, but Conley was not minded to submit to the demands of what he regarded as a rival trade union. I hoped for his sake that common sense would prevail, but I heard that he had tried his luck, with dire results. His entrances were booed, his arias were punctuated with catcalls. Fortunately it was only a matinée début, and after that he learned his lesson. Joseph Hislop had defied the official body as well, to the detriment of his career. The claque could not only ruin an opening night, they could influence critics as well.

There were also supposed to be maverick claques, allegedly organised by factions favouring certain singers and operating against their rivals, but I never encountered any of them, and don't know if they really existed.

Mario Labroca, who was artistic director of La Scala, told my friend Germaine Lubin that the official claque was integral to the world of opera, but she, being French and in any case much in demand for Wagnerian roles, took a dim view of being expected to pay for such a service.

"Diana, I pay my agent, my dresser, my manager, my pianist etc. etc. But I am paid to sing, not to maintain an applause machine, which I do not need."

Germaine was a great star, so I didn't like to say to her, 'Better do it in Italy, or else.' I myself plucked up the courage to ask Antonio Ghiringhelli if it was necessary for all to shell out for the claque, and received no response but a half smile, which I took to mean 'Yes'. I got the same answer, though more explicitly, from Mario del Monaco,

Paolo Silveri, Luigi Infantino and Raimondo Torres, who all said it was a tradition, and one must toe the line.

Franco was getting to be more and more in demand, and had signed up for a tour of New York, Chicago and San Francisco, before setting off for a season at the Teatro Colon in Buenos Aires.

"You have one year, Diana, in which to decide whether to come with me or not."

It was an ultimatum. What was I to do? For all his marital ties, Franco and I had a very strong bond. He could be one of the sweetest characters I've ever known, when I wasn't teasing his jealousy, and we could laugh together as well as love each other. But this was Italy, where divorce was out of the question, and in any event, I could not have let him leave his family. The children were of the utmost importance to him, and as I could never have given him any myself, it would have been doubly unfair to split his marriage.

I had started the affair knowing perfectly well that Franco was married. For that I can be criticised, and I accept it. In fact I had never expected it to last; Franco's reputation as a womaniser was equal to his reputation as a singer, and both were growing, so I had seen myself as a passing fancy. Moreover, I was not unhappy to be regarded as such. I was not looking for a permanent relationship - I could bring nothing permanent to one. I was in a kind of No Man's Land. I had been burying my head in the sand of my smallholding, looking no further than the day. Then, suddenly, everything happened at once - Torres and Erede, Milan, the world of opera, a married lover. None of these had been in my scheme of things, but now I had to face up to the future and I remembered another narrow world where I had once had a part - Intelligence, with all its curious inhabitants.

While I was trying to envisage some sort of future, I heard from a Yugoslav whom I had met a few times in London in the later part of the war. I knew little of him, other than that he was a Communist and close to Tito, whom he idolised. Vlado Matacic even seemed to idolise Stalin as well, at that time. I don't know how he knew I was in Milan; he was secretive, but he admitted that he had come to Italy to meet Togliatti, the leader of the Communist Party, now that he was back from his wartime sojourn in Moscow. What they were cooking up together was not my business, but I suspect it was significant. Milan was a Communist stronghold at that time, and I must confess that the current extremes of poverty and desperation in the south, when contrasted with the displays of wealth I had seen in the north, made me more sympathetic to his dream of equality and social justice for all.

Vlado also brought me news of Marko Pavicic, and it wasn't good news.

Marko had returned to Yugoslavia to rejoin his parents. He found his father had been killed, while his mother and uncles were under something close to house arrest in their villa at Rab on the Adriatic. Their conditions were harsh enough, but Marko himself had been sentenced to several years in jail for the 'crime' of serving his country - but as a loyal subject of King Peter's Government-in-Exile, rather than a Communist partisan.

"What can I do for him?"

Vlado's reply was direct. "Nothing - don't try. Our country is like Poland, like Hungary - in turmoil."

Why had he sought me out? I was no longer naive enough not to suspect an ulterior motive.

"You could draw attention to what is happening. The Americans are helping Nazis to evade justice, the Vatican is protecting war criminals. The French and British, if not actively conniving, are turning a blind eye. You could alert the press in England and France. Why should millions of people who fought for justice and freedom be betrayed?"

I had no power to alert the press in any country, as Vlado must have been well aware. "Perhaps you know some people of importance?" he suggested.

I didn't. Since 1945 I had first been too ill, then too preoccupied with other things to keep up with anyone influential. I hadn't cut all the threads to my wartime chiefs, but what little contact I retained was peripheral. Yet as I listened I felt a buzz of excitement begin to stir deep inside - Poland, Yugoslavia, Germany itself beckoned. Even if I could do nothing, I could see for myself if Vlado was telling the truth.

But if I did, then what? I was twenty-seven years old, with a promising career, and one which gave my mother untold pleasure and a modicum of financial security. Could I walk away from that, evading my responsibilities, just to travel into the unknown heartlands of devastated Europe? And what could I do when I got there?

My mind was troubled and unclear, but as had so often happened before, it was Mama who made the decision possible. "Darling, would you mind terribly if I went back to London?"

The suggestion came out of the blue. "Oliver." It wasn't a question.

"He's not at all well, back from the Gold Coast on sick leave - Bridie has just written." She handed me the letter.

Bridie made it plain that she could cope with the flat, the animals etc. but not Mr Rigold. He was as usual drunk one day, ill the next, and had been thrown out of his bedsitter. He turned up immediately at

Luxborough Street with his baggage and his tale of woe, which was nothing new, but I knew Mama would not be happy until she could be on hand to curb his excesses. In any case, I wanted to spare little Bridie from having to deal with one of his furies. She was a devout Catholic, and an aspect of Oliver's religious mania was a deadly hatred of Papists.

Mama went back to England, and I agreed to visit her when my course was over. I had in any case to arrange a discussion with Ibbs and Tillet about my first London recital at the Wigmore Hall, which was getting close. Franco was torn between delight at being able to claim all my free time, and jealous tantrums when I showed signs of having a life of my own. His own was very complicated; he was a serious artist, a diligent worker with an ever-increasing repertoire, travelling, singing, philandering wherever possible, keeping his Roman household calm, and me in Milan. It was more than enough for anyone, and I was expected to fit in with it.

Instead I applied for a visa to Titoland. The Yugoslav border wasn't far, and I had Vlado to smooth my way.

A young singer, seeking to bring a programme of folk songs in Welsh, Irish, French etc. for the benefit of students, who would find a marked similarity between the cadences and sentiments of each country's longing for self-expression: as a ploy it worked, and musically it was true. The plaintive, and often sad, sounds of folk music had a uniform voice, just as folk dancing has a uniform lilt. Many Irish friends of mine held the view that repression, in any context, produced the need for expression through song, and certainly I found as I travelled in the Eastern Bloc that every country's folk music could be easily interpreted and absorbed into the culture of western Europe.

I crossed into Yugoslavia with some trepidation, but Vlado made my first few days there enjoyable, and introduced me to several useful contacts. A conductor from the Zagreb Opera showed interest, the Head of Broadcasting in Titograd agreed that I should record a series of Welsh and Irish songs, and I returned to Milan with my tail up. It would be a piece of cake, if I could only decide which way to go. I had friends and acquaintances in several countries, so all I needed to do was call on them.

A very heavy cold which I could not throw off made a few days' break from singing essential, and on the spur of the moment I called Stockholm. Lars Gunnarsson, an old contact from the Red Cross, was surprised to hear me suggest a visit, but very cordially agreed to put me up for a few days. Much to Franco's fury, I set off.

I knew that once in Sweden Lars could help me get the ferry from Malmo or Ystad, to Gdynia or Gdansk, but it was essential to enter Poland with neutral papers. The country was still in upheaval, but it drew me. Many of my Polish friends had returned to their country after the war feeling disillusioned and betrayed by the Yalta and Potsdam treaties, and wondering if any of their families had survived the successive invasions of the Panzers and the Red Army.

I was determined to reach Warsaw, whatever it took and whatever the consequences, and even if I could only stay one day. I wanted to see the ruins, and if possible find out through the Polish Red Cross what had happened to certain friends of mine who I feared must have faced the worst imaginable homecoming. There was neither justice nor stability in Polish politics at that time, and jail or worse could have been the fate of people in the *Armia Krajowa* and the Polish Forces in the west.

Lars, always a very quiet and reliable man, grinned at me when I asked him if he could get me into Poland. "You are quite mad, Diana."

"Only for a few days, Lars, I want to see things for myself."

I explained my predicament, how I was torn between my need to earn, my desire to spend some time in eastern Europe, how I wanted to follow my singing career but at the same time be free to follow my nose. I knew Lars could open certain doors for me if he chose.

"For what purpose? What do you want to do? The war is over."

"Is it? Or has it begun again, in a political sense?"

"You have been listening to Cold War voices, Diana, be warned. Politics are even dirtier than conflict."

I could see Lars was serious, but he hadn't turned me down flat.

"I'll take you into Poland for a few days, I go there regularly and you can pass as my wife. But think of the journey as being one undertaken in wartime. The situation is perilous and the Stalinists have taken off their gloves. They give no quarter."

"I've been in Milan, Lars, there's a lot of talk from the Communists about changing the face of Europe. I've made a contact in Yugoslavia, and I want to get in there and find some friends. But first - "

"Hold on! Before you go rushing into Communist countries without having any plans, stop and think. Do you want a career or do you want a cover? If the latter, whom will you work for, assuming anyone is interested in employing you?"

I had no answer to this. I had given the question no thought. "I don't think anyone would offer me a job, Lars. As you say, the war is over, the professionals are in charge, and I'm told amateurs have no part any longer."

I felt his eyes on me, shrewdly appraising, before he replied, "Hardly an amateur now, Diana, you learned quickly, you listened carefully. There might be an opportunity for you as a freelance 'cutout' [trade slang for an observer or informer]. Would you be interested?"

Without a moment's hesitation I leapt in, stupid idiot that I was. Mama, home, career - all were pushed aside at the thought of covering the eastern countries that were already showing signs of the ideological war to come, even if relations had not yet frozen into open hostility. "When can we leave for Poland?"

"Give me a couple of days to arrange things. Remember, you'll travel as Christianne - and you'd better notify Milan of the delay in your return."

That was no problem, my cold still offered an excuse, so they suggested I take another week before going to the doctor for a check-up. There was no problem about taking Christianne's place either. Theirs had been a very turbulent marriage, and in 1945 she had returned to France. Lars was now living with a Norwegian Red Cross worker.

I had never felt so scared in my life as on the ferry from Ystad to Gdynia. The sea was rough, and I felt sick, which made my nerves worse. Once we were docked we found the place teeming with soldiers and police, and scenes of destruction wherever we looked. The buildings were pitted and scarred, and the people, grey-faced and undernourished, seemed constantly to be moving like wraiths from place to place, looking for food or a place to sleep. The children looked haggard and prematurely old, the old people behaved like ill-used children, and I was only on the fringe of devastated Poland.

'One vast killing field'. I remembered Marian Rejewski's words about his own country. The Poles in the West had known about the concentration and extermination camps that had spread like a blight throughout their country. Several million of their own men, women and children had fallen victim to starvation, disease and murder (with or without accompanying torture). Oswiecim, which west Europeans call Auschwitz, became the major site of Hitler's 'Final Solution to the Jewish Problem in Europe'.

Chaos reigned, and although the Red Cross and other agencies were trying to recreate something like order and normality, it was an epic task. The few days I spent with Lars left me shocked and shaken, but I was even more determined to find a way which would help me return to the 'Killing Fields', and find out if possible how much truth lay in a rumour which had been circulating since the end of the war. This was that the crimes of certain 'useful anti-Communist' Nazis were being covered up, and they were being given new identities and safe conduct out of Germany, thereby evading Polish, Yugoslav and Russian requests for their extradition.

Lars's view of this was forthright. "Go back to Milan, Diana, advance your career, you cannot alter anything. The big powers will do as they wish, nothing can stop them."

I should have heeded him. He understood politics far better than I, and the Machiavellian deals which would allow SS and Gestapo men to be reinstated in the Security Services, never mind judges, bankers and industrialists - all guilty as Hell, though without the same physical involvement - who were 'de-Nazified' and confirmed in their positions of authority.

Lars also foresaw the Cold War, as clearly as he could foresee me blundering into dangerous situations with no better protection than my childhood belief that *Le Bon Dieu* would always protect me. I had hung onto this, even though by this time I was little more than nominally a Catholic. On this slender basis, by the time I returned to Milan I had decided that my future lay outside the world of opera. I was still unsure how to go about it, and I said farewell to all my friends at La Scala with deep regret. All would leave gaps in my life. I had listened to so many brilliant performers - Callas and di Stephano, Tagliavini, Corelli, the list is endless. I would miss those glorious sounds, the thrill of being backstage, waiting for the curtain to rise, the applause and flowers, the flow of adrenalin as the houselights dimmed, but in my heart I knew I wasn't coming back. Where I would go, and how I would get there I still didn't know, and Franco did nothing to make my departure any easier.

He sulked for days, and picked quarrels whenever he could. "You are leaving me, you don't love me, you are selfish, you are cruel." And so on. Italian opera singers develop an extensive vocabulary of reproach.

"Don't be childish." I was really vexed and hurt by his behaviour. "I'm going home for a short while to prepare for my recital. Stop acting the idiot. You are too egotistic, and I'm sick of your accusations."

We had quarrelled in the past, but never seriously. Now I felt trapped, and found myself dreading the scenes that were becoming more and more frequent.

My last act before leaving Milan was to go once more to the Duomo, there to give thanks for my safe journey through Poland, and to pray for all the people I held in affection and esteem. When I had first seen it the vastness of the cathedral had seemed to me too impersonal, too grandiose to offer solace or strength to those who passed its portals. Now I understood what drew almost all the singers who thronged it prior to their performances. Its magnificence was the magnificence of a huge operatic stage - the candles, the incense, the atmosphere sent tingles down my spine as I knelt before the high altar.

I remember the wonderful Eva Turner telling Mama and me how she had prayed there prior to her very first appearance at La Scala (as Sieglinde, I believe) and was rewarded with a huge success. I'm sure it owed more to her own efforts and qualities than any divine intervention, but who can prove that? Anyway, I lit a fistful of candles, and hoped the Good Lord and the Holy Virgin would guard my friends, and fulfil all their hearts' desires.

Chapter Ten

America

I told Mama about my time in Stockholm, but not about Poland. I also told her about Franco's rages and my reactions, and she understood us both far better than I did.

"Darling, be honest. I know you care for Franco, but in your own way. You don't really love him, and I sometimes wonder if you ever will find a man who is more important to you than a cause."

A cause? What's that? I didn't understand her, then, but she had, as usual, seen through me. She saw my essential detachment from people, and my tendency to distance myself from emotional involvement.

"You tend to shut people out, walk away from them."

"Is that how you see me? Do I shut you out?" I asked with horror.

She laughed. "No, my darling daughter - it's because you and I are so close. That enables me to see how you treat other people. You keep them at a distance as far as you can."

I hadn't thought of my emotional character in any specific way until now, and I found it uncomfortable, weighing my faults and inconsistencies. I remembered from long ago the gentle words of the Mother Superior of the Convent of Marie Reparatrice in Dublin. "Diana, dear child, always face yourself in the mirror. If fault there be, accept that part lies with you. Never place the blame entirely on others."

The conversation had occurred after an angry discussion, when I had been exchanging harsh words with a girl called Agnes Coughlan about the neutral stance of Ireland and the border dispute. We both lost our tempers, I lost the argument, and I was grousing to the nun, demanding credit and sympathy, and support for my denigration of the other girl.

Since then I had learned to bridle my tongue, and resist the temptation to plunge headlong into a row, whatever the provocation. If anything, my feigned indifference to people's opinions seemed to infuriate them more than my arguments had done. A fact well known to psychologists, but I worked it out for myself.

Back in London I contacted Idris Lewis of BBC Wales, and made a few broadcasts from Cardiff. Meanwhile I was back with Spencer Clay, preparing for my Wigmore Hall recital. He was old and frail by now, but still a marvellous teacher - enthusiastic, critical, but with the gift of being able to explain, to show me exactly where I was going wrong. His insight into what are called 'little songs', which exist to express a thought or an emotion rather than the singer's range, staying power and virtuosity, was amazing. A phrase, or sometimes just a word, can carry mystery, pathos, longing. I prayed I could do him justice, and in this I had the added joy of working with Ernest Lush as my accompanist.

At our first meeting I was petrified by his austere and remote manner, but by the second rehearsal I realised that here was a shy, retiring man who spoke through his music. Kind, amusing, with a dry humour, he worked miracles - chiefly on my tendency to treat art songs and lieder as operatic arias. He would grin, and say, "Wigmore Hall, Diana, not the Albert! I'm a piano, not an orchestra."

As my début approached I found my opening song, 'My heart is ever faithful', was driving me to distraction. I could find no way of bringing it to a proper conclusion. Over and over, I made the same mistake, and over and over Spencer and Ernest would assure me it was only nerves. Maybe so, but what help was that?

"I shall carry my music." I was quite determined to do so, damn the sneers, and no more was said.

I had a lovely dress for the occasion, a white lace crinoline, off the shoulders, simple and uncluttered. The hall, which never has the kindest lighting, looked inviting, with the platform decorated with ferns and a few potted plants. The place was packed as well. I could hear what seemed a hubbub from the audience, and I could feel my knees knocking. I was to perform Bach, Handel, Pergolesi, Verdi and Bellini in the first group; Debussy, Poulenc, Duparc and Auric in the second. Then groups of Spanish and English songs after the interval.

Suddenly I was due on, and as the door began to open, Ernest slipped my few miserable pages of music from my trembling hand and said, "Get on, Diana, just sing - you'll be all right."

How I acknowledged the ovation and bowed to the audience without falling over, I'll never know, and to this day I can see the little smile on Ernest's face as our eyes met, and we began.

A success? Yes, in the main. I was praised for my musicianship, diction, languages and choice of programme. Also for my composure. Ye Gods! Little did anyone know how I longed to swallow, to breathe where no breath was allowed, how I feared to fail to sustain the legato flow of 'Chanson Triste' or fade on my pianissimo notes in 'Les Ponts de C'. (This is a song of sorrow for France by Poulenc, very expressive, and sung to perfection by Pierre Bernac, the famous French baritone.) Altogether the critics were very kind. Ernest Newman advised me to allow my Italianate tone to take precedence over my French production, but even he was gentle. Everyone was pleased, and I forgave Ernest his trick. We worked together several more times before I went to the United States.

Then came a new development. The colds I had suffered in Milan, which had been put down to the misty damp weather, had left me with a dry aggravating cough. Now X-rays found a shadow on my right lung. Nothing very serious, but Mama wanted me to take a few months' rest in a warm climate, and so did the doctors. My father suggested that I join him at Menton, and I was considering this when Pam, by now married to James Mason and living in Beverly Hills, offered me a holiday with them.

There might be opportunities to work if I was fit enough to take them up. Community concerts were very popular at that time, and there were music clubs, voice-overs for radio and television commercials, even some television chat shows might be arranged. With luxurious living in a sunny climate, altogether far too good to miss. In the spring of 1951 I sailed for New York on the *Caronia*. I remembered that Kim Philby had travelled to America on the same ship.

It meant that my visit to eastern Europe must be delayed, but by this time I was sensible enough to realise I must have my health as well as my wits about me if I was to bum around Belgrade, Prague, Warsaw and Sofia. The United States also offered the possibility of contacting some people who had worked with and for Allen Dulles, and others who had been on the War Crimes Commission and the Nuremberg Trials in Germany - old hands, who might prove helpful.

Mama refused to accompany me. "No darling, I'll stay in London and look after the animals. Bridie will be getting married soon, and I don't think her husband will stand for her living here as a dog-sitter."

Cunning Welsh witch! Oliver was around, needing a nanny, whereas I could manage without one. In any case, Mama's memories of New York had not endeared the American way of life to her. Pam and James had made her very welcome, and she had found their house on the river quite lovely. There was abundance of parties, hospitality and general kindliness, though after the austerity of wartime England it all seemed over the top and unreal. Her main complaint was about the police.

"There I was, in the middle of Park Avenue, arms full of boxes and packages, the traffic moving at lethal speeds or jammed bumper-to-bumper. The rain was pouring down, and when I asked the policeman where I could find a taxi, he just glared and said, 'Call one, sister!' So rude!"

Darling Mama, she was always so well-mannered. She found any brusqueness or lack of courtesy deeply offensive. For all her rule-breaking, she was a great believer in Grandmama's old values of a polite tongue, so signally lacking in New York.

My experience was to be otherwise. I arrived on a beautiful spring day, marred only by losing the keys to my baggage. In fact they weren't truly lost. I had absent-mindedly placed them on top of a layer of clothes, then banged down the lid of the self-locking trunk. I found a Customs Officer, and led him to my stacked collection of twelve cases, babbling about the loss of my keys. He listened in stony silence while my heart sank. I had been told that the law required that each and every piece of baggage must be open for inspection.

He stood contemplating them for a minute before he asked, "Where's your porter?"

A man appeared with a trolley waggon. "Get this stuff the Hell out of here!"

Then he looked me up and down, and grinned all over his face. "Fine day, pretty chick! Enjoy your stay!"

I could have kissed him, but in fact I got this sort of treatment everywhere I went. The women were charming, friendly and welcoming, the men full of compliments (and sometimes a little too friendly) but pleasant and protective. Maybe I was lucky, but I had no word of complaint even after spending nearly a year in America, except about Hedda Hopper, the gossip columnist. But she was a professional bitch, and in any case, I was hardly big enough game for her sights. She didn't count.

I hadn't liked Yanks much during the war. I'd found them brash and condescending, in the main. Afterwards, I hadn't liked them in Italy either. They were full of themselves and their country, and bragged of both incessantly. But now I met them on their home ground they were very different.

I had booked into the Alrae Hotel, a charming little place just off Fifth Avenue, owned at that time by a Viennese couple who managed to convey the kind of family atmosphere so often found on the continent, but with all the comforts Americans expect as a matter of course. I had a first-floor suite with patio - a delight until I tried to open the window. It was hermetically sealed, and the heat was stifling. I rang for the floor-waiter, and collapsed with laughter at his horrified expression when I asked him to call someone to attend to the windows.

"Madam, it's far too cold outside, it's only April. I can arrange for the air conditioning to come on if you wish."

Madam did not wish. I don't like air conditioning, or more than minimal central heating, and I don't believe either is good for the voice. In response to my persistent proddings an odd job man appeared, and I was able to stand outside and view New York from what must have seemed like ground level to the natives.

On my first visit to the Pierre, to have cocktails and dinner on the thirty-sixth floor with Joan Bennet and Walter Wanger, I was able to enjoy a more traditional aspect. Certainly, there was an impressive panorama from that suite, and I felt very much the country cousin among all those lovely, elegant women, and their escorts, so obviously accustomed to the enjoyment of the good life, and the exercise of power.

"You've only seen one side of New York life so far," Joan said. "Before you leave we'll show you how the ordinary folk live."

In fact I saw it with my floor waiter, who was Greek American and his Czech American wife. It was great. Chinatown, the Bronx, Coney Island, delicatessens, dinettes and best of all, breakfast at the Zoo. This was the real highlight, and I was truly grateful to the kindly couple for giving up their free time so that I could be a tourist.

I was invited to visit the Metropolitan Opera House, and given a tour of the whole place. I auditioned (disastrously) for CBS, and sang to no good purpose for a representative of Sol Hurok, the great operatic impresario. It turned out that he was looking for a Gilda, and asked if I was still interested in that role. I told him, 'No thank you', as I was already moving away from the coloratura repertoire towards the lyric. He had none of those available. But for me the *pièce de résistance* was to see Rocky Marciano fight. I've forgotten who was on the receiving end, but I was sorry for him. Marciano fought like the Devil, rough and crude, but quite fantastic. I had always been a boxing buff, and one of my best friends in Ireland had been the playboy, singer and boxer, Jack Doyle. Though he clowned around and played to the gallery, in his early days he could use his gloves well, but even in his prime he could never have lasted a round against Marciano.

I left New York for California by train, the *Super Chief*, in a drawing-room suite with every comfort and service built in. You could have your hair dressed, eat in style in the dining-car, enjoy the desert crossing in the observation car, take cocktails in the lounge and so on. A first class hotel on wheels.

We stopped in Chicago, where we were delayed for a couple of extra hours by an engine fault, so I grabbed a cab and asked the driver to show me the city - just bear in mind my departure time. He was marvellous. I had to see the Opera House of course, but the flop-house district was on the agenda as well, with its sad wrecks of people, homeless and for the most part alcoholic, in the cold air of the Windy City. It deserves the nickname; the north wind blows cold off Lake Michigan. The sight made me feel quite guilty as I tucked in a delicious breakfast, which my driver insisted on buying as my first meal in a drug store.

I took his name and address for when I reached California, because not only had he fed me, he refused to let me pay the fare.

"My pleasure, lady, you've made my day."

I wrote him a thankyou note from Beverly Hills, and got a card back wishing me a happy stay in California.

The Mason house in Beverly Hills was spacious, cool, and marvellously comfortable. They were very prosperous, with James much in demand as a film star, and Pam as a writer, chat show hostess, and amanuensis to James. There were plenty of animals, a glorious garden, and for me a sybaritic round of gaiety and entertainment - swimming-pool parties, musical evenings, cinemas, drug stores and wonderful restaurants. Meeting old friends was a bonus.

Roy Kellino was living in their guest house, which was a lovely surprise for me as we renewed our wartime friendship. Vivian and Judy, with three children by then, were also in Los Angeles, and some other old friends, not least Baron von Kettler.

He had returned to Berlin at the end of the war to find both his parents were dead. His mother had left him jewellery and some money, but his father's estate was in the Russian zone, and the final decision about its disposal was still a long way off. I assumed he would have been shocked and horrified at the sight of what had been done to his homeland, but he surprised me. "We deserved everything we got," he said. "We plunged the world into chaos. Perhaps Germany will have learned a lesson."

Having applied for US citizenship, he had renounced his undemocratic title of nobility, and was now known as Gary Kettler, though not to me. Gunther he remained, and I was thrilled to find him in Hollywood, where he had started a real estate business, and was doing well. Our reunion was only as affectionate friends, which was just as well because Pam took a fancy to Gunther, and began a very obvious flirtation. It ended abruptly, and with a certain rancour on both sides, but I refrained from asking why.

Gwen Knox had settled in Hollywood, in an entrancing little house on Beechwood Drive. There she was enjoying a quietly satisfying social life working with animals and singing in her church choir. Hollywood isn't tinsel exclusively. It was another grand reunion for me, as there was one more wartime chum - Scott Forbes, whom I had met when he was invalided out of the RAF. He was an exceedingly handsome man, and was quickly snapped up by an agent, who changed his name to Julian Dallas, and launched him into films. He caught the eye of Twentieth-Century Fox, who gave him his old name back and a three-year contract. There he was having a high old time, being chased by many ladies, and somehow never running fast enough not to be caught.

The Mason household was very busy, and I could not always expect someone to be there to ferry me about. To become more self-sufficient, I tried to learn how to drive, as Pam had done. It was not a success; I lacked the temperament. The police objected to some practices of mine, including (1) driving down Santa Monica Boulevard alone on a learner's permit, (2) trying to outrace a motorcycle cop who caught me speeding, (3) while practising parking, I managed to graze a police car.

After these brushes with the law, I gave it up. Sooner or later I would have killed myself, and quite possibly several other people. I simply had no sense of speed. To sustain my independence, I reverted to Yellow Cabs, friends and James's factotum, Johnny Monaghan.

I have already written about many of the more interesting things that happened to me in Hollywood in my biography of James Mason. I do not propose to repeat myself now, nor to scrape that barrel, but I was amused by the gossip surrounding Roy Kellino. To have a first husband living on the premises was enough to keep tongues wagging, even in Hollywood, and of course, many people were unaware of my connection with the Masons. Consequently I heard a number of prurient or spiteful remarks to the effect that James must be either a cuckold or a fag, though as it happened, Roy had married again and divorced before arriving in the United States. He was by now involved with Barbara, another delightful lady whom he married a little later.

He, Barbara, her two sons from a previous marriage and I spent a few days together on Catalina Island, where we could explore the seabed from a glass capsule rather like a diving-bell, capable of holding up to six people. I had never regarded the sea as either friendly or interesting, but as I watched the extraordinary shapes and colours of the fish and plants, I realised how ignorant I was. The marine life was incredible, and I particularly enjoyed watching the divers feed the fish from the glass-bottomed boats.

Roy, with his photographer's eye, had the idea that underwater documentary films would be of interest to schools and colleges, but first he needed to find backers for the venture. Unfortunately he was ahead of his time, nature films were not so popular then as they have since become, mainly under the impact of colour television. Roy gradually lost sight of the idea. In the end it was Cousteau, and the team of Hans and Lotte Hass, who made the breakthrough. Meanwhile, Roy became more and more involved with the Hal Roach television movies, and was unable to spare the time to make the conservationist and educational programmes he would have liked.

I enjoyed many concerts in the Hollywood Bowl, though I didn't perform there. But I met Franz Waxman, Miklos Rozsa, Dmitri Tiomkin, Alfred Newman and André Previn, among others. They were all top-class musicians, who could play several instruments and conduct, as well as composing scores for films. André Previn in particular was a quite beautiful pianist, having been a child prodigy.

Mikki Rosza's studio bungalow at MGM was quite splendid. It was fitted out as a luxury apartment, centred upon a magnificent Bechstein. I could have lived in it, it was only a workplace to him - but he was their top composer and winner of several Oscars.

Apart from the conductors, I had the enormous privilege of meeting Igor Stravinski and his wife. We talked mainly about music festivals, and how they were arranged in different places including Berkeley, Dubrovnik and Bayreuth. They lived very simply, and entertained in their kitchen dining-room, where she cooked. I found them both very charming, as were Ray and Prima Sinatra. Ray used to accompany me on piano, and it was through him that I met Mario Lanza. He appeared on 'Coca Cola Hour', a musical and variety programme, which Ray conducted and where many well-known artists appeared.

Mario and Betty Lanza often came to the Sinatras for Italian Sunday lunch, and Mario would tuck into pasta and wine with great gusto, though he knew he should be watching his weight. I liked him, though he had a reputation for arrogance and vulgarity. I think it must have been largely nerves; he was worried about his increasing weight, and his voice as well. It was a fine, natural voice with élan and energy, but it brought him too much fame, and too quickly. Consequently he had insufficient technical skill to deal with the problems that will arise from time to time. Singing through a cold, for instance, can be taxing psychologically as well as vocally, and on this sort of occasion an assured technique is essential.

Lanza lacked this, but he was hailed overnight as 'a great singer', when he was really only a singing movie star. Yet people who should have known better were comparing him to Enrico Caruso, which was not only gross flattery in terms of his talent, but wildly inappropriate in terms of his vocal timbre. It wasn't even the same kind of voice, but the name was brought up because Caruso was in everyone's mind as the greatest tenor of all time. A God-given voice, disciplined and enriched by years of training and study, which Lanza had not yet had the time and never had the temperament to apply.

He told me that his parents had been very indulgent, and spoiled him as a child. Now he was self-indulgent, and to diet was a burden. He enjoyed his food, not to mention his wine and beer, and had no enthusiasm for the battle against the bulge. Moreover, when he tried it seemed to affect his voice, leaving his intonation unreliable, and dulling or making him miss altogether the ringing top notes for which he was famous.

This is terribly destructive for any singer, but for Lanza it was worse than most as he made the fearful error of believing his own publicity. He had a genuine ambition to conquer the world of Italian Opera, which was ludicrous when you consider that it would have meant direct competition with Ramon Vinay, Mario del Monaco, Franco Corelli and Jussi Bjorling. He would have had to take intensive coaching to prepare for the major rules he wished to carry.

In fact his career ended suddenly and tragically, leaving his millions of fans heartbroken. He was never put to the test, but even so, his recording of 'Be my Love' outsold every record of its era; no small achievement. I was never famous, but I know from experience how difficult it is to re-adjust oneself to facing impartial criticism from an unsympathetic press. A young and pleasing personality, with a new voice, is excused much, but it will not be excused for long, and a career as it progresses will attract ever more rigorous criticism.

I really only disliked a single aspect of life in Hollywood. I attended the Sheriff's Rodeo, a grand display of riders and horses, resplendent in silver bridles and medallions, and I admired the beautiful and in some cases unfamiliar breeds, such as the golden palomino and the spotted horses. But I was shocked and sickened by the bronco-busting, bull-riding, steer and calf-roping, with their quite unnecessary displays of violence. The furious efforts of the animals are based not on ill-temper or love of the contest, but a tight cinch round their tenderest parts. They will do anything to rid themselves of the pain which this simple device inflicts. I went to the paddock after the display, and saw how wretched and exhausted they were. There was no fight left in any of them, they were simply pathetic creatures, soured by ill-treatment.

I suppose it was my knowledge of wartime cruelty that had made me sensitive to this deliberate and calculated inhumanity, purely to gratify human blood-lust and the quest for vicarious excitement. I was appalled then, as I still am, by performing animals, hunting, especially of stags, the breeding of game for the shoot. All totally unnecessary means of amusing humans, by gratifying those baser instincts which they ought to be trying to vanquish. I realise that culling is necessary at times to preserve the natural balance. We can hardly have wolf packs, grisly bears and lynxes running wild in areas where people live, so Man must take on the role of predator. But to me, shooting for trophies is as abhorrent as bear or badger-baiting, or bull-fighting.

I enquired of the ASPCA if they had inspectors at rodeos and similar gatherings, but their replies were evasive and disappointing. On a later occasion, when I reported a distressed St. Bernard I had seen, I was told that the owners were within their rights to keep the dog chained in a small yard full of excrement, and only watered and fed at infrequent intervals. "Maybe so," I was told, "But there is dog food in the house, and the animal is not starving."

I was also disgusted by reports I read of people killing wild horses by driving them over ravines, shooting them at random and so on. I could associate none of the people I met with such violent practices, but every society has its brutal fringe, and I must restrain myself from tarring everyone with the same brush.

Van Heflin and his wife, Francie, James Stewart, Frank Sinatra, Burt Lancaster, Andy and Mary Stone, Faith Domergue and her husband Hugo Fregonese, the Rozsas, the Negulescos and many others were frequent visitors to the Masons, and in return they offered lavish parties at their own homes. Pam had an entourage of adoring friends, and James a rather more laid-back circle of cronies. I found it easy to mix with both groups, but I was coming to miss Mama.

My wartime journeys had never taken me away for long, and though we wrote to each other daily I was beginning to become sated with the good life. I ought to be furthering my career, but I was always lukewarm over any approaches I got. I had lost impetus, and had I not met Paul Gregory I think I would have cut short my stay in California. But Paul had formed his Drama Quartet, with Charles Laughton, Sir Cedric Hardwicke, Charles Boyer and Agnes Moorhead. They had had a fabulous success touring the United States where they performed Shaw's 'Don Juan in Hell'. It was done against plain black velvet back-cloths, the men in dinner-jackets, with their books on lecterns, and Paul had booked Carnegie Hall for Laughton to do Bible readings and recordings of Shakespeare and lyric poetry. Boyer recorded the love-letters of

Napoleon to Josephine. He was a sweet, kind man and a devoted husband and he also ran a bookshop in Beverly Hills. He often served his customers in person, and was more amused than hurt if they failed to recognise him.

I still heard regularly from Franco, cajoling me to join him, and I was tempted to take him up on it. I could give up any thought of a career of my own, and let him shoulder the additional burden of maintaining me as his mistress. But it would have solved nothing, as I would still have felt cut off from home and Mama. I could not in fairness be a kept woman, and at the same time always be skiving off back to England.

I must solve my own problems, and face the decision which had been implicit ever since I gave up the small-holding and trundled off on the Simplon Express to Milan. Besides, I was getting worried. I had written on several occasions to Prague, Warsaw, Torun and Zagreb, but got no answers, which boded ill for my wartime friends.

It was common knowledge among the security forces even before the war ended that elements within the Allies felt that we had fought the wrong enemy, notwithstanding what Hitler stood for, nor taking into account the immense suffering and sacrifice of the Russian people. I personally have heard it said by rightwingers that 'the poor bloody peasants were cannon fodder either way.' Stalinism did nothing to give the lie to such statements.

I had no pre-conceived ideas of what I should do, but the reactions I got encouraged me to start digging into the rumours that were circulating at the time, about ratlines and cover-ups being made available to Nazis who might be on the run, but who still had the knowledge to trade with sundry governments, but principally the United States.

The months passed, my lung was declared clear, and we started serious negotiations for singing engagements. Pam and James had made it clear that I had a home in California for as long as I wished, Mama would be welcomed with delight. The guest house would always be open to us and any animals we could smuggle in or acquire on the way. Paul had some brilliant ideas to further my career. I had my work-permit, my Social Security card, and the doors were all open. What went wrong?

Me. That's what. The call of Europe was too strong, London was too much my base. I couldn't cut the ties. In a flurry of jubilation I packed my bags, kissed everyone goodbye and took the train to New York, where Paul Gregory gave me a long lecture on my want of good sense over a farewell lunch at the Pierre Hotel. He said I was throwing away opportunities that might never come again, and of course he was right.

He was shrewd as well as artistic, and advised me to take my time, and decide what I wished to do, and where. A tour of the lesser cities of the United States would give me a chance to test myself, not vocally, for that was not the problem. The problem was my indecisiveness, my feelings of homesickness and lack of ambition.

Nonetheless, I boarded my ship, the old *Mauritania*. It was quite a trip, with seventy men and only four women aboard. The men were coming back from a trade delegation, and the other women were a pretty American girl, rejoining her French husband at Le Havre, an elderly ex-hospital matron who had been visiting her daughter in Maine and a twittery, nosy, Irish Catholic spinster in her forties who regarded all men as ravening beasts who had somehow failed to be ravenous for her. In a few days she had managed to offend nearly everyone on the ship, and had we arrived in Cobh any later, I swear there'd have been a cry of 'Woman overboard!'

The American girl and I had a fabulous few days, and reeled off the ship with our handbags bulging with cards. There were invitations to lunch, to dinner, to do a show, to stay overnight - all good-humoured flirting, with enough champagne flowing to ensure no one came sober down the gangplank. In five days I had equalled my customary intake for about ten years, and I looked ghastly, but it had been great fun.

Southampton was wet and scruffy, but I could have kissed the ground. What seemed like a toy train after the *Super Chief* trundled us to Waterloo, and we squealed with delight over buttered toast and fruit cake in the Pullman, as if we had been quite starved of creature comforts in the United States. England is *home*.

Chapter Eleven

London, Yugoslavia and Menton

A second London recital was planned for shortly after I returned to England, with a new programme and, to my regret, a new accompanist. Ernest Lush was now working exclusively for the BBC. Emmie Tillet suggested Gerald Moore.

I had met Gerald only once, in a Dublin pub, and found him very charming and amusing. I admired his talent, but somehow felt less happy with the idea of him as a partner, an attitude that got me on the wrong side of Emmie. She felt it was in my best interest to be guided by her expert knowledge, and I'm sure she was right, but trusting my instincts, I invited Daniel Kelly to play for me. It was a momentous and lucky decision.

Dan and I tuned to each other at once. He was tall and spare, with heavy glasses for his very poor eyesight, bashful and shy. Primarily a self-taught musician, he had a remarkable intuitive understanding of my strong and weak points. His mother, a tiny little woman but with the heart of a lioness in defence of her son, attended every recital he gave. They adored each other, and she saw to his every need, particularly seeing that he remembered to eat.

We were friends from our first meeting. We enjoyed every minute of our rehearsals, or any other time spent together. He was gentle in pointing out my numerous mistakes, supportive with volume, delicate in his touch, and altogether the perfect partner. He encouraged me to make a real effort, and build on the promising début which I had allowed to dwindle into a sort of 'Shall I? Shan't I? Could do better!' attitude. We decided on a programme and set to work in earnest, while I took up a few long-standing engagements in Wales, Dublin and music clubs.

The lease on our flat had expired by now, so we took a short lease on a house at 28, Pembroke Gardens, Kensington. The lease was being sold by Nevill Foulkes, QC, but the ground landlords were the Prudential

Insurance Co. and the triangle of houses was earmarked for future development. I may say that more pleasant or efficient landlords could hardly be found. The house was really too big for us, with two rooms on all four floors, like Trevor Place. But once we had seen the garden we looked no further. It was edged by trees, and wonderfully quiet and secluded - as good as being in the country. It also had a basement, where we installed Bridie, by now married to Bill.

We turned a small garden room on the ground floor into a kitchen for ourselves, and let the top floor to Dennis Edwards and an Irish friend of his, Desmond Jordan. They had met while working for Lord Longford at the Abbey Theatre in Dublin, and decided to share a flat in London while they looked for work in television. Desmond was smallish, very good-looking, and with a most delightful singing voice. I never tired of his rendition of 'She passed through the fair'. Between the two of them they made enough to enjoy themselves, though it was a hand-to-mouth existence, so I was glad to have them as lodgers. When I was away, I knew Mama would have people in the house who, apart from being friends, could protect her if the need arose.

I resumed my singing. There was the opportunity of a recital in Vienna, and a tour of Scandinavia. Yugoslavia, Poland, Czechoslovakia were possibilities for the future, where I could pursue my other interests, but they needed to be defined.

Should I do research and write it up as a book, taking the lid off postwar scandals and the deception of the British public over the non-prosecution of war criminals? Would I be free to do so, or capable of uncovering sufficient material? Who would open doors and archives for me? There were so many unanswerable questions. Could I gain the support of an official agency? Most likely not - I would be pointing the finger at many of them. I knew I had little chance of being co-opted into those departments. My intentions would be suspect, and in any event I had no wish to be bound by their rules.

I was not motivated by disloyalty to France or England, but by a desire to know if the rumours of cynical cover-up and suppression of reports were true. I was uncertain where my delving might lead. I would have no protection, despite my former connections, and no one would claim me if I got in too deep. So what was I looking for, and in particular, why?

The answer to that lay in the past. From 1942 onwards I had known of the mass murders taking place in Poland and Russia, and to a lesser extent in other countries. I knew of the concentration and extermination camps, the butchering of POWs of all nationalities, the *Kugel Erlass* and *Nacht und Nebel Erlass* ('Bullet' Decree and 'Darkness and Fog'

Decree) that cost the lives of thousands of people.

The *Nacht und Nebel Erlass* was issued by Hitler himself in 1941. Under it, people convicted of offences against the Reich or the German armed forces in occupied territory were to be deported to Germany and there handed over to SIPO (the security police) for punishment. The families of deportees were never to be informed of where the prisoners were, or what was their ultimate fate. This decree was not applied in cases where the death penalty could legally be imposed, but it cost untold thousands of deaths for people who were picked up and instantly became 'unpersons'.

Kugel Erlass, which came into force in March 1944, included an order that all escaped officers and NCOs were to be handed over to the chief of SIPO and SD (the Security Service). The code name for this procedure was 'Stufe III', and it was by the direct order of Field Marshall Keitel that the lists of shot POWs was posted on notice boards as a deterrent to others who might be contemplating escape.

I knew of the atrocious aftermath of the breakout from Dössel. On that occasion forty-four escaped, of whom thirty-seven were recaptured and murdered in Dortmund or Buchenwald. Two friends of mine were among the lucky seven. Wincenty Kawalec, who is still alive, and Jan Zieleniewski, now dead. Then there was the gratuitous killing of the RAF men at Zagan, and many other occasions when men and women, ostensibly protected by the Geneva Convention, were murdered in cold blood. The silence from Poland and Yugoslavia was a persistent torment; I needed to know what had happened to Marko in Zagreb, to Stachu in Warsaw, and others in different parts of eastern Europe.

The Cold War was growing ever more icy, and I would certainly find myself in deep trouble unless I moved carefully. Fortunately I knew a few key men who had taken part in the Nuremburg prosecutions, as well as Colonel Manuel and Jacques Soustelle who were still highly placed in France. I could also expect a sympathetic hearing from those who had fought to see justice done, and failed through no fault of their own. There were Lord Simon, Aidan Crawley, who had himself been a prisoner at Zagan, Lord Russell, Sir David Maxwell Fyfe and a number of others less well known, who must have been discomfited and disappointed at the outcome of the War Trials.

Meanwhile my music programmes needed careful thought and much preparation. The Viennese would be a very tough audience, especially as I intended to avoid the German repertoire entirely. German was a difficult language for me to sing in, and rather than suffer by comparison with such magnificent exponents of lieder as Sena Junirac, Victoria de los Angeles, Elizabeth Schwarzkopf and Irmgaad Seefried, I chose

Italian songs, such as Pizzetti's 'Tre Canzoni', Turina's 'Saeta' and some rarely-performed songs by Guridi, Santoliquido and Respighi. I also had three particular favourites which were the mainstay of my recitals: George Auric's 'Quatre Chants de la France Malheureuse', written during the German occupation, Milhaud's 'Catalogue des fleurs' and a satirical piece by Henri Sauget, 'La Voyante', which is about palmistry. I wanted my encores to vary, but Ravel's 'Air de l'Enfant' and Faure's 'En Prière' were two more favourites.

On those occasions when I met with an exceptionally enthusiastic reception, I dared to indulge in Irish or Spanish folk songs, which were very well received. This meant I could 'mix and match' as recitals in the same city or town rarely fell at close intervals. In the United States I had learned the trick of keeping a 'dress book' (very important not to be seen in the same gown twice in the same city) and I found it useful to do the same with my songs.

I think every singer or pianist has a favourite pot-boiler, and my encores were invariably Bax's 'I heard a piper piping' and 'I know where I'm going'. This last left one Viennese puzzled at the words 'some say he's black' i.e., black-hearted. How could there be any argument about whether or not he was a negro? It took me a while to explain.

"Darling," I said to Mama, "would you mind if I flew from Vienna to see if I can find Marko? Zagreb is only a hop away."

"Will you be safe?" That was her sole concern. "The conditions may be pretty awful. How long do you intend to stay there?"

At this stage I didn't know. I had sent a letter to Vlado, and his reply had been reassuring. Marko had been released from prison, and was teaching English for a living. I had also been in touch with Lars, and he seemed willing to help get me into Poland - quite legally on this occasion.

"You will have to proceed with caution in all the Soviet Bloc, Diana, but if you gain any special insight or information, I think I can find you a paymaster." Lars was always very vague about his position; he was a Red Cross official, but how much else? I never enquired. He had always been my good and trusted friend, and what he did was his own business. His words buoyed me up, and when I reached Stockholm he was able to give me some valuable advice, and several very useful names.

In 1953 the senior British representative in Warsaw was Sir John Rennie with ambassadorial status, though his official position was vague. He had been in charge of the British Information Service in New York from 1942 to 1946, so he must have been a security chief already. He later became head of MI6, prior to Maurice Oldfield. He was not an unqualified success in that position, but he was a very clever man, and needed to be as Poland was an extremely difficult posting for anyone, and demanded a delicate and experienced hand. The Soviets were suspicious of the Allies, and while they claimed to enjoy the warmest fraternal accord with their Polish neighbours, these sentiments were not entirely reciprocated. To achieve my purpose and gain worthwhile information, I would need to cultivate people in authority, and steer a non-aligned course.

As Lars pointed out, "You will find it easy to gain access to officials, Diana, but then you will have to make your own opportunities. Red tape and bureaucracy abound, but you, as an artist, will have a certain amount of freedom. Just observe the rules, however petty, expect your hotel room to be bugged, and remember the sort of discretion we all used in the war."

I installed myself in the Bristol Hotel, originally owned by Paderewski, and used by German officers during the occupation. It was a noble building, but now its splendour was faded, its fabric pitted and scarred by years of war and neglect, but full of atmosphere and the ghosts of the *belle époque*. Warsaw was very cold, even in autumn, and the general dilapidation seemed to fill the air with despondency. Pinched faces, drab clothes and masses of anxious-eyed soldiers passing through the streets gave me a sense that a dreary tragedy was being played out endlessly in the heartland of what had once been a beautiful and gay capital.

Lars put me in touch with the Polish Red Cross in Warsaw, and the Historical War Institute, which had re-opened its archives in 1945. In this way I met several people who remain friends to this day. One was Witold Lokuciewski, an ex-RAF squadron leader who had reached England from France in 1940 as Flight Leader of the Polish 303 Squadron. He was a much decorated officer, holding Croix de Guerre, Silver Cross *Virtuti Militari*, Croix de Valeur and Polish Order (all 1940) and DFC (1941). He accounted for nine or ten German aircraft before being shot down himself in 1943. After several months in hospital, he was transferred to a POW camp, from which he made two unsuccessful attempts to escape.

It was he who told me of the infamous murder of RAF officers at Zagan (Stalag Luft III Sagan). Of the seventy-six escapees, only three got away. Fifteen were recaptured by the Wehrmacht and sent back to the camp, eight were detained by the Gestapo, and fifty were shot 'resisting arrest' or 'attempting to escape'. He himself was to have taken part in the mass escape on the night of 24-25 March 1944, but the order was decided by lot, and he was in one of the last groups, which in effect saved his life.

There was no doubt in his mind that the murder of the RAF men (who included British, Polish, Canadians, Australians and New Zealanders in their number) was carried out under the *Kugel Erlass.*

Aidan Crawley, giving evidence to the International Military Tribunal at Nuremburg, said that under *Kugel* recaptured British and American officers and NCOs should be handed over to the Wehrmacht. This order was often ignored, and though Zagan claimed the attention of the War Trial Judges, many similar murders took place elsewhere.

Meanwhile, Lokuciewski had returned to Poland in 1947, where he was recalled by the Polish Airforce to study jet aircraft. He was able to give me many details about how the Poles were battling to re-establish themselves and the new order, and I, in turn, was able to draw certain conclusions about the general situation. It was fraught, to say the least, not only for those who had fought for their country in the West, but for those who had organised and fought in the *Armia Krajowa*, which had taken its orders and given its loyalty first to General Sikorski's Government-in-Exile, and after his death to the new Commander-in-Chief, General Sosnkowski. Some of General Anders's troops, who had fought so bravely at Monte Cassino, had received nothing like a hero's welcome on returning home, and many had suffered terribly under the Stalinists.

Dr Szymon Datner was a Jewish historian who had survived the Holocaust. He offered me the use of his research papers and private memoirs of the years 1939 to 1953. They were horrific, but I was amazed at his lack of hatred or desire for revenge. Both his sons were victims of the Bialystock Ghetto, when they had joined in an attempted breakout. It failed, and the SS moved in to massacre everyone of fighting age. His own survival was little short of a miracle. Yet through his intelligence, his ability as a logician and above all his good-heartedness, he could speak about the unspeakable without apparent anger or melodrama.

One of the bravest and luckiest survivors of the notorious Pawiak Prison was Regina Domanska. She gave me understanding of the plight of Polish women in wartime, and the mental and physical diseases which were the continuing legacy of their trauma.

Tomasz Sobanski, sentenced to Auschwitz at sixteen, and a survivor after four years of that Hell, did much to fire my interest in the events of the Polish Holocaust and in the travesty of justice inflicted on the Poles from both sides of the Iron Curtain. His story forms part of a collection of escape stories which I still hope to see published, though they make appalling reading. So far, western publishers have blenched at recording the treachery which did not 'just happen' to Poland in the aftermath of war, but were part and parcel in the agreed carve-up of the country by the Allies.

The destruction was well-nigh total. The country was left without an industrial or agricultural base, just a crying need for economic aid in every sphere. The need for medical aid was unassuageable as well, for the traumatised general population almost as much as to rehabilitate the camp victims, yet such little reparation as was forthcoming was siphoned off by bureaucrats. From 1954, and ever since, the Poles have been fighting for their spiritual freedom and national identity against all the odds. At that time there were plenty of political divisions, but it was the poverty, and all it entailed in lack of such basic human needs as housing, that was most painfully apparent. Yet in the midst of misery and deprivation, the insuperable fighting spirit of the people could still be seen.

Tomasz, and others who had survived for years in one or other of the camps, were my mentors. Through them I learned how most, though not all, Nazi war criminals had evaded justice. The hunt for them, and the demands of the Poles for specific Germans to be extradited, were blocked at every turn, and it is shameful to think that perpetrators of some of the most monstrous crimes against humanity ever recorded went unpunished - then and now.

Children had suffered the same fate as their elders - beaten, gassed, worked to death, starved, used for medical 'experiments'. To that can be added the very conservative estimate of 250,000 taken for 'Germanisation', of whom very few were recovered after the war to be returned to their rightful parents, even if still alive. But at least a million children were orphaned as a result of the Nazi occupation, and the national death-toll lies between three and a half and four million - not counting the two million Polish Jews.

The distinction should perhaps receive greater emphasis than it usually gets. There was a Polish Holocaust as well as a Jewish one. Of the Jews who fought throughout the war I would like to bring to special notice a very brave young man, possibly the only survivor of the Ghetto Bunker (now preserved as a memorial). Marek Edelman, a Jewish socialist then aged twenty-one, was one of two ordered to escape before the remaining fifteen individuals killed themselves rather than fall into German hands. Thereafter he led a group of Jewish partisans, fighting from within Poland as a Polish patriot. Later he aligned himself with Solidarity when Martial Law was declared in 1980.

During the Nazi occupation of Poland there were several partisan units recruited entirely from Jewish fighters, but they were often ostracised or even betrayed by other factions, doubling the odds against their survival. Latent and open anti-Semitism had always been a feature of Polish life, though the antipathy was as likely to be political as racist or religious. Poland had been a refuge for Jews, but their failure to integrate was often misunderstood, and taken as evidence of something to hide rather than a simple determination to preserve their integrity, religion and way of life. It did not prevent Edelman and those like him from fighting the common enemy, nor did it prevent many Poles from risking, and sometimes sacrificing, their lives to save those of Jewish people.

You may wonder, what was Poland to me? Anton was well in my past by now, and I had no direct interest. But I had friendships forged in conflict, and others who might not be friends but whom I still admired. Moreover, what I saw answered the question that had been troubling me: did I seek a career for its own ends, or did I want only to follow a career, to cover my real interest? Why were we in the West, and why were the Soviets, so lukewarm in pursuing the demands of the Poles to put war criminals on trial?

Now I knew: the career was secondary. Naturally, this decision entailed certain problems, principally the financial one. Nevertheless, I knew I could make enough for my needs by 'singing for my supper', and by peddling information to press agencies or governments. There is always a market for information.

Trained agents have their jobs to do, and no time to waste on minor matters. Pressmen must be circumspect, and stay within the briefs laid down by ministries of information. I, still quite a young artist, was able to look for opportunities to perform in countries for which I had sympathy, nor was it as difficult as I had feared to meet the people in charge of broadcasts and recitals.

From Warsaw I went to Krakow, Torun and Gdansk, then by ferry to Malmo and Stockholm. From there I flew to Paris to bend the ear of a noted spymaster. I was disappointed. He greeted me with mild warmth, and we chatted about General de Gaulle and some other mutual friends and friends of friends including the famous Dédé Mainguard, who with Pearl Witherington maintained Squadron Leader Maurice Southgate's circuits after his arrest by the Germans. These were people of great distinction, who had done France the highest service by their dedication to duty, but even so he showed no interest whatever in my proposition, but sent me on my way with a few compliments to sweeten the pill. I left downhearted but not dissuaded, and returned to London.

Mama had worked wonders on the house and garden. We now had a rose walk and a marvellous horseshoe rosebed. She had planted lilac, laburnum and flowering cherry trees, and in the paved area azaleas and rhododendrons in raised peat borders. But best of all, in a remote corner there was a wendy hut, where a pair of hedgehogs had installed themselves for hibernation. They had a warm, dry bed of withered leaves, straw and soft hay, but with the hut door open it stayed cool enough to keep them sleeping till spring. In another secluded corner she had erected a half shelter and filled it with hay. Here several stray cats took refuge.

My seven tortoises, Florian, Eloise, Tosca, Alberto, Dominic, Jo-Jo and Loulou were in their boxes in the greenhouse, dozing the chilly months away, and I found Olivia had had three gorgeous puppies to add to our dog family. How long had I been away? It seemed like years, but had only been seven weeks.

The transformation of our garden was very largely due to Tom, our odd-jobber, who at that time was working as a caretaker in a small block of flats nearby. He had appeared one day looking for outdoor work, and Mama had set him to weeding and digging.

After several months of this really hard labour, Tom said he had decided to leave London to live in the country. A windfall win on the football pools had given him the chance to indulge his two passions - breeding German shepherd dogs and dealing in antiques. We were going to miss his strong arms and laconic wit, and made him promise to keep in touch.

So he did, but the first letter we got left us open-mouthed with astonishment. Our gardener-handyman was now a guest of the Crown in HMP Dartmoor, serving his *second* sentence for robbing a bank. He was, and had been since his late teens, a 'jelly-man', and highly proficient at this skilled but disreputable calling.

Apart from explaining about his true life-style, he admitted to having known nothing about gardening. When he was asked to prune roses, or whatever, he would first visit Kensington Lending Library to read up on the plants he was about to encounter. He must have had a natural talent for our garden at 28 Pembroke flourished.

During his years on the Moor Tom made me literally dozens of teddy bears and other soft toys, all of which were sold to raise funds for animal welfare societies. They were quite gorgeous, and I had to tell Tom I was almost sorry to learn he was to be freed, and deliveries would cease.

They didn't cease for long. Tom was not a reformed character, and we soon heard from him again - a long stretch at Long Lartin this time, but thankfully his very last. He now enjoys a quiet retirement in a country cottage with his dogs, a number of relatives, and many friends, including myself; a nicer, gentler man you could hardly meet.

I told my paymaster about my 'marvellous odd-jobber', to which he replied, "It would seem, Diana, that your friends have a propensity for prison - I begin to feel wary of you!"

Bastard! He was the man indirectly responsible for the incarceration of my 'husband' in Lewes and the Isle of Man, while I certainly had no hand in Tom's career.

I was delighted to be home again. Mama and I spent weeks entertaining and being entertained, and I took on an improbable new lover. I met Stanley Ellis at a party. He was a doctor, separated from his wife, and a Geordie, which did nothing to make communication easy. Our first meeting was marred somewhat by my asking him if he was a Welshman, as he had such a lovely lilt to his voice.

"I'm a Geordie," he said frostily.

"What's that?"

"I come from Newcastle."

"What a pity!" I meant it was a pity he was not Welsh. Fortunately our other differences were not immediately apparent, though we certainly argued vehemently throughout our first date (which was to watch the Barbarians play at Twickenham, I forget against whom). We were strongly attracted to each other, and our affair took a natural course until we realised how very incompatible were our views. Stanley was a radical rightwinger, and liberalism inflamed him. I must confess, I enjoyed teasing him, and often threw down the gauntlet just to see him explode.

One occasion, in the Bunch of Grapes in Brompton Road, a persistent drunk tried to chat me up, and never mind who I was with. Stanley got more and more irate, and threatened to 'do him over'. It was only at this point that I learned he had the highest possible belt at Judo!

I found him spoilt but very attractive, he called me a 'bloody socialist', which I took as a compliment. In fact, we had nothing in common apart from a love of Rugby football, which is an inauspicious foundation for romance. Nonetheless, I'm glad to have known him, and I felt a little sad as I set off for Belgrade in 1955.

I was weighed down with coffee, tea, soap, chocolate and loo paper - all like gold over there at that time - for my own use, as gifts and for bribes. What with warm clothes, my excess baggage cost an arm and a leg, and made even the blasé JAT Airline staff raise an eyebrow. I carried my music as hand baggage - forty songs take up little space, and I had brought along Malcolm Arnold's Overture, 'Tam O'Shanter' with full orchestration, as a gift for whoever was in charge of broadcasting.

In Belgrade I struck lucky. I was met by 'Frank', a friend from Associated Press, who warned me literally against everything, starting with the weather, the people and the food, and whose principal advice was to get out as soon as possible. Having just set foot on Serbian soil, I was less than enchanted, but I let him rattle on because he was a link with the past who might well give me a shove in the right direction, if only to get rid of me. He had good connections, but he guarded his back in a way which led me to believe he was involved with Intelligence one way or another (in fact I found out later he was with the CIA). Yugoslavia was full of opportunities for mischief, with the antagonisms between Orthodox, Catholic and Moslem cutting across those between Croats, Slovenes, Serbs, Montenegrans and the sundry leftover minorities of the Illyrian littoral.

Tito was a unifying force, but memories of wartime fratricide, and the usual misuse of the national emergency to settle private scores, still lay very near the surface. During the war Frank had been a close friend of James (Jesus) Angleton, and was quite as virulent an anti-Communist as he, so I questioned the wisdom of his appointment. A news agency should be unbiased. Still, this was not my problem, and in my own case he turned up trumps.

I made two key contacts through him - Zivojin Zdravkovic, Principal Conductor of the Belgrade State Symphony, and Aleksander Rankovic, a personal friend of Tito, and for many years Chief of State Security. Zivojin reminded me strongly of Malcolm Sargent; he was dark and saturnine in appearance, but full of vitality and wit, and with an eye for a pretty woman. He was an excellent musician, with a fine repertoire, but the Malcolm Arnold overture was new to him, and it sealed our friendship. Later on I was to take him other music, including Walton, Tippett and Britten, as well as Italian and French composers. In return he introduced me to Shostakovitch and some other Russians of whom I knew little.

It was a useful link, which over the next few years helped me to meet a number of highly-placed officials and perform at a concert in the open air amphitheatre at Pula, attended by Tito, Nehru, and General Nasser, who came over from the meeting of 'non-aligned' heads of state at Brioni. I remember in particular Nasser's gorgeous teeth, and Nehru, very elegant in his formal white. They were very unlike each other, though both had very courteous manners.

Rankovic was different. He looked, and was, a man whom anyone would do very well not to annoy or offend, though to me he was very helpful on my later visits to Yugoslavia and I found him a congenial contact.

From Belgrade I went to Zagreb, where I was reunited with Marko. We fell on each other's necks like lost children, and tears were near the surface for both of us. I knew he had had a hellish time in prison, yet he never griped about the punishment he had so unjustly received. He laughed describing the rats, the filthy water that seeped continually into the cells, the rotten food. No grumbles, no curses, he'd taken the bad times as in the past he'd enjoyed the good, and now things were better. He was a professor of English, married to a lovely young actress, Lila Andres, part Greek and very passionate.

They lived with her widowed mother, Nada, a sweet woman, made old before her time by overwork and deprivation. The apartment in Marulicev had large rooms, parquet floors, and fine old tiled stoves to heat each room. Electricity and gas were supposed to be available for cooking, but in practice were only on for short periods most days. The lifts were permanently out of order, and there had been no materials for building repairs since the war, though every building needed them. There was no toilet paper either, the only soap was made from pigs' fat and smelt rancid, and like everything else must be queued for. In winter, when the temperature dropped below freezing, and stayed there for months on end, there was no fruit, and few vegetables. Icicles hung like bars across the windows, and Marko ordered me not to get out of bed before the maid had arrived to light the stove in my room.

The maid was a peasant woman in her late twenties, though she looked fifty. She walked down the mountainside each morning at 5.00 a.m., bringing with her a basket of twigs and small branches to use as kindling, her hands and feet bound with rags as protection against the cold. The skin was no less cracked and raw on her face. I was shocked by the desperate poverty, as I had been in Poland. The lack of everything in the mid-fifties was far worse than we had had to endure in England at any time during the war, but these were countries that had been invaded and defeated, and seen civil war as well.

She simply adored my toiletry, and face creams of all sorts disappeared at an alarming rate, hand cream and lotions likewise. Marko was for admonishing her but I hadn't the heart to forbid her these small pleasures; after all, thanks to her I could get out of bed each day with a warm stove in my room.

I noticed that among her other afflictions her teeth had been worn down virtually to the gums. Nada explained that with the partisans she had existed for weeks and months on weeds and grasses, a few frozen or mouldy root vegetables, even sucking and biting on stones to keep the flow of saliva.

"Those were hard and difficult years to survive," Nada understated, and

I could only salute the courage and endurance of these people, the women as much if not more than the men, for many of them had the added burden of children to keep fed and safe.

The only cars I saw during my first few weeks in Zagreb carried diplomatic plates, otherwise goods went by horse and cart, people went by tram, occasionally by taxi, but mainly on foot. Even so, Saturday nights at the Esplanade Hotel were fun. We ate, drank and danced, and the place was always full. So were the bars, restaurants and coffee houses, if only because, being government-owned, they were warm and well-lit. Those who could afford them went there to read the local papers, and drink the strong, sweet, cheap Turkish coffee.

Despite all the cold, shortages and hardships the atmosphere was amazing. Everyone was kind, friendly and helpful, and I enjoyed a lot of laughs when, to save Nada from standing by the hour in freezing queues, I would go to the butcher or the fruiterer. There I was once (just once!) offered the priceless gift of two bananas and two oranges. A present for the *Franzsuski*, as I was called. Where they had come from I knew not, neither did I care to ask. Nada had a grandchild through her other daughter, Vera, and they nearly wept with sheer delight when I handed them over.

The butcher was a poppet as well, and sometimes gave us a bone with a little meat or fat for the Irish setter. Because I had only about ten words of Croatian, and no grammar, he and the queue would fall about laughing as I gestured, pointed, and used my pathetic vocabulary till I got what I wanted. *Pol Kile, Molim, dinstani snitzel*, was my stock phrase, meaning, 'Please a pound of steak' (or veal, or whatever). I never got it right but nobody minded. I would return to Nada's kitchen with many little extras for the pot. A tiny piece of pork, liver, kidney, dripping, plus a few gruesome bits of God-knows-what for the dog.

Marko had a favourite little fish restaurant, which was always packed. I didn't know what fish we were eating a lot of the time, but it was always delicious and the business was thriving. The only drawback was the smell. We came out with our clothes literally stinking of fish oil. The only way to get rid of it was to hang them from a window, and let the biting cold fumigate it away.

Through Jim Lambert, the Vice Consul, I was able to get a few bottles of whisky before I left for England, which I distributed as gifts to the shopkeepers who had been so generous. They were most gratefully received, though hard liquor (mainly raki or slivovic) was one thing that didn't seem to be in short supply. One could often see drunken bodies huddled in doorways late at night. They were generally picked up by friends or the police, which was as well, since otherwise they had only their vast intake of raki to keep them from freezing.

Jim was a great, shambling bear of a man, who seemed utterly unsuited to diplomatic work. He was so shy that for several days I was unable to understand what he said to me, because he half turned and covered his face with his hand while speaking. It was pure shyness on his part, and a desire not to inflict his whisky-laden breath on people. He had originally been an historian in the Houses of Parliament before being posted to Yugoslavia, where the people had taken him to their hearts. They realised that his odd appearance and uneasy manner cloaked his timidity, and a warm, generous heart. They also admired his capacity for drink, which is a distinction not easily come by in Yugoslavia.

Jim's aide was a delightful lady called Karla Kunc, whose husband had been a relative of the great diva Zinka Milanov. He had accompanied her to the United States, and never came back, leaving Karla virtually penniless. But she had a fine command of English, which found her a niche in the consulate, where she was well established by the time I knew her. A prodigious worker, she had like so many others gone through a gruelling war and postwar period. There was a certain air of unreality, meeting, in the civilised and relaxing atmosphere of an embassy party, people who had suffered the most hair-raising adventures and appalling deprivations. The effect was a little like being on a film set between takes.

When the time came to go back, Jim kindly offered to drive me to Trieste, where he was going on business, and offered me the protection of the diplomatic bag if I had use for it. It was typically kind, but also unworldly, as many people were looking for opportunities to smuggle gold, coded messages or other forbidden exports. I had been approached several times by people who hoped I might have access to special channels, and I always feigned surprise, and gave them a flat no. It is easy to get trapped that way, and I had become wary over the years.

I greatly enjoyed the journey to Trieste, though the roads were none too good. Jim's car was comfortable, and he was very good company, with a lot of interesting opinions on the possible future of the Soviet Bloc, now that he was no longer tongue-tied. He knew a lot of history, and had a natural curiosity, both of which made him a favourite with the Yugoslavs, though his untidy appearance and lack of sophistication did not endear him with the embassy in Belgrade.

When Anthony 'Puff' Asquith came to lecture on the films of Laurence Olivier, he and Jim appeared on the platform with hair and ties awry, unpressed trousers, and a general impression of being kitted out from jumble sale remnants, to the annoyance of the career diplomats among whom he found himself. Asquith was an excellent speaker, but on this occasion both had obviously been drinking for several hours before-hand. My great fear was that Jim had forgotten to check his flies - it would not have been the first time! He could very easily have been taken for a flasher.

Accounts of heavy drinking and its effects are a mainstay of English comedy, but in Jim's case it masked a deeper tragedy. He had loved but failed to captivate a Yugoslav girl, probably because of his shyness and diffidence. Doubtless she was right to follow her heart, but for him the light was gone from life. The only remaining interest lay at the bottom of a bottle. I have seen him literally pour whisky down his throat, straight from the neck, impatient that anaesthesia was so long a-coming. Shortly after his return to England he succeeded in drinking himself to death.

My original intention had been to fly home via Trieste and Vienna, but instead I took the Simplon express. My head and my music case were stuffed with notes and information about economic conditions, and sightings of Soviet troops in and around Belgrade and Zagreb. Some of it was on-the-ground economic information, about shortages of consumer goods and materials, their cost, the numbers of families sharing a single room, people who had come from the country keeping their hens or goats in their apartments. This was sensitive only in so far as it contradicted the Party Line. Then there were incidents of favouritism and receiving bribes by Party members who had patronage to dispense, in which connection some were not above blackmailing or denouncing each other to gain advancement.

In isolation, my observations had little immediate and individual importance, but once I had collated them, a balanced and comprehen-sive picture of Titoland appeared, susceptible to economic and political analysis. I had managed to do much the same in Poland.

Armed with my 'diaries' I approached my few remaining contacts from Curzon Street, and some other places where Eastern Bloc countries came under scrutiny. To my surprise and pleasure, my comments were well received, and I was told that informants were always welcome providing that they could produce clear, unbiased factual statements. No doubt they would be verified by agents in posts at embassies, but they would at least have something to start from.

As I had suspected, people like myself could see more of the game than those with official standing. Even businessmen came under very close scrutiny, as the case of Greville Wynne, a British agent picked up and imprisoned for spying, subsequently exchanged for Gordon Lonsdale, was to prove, but a daft female looking up wartime friends and singing to earn her keep would arouse few, if any, suspicions that I was not as simple as I looked.

One of my less admiring masters once exclaimed that I was a "Damned little serpent. You may seem innocent enough, but God help anyone who falls for your wide-eyed look." I was rather hurt at the time, but truly, this was praise from Caesar.

"You look like a girl, but you've a man's head on your shoulders!" Another backhander, yet with hindsight I think he was correct. I was good at detaching myself from people and events, and this 'semi-detached' attitude, which makes life so difficult for someone who wants a deep personal involvement, is fine for an agent. It was fine for me as well. The fact is, when the chips are down I like to go solo.

In 1960 I was in Dubrovnik, preparing for a recital at the Festival of Arts, when the shocking and unexpected news came that my father had suffered a heart attack. Mama immediately flew to Nice and alerted me from there. The Festival organiser, Professor Josip Depolo, was a delightful man, very good-looking, with impeccable manners, and an Italianate love of women. He could not have been kinder or more understanding when I told him I must cancel at short notice and leave at once for Menton. It meant a great deal of trouble for him, as another singer must be found, new programmes printed and so forth, but Josip, apart from making me promise to appear the following year, helped me on my way without a word of complaint.

Louis was very ill indeed when I reached the Côte. His doctor had warned him time after time to cut down on his cigarettes and gambling, but to no avail. His partner, Loulou Bourgoint, told me that a few days before the attack he had suffered heavy losses at the Sporting Club, and had complained of feeling off-colour after going to Confession on the Saturday. On Sunday morning he was shaving before Mass when he collapsed. Had old Marie, our housekeeper, not arrived with some shirts she had ironed, Louis would doubtless have died.

In retrospect, I think it would have been better that way. His doctor ordered him to live at his brother's house in the Val du Carei, where he was put on a regime which deprived him of smoking, drinking and gambling. Even sex with his current mistress, a married lady from Paris, was out, as being too much of an exertion. He developed a sharp and malicious tongue, and used it to torment poor Uncle Jo's wife, though she did all she could to please him.

Even my Cousin Danielle felt its rough edge, and was often reduced to tears by such uncalled-for remarks as "*Veau devient vache!*" (calf going on cow!) as he looked at her. She was in fact a pretty girl, but she had come late in Jo and Louise's life, and was not the sort of delicate and chic creature that had always pleased Louis. She was rather plump, gentle, and timid in the face of his repartee. I took him to task more than once, pointing out that he was living at Jo's house, and that Louise was preparing his special meals without complaint. He replied that he was making it worth their while.

He also felt slighted because Mama would not move back to France to take care of him, and even more angry when I took over the apartment in Palais Viale. He could not have remained there himself, it was on the fourth floor, which meant a hundred marble steps every time the lift failed. "Why don't you give up Palais Viale and take an entrance floor apartment? Then I could live with you."

Poor father, I tried to explain that I would never be resident anywhere for more than a few weeks at a time, and I certainly had no intention of coercing Mama into a change of life-style.

It is always sad to see someone you care about deteriorate, but Louis had always lived his own way, and was still doing so as far as his health permitted. Loulou his partner and Andrée, his enchantingly pretty wife, visited him literally every day with newspapers, keeping him up to date with the business, and driving him to and from church every Sunday, as he chose not to attend at the same time as his brother.

Mama came several times, though to no good purpose. Louis resented her indifference to him, which she felt was unfair. They were two people who had little in common by this time, and if love cannot be commanded, it should not be feigned. Between my other journeys, I flew in to be with him whenever I could. He and I got on well whenever we met. He knew I wouldn't stand for being treated as he did the rest of the family, and it amused him when I told him off for being beastly.

"You understand me, Diana, Louise and Danielle do not. They are stupid, and cry if you frown at them."

I understood him. They were sensitive, and one had to crack back at him, which they couldn't do.

"My brother married a peasant!"

This was no way to speak of a woman who was always trying to be kind. "She's a silly ass," I would reply, "and if she is a peasant, you be thankful - no one else would be so long-suffering."

He would laugh then, and call me hard-hearted. "No time for your father, a husband, or even a lover. Diana, you were always a strange girl."

So be it.

Chapter Twelve

Yugoslavia and California

During 1957 and 1958 I travelled extensively in eastern Europe, taking in Belgrade, Rab, Split, Zagreb and Dubrovnik, as well as Vienna, Prague and Warsaw. I was in Budapest briefly, after the uprising, but I had mixed feelings about the Hungarians. I remembered how they and some of the Bulgars had fought alongside the Croatian Fascist Anton Pavlecic's *Ustashi* autonomous army group to crush their fellow Yugoslavs. They had also lain in wait for Polish couriers and escapees coming via Zakopane and the treacherous frontier mountains and turned them over to the Nazis.

Even so, in that sad time, with the repression and bloodshed that followed the murder of Imre Nagy by Khruschev, it was impossible not to want to help. Whatever some of them might have been doing before, now they were fighting to free themselves from an alien system imposed on them by war. Many innocent people paid with their lives doing that. As I travelled my prejudices lessened, and I tried to put myself in the place of people on both sides whom I knew to have committed the most heinous crimes. They had seemed, to themselves and others, to be like other people, yet they had done things horrible past belief. What had impelled them?

It required great and continuous efforts to keep sentiment from clouding my assessment of political situations. If I was to return with worthwile information of any kind, it must be unbiased. Not easy, especially when I was confronted with my friends' experiences in Poland, and the Italian atrocities in Yugoslavia.

In Zagreb I met Vishnja Serdar, who was in charge of radio pro-grammes. She immediately signed me up for a series of recordings to be broadcast later, and found me a delightful accompanist called Freddie Dosek. This was far better than going to the hassle of getting a visa for Dan Kelly, who in any case preferred not to fly, and would not have enjoyed the countries of eastern Europe.

An excellent rapport grew up between Freddie, Vishnja and myself, and I made recordings for all the major stations, principally of folk songs. I was already tri-lingual, Spanish came easily, and Croatian is pronounced as it is written. I was therefore able to sing a few songs in this language as well, though not as major numbers, and certainly not in public, but I was able to make and illustrate interesting comparisons with Welsh and Irish ditties. There are certain folk cadences which strike a chord wherever they come from.

It seemed to me that Split bred a race of exceptionally handsome men, and I could have believed that the authorities hand-picked them to parade the streets, beguiling and impressing visitors from abroad. Amazingly, these included droves of Germans, keen to enjoy the Adriatic coast. They seemed quite oblivious to the open dislike of the locals, though there were still places in Yugoslavia where no German dared show his face.

My old Polish friend, Wilhelm Rotkiewicz, who was Tito's chief signals officer throughout the war, told me of a small town where a banner was prominently and permanently displayed, reading:

NO GERMAN MAY SET FOOT WITHIN THIS TOWN

The Italian reputation had also suffered a well-deserved knock. It is true that certain officers were so sickened by the brutality and repression in Slovenia that they mutinied rather than take any more part in the atrocities. They paid the price of their heroism in the cause of minimal decency. But in general they behaved no better than the Nazis, the *Ustashi* and General Mikhailovic's Serbian *Chetniks*, who helped the Germans against Tito. But if anything, the latter two groups were the worst, as they committed atrocities against their own kind.

The Adriatic coast in summer was like the Côte d'Azur at a bargain price, with a sea so blue and clear that you felt you could touch the bottom, islands shaded by trees and shrubs, others barren stretches of rock. Krk combined both aspects, one half being stark rock, the other thick and inviting with green and perfumed vegetation.

Rab was then, as now, haunted by the horror of the Italian-operated concentration camp, but it had all the appearance of a sleepy seaside island resort, with boats for hire and a comfortable hotel on the quayside to accommodate tourists - and yes, they were mainly Germans. They were attracted by the nudist beaches, and seemed to spend the whole night moving between each others' rooms. When I complained to the manager, he explained conspiratorially, "Madame, you will understand, they are very uncivilised - they exchange wives and lovers when on holiday."

Did they? I've no idea, but I cursed their rompings. I'm a poor sleeper at the best of times, and the slightest sound could not only wake me but prevent me from sleeping again.

One young, rather flashy man singled me out. He began by approaching our table on the patio, and after a smirk or two at me, placed his gold watch, bracelet, medallion and chain, signet rings and gold cigarette lighter in front of me. Marko, who fortunately was staying with his mother and uncles at their old villa, acted as interpreter.

"Marko," I asked, seeing that he was laughing, "What does this idiot want? Is he trying to sell me these things? If so, tell him to get lost."

"No, Diana." Marko began a rapid conversation in German, to which the man listened avidly. Then he turned back to me.

"Not selling, buying!" He grinned at my obvious puzzlement. "This fellow comes from Hamburg, where he owns a big sausage factory. He is married with two children, and quite wealthy. He is looking for a mistress - a woman of chic, intelligence and charm. He has been observing you carefully these last few days, and wishes to know if you will consider his proposition. He offers a nice flat, plenty of spending money, and as much freedom as you wish, within reason. The gold is to show you that he is a man of substance."

I was amazed. As a young woman travelling alone I was considered fair game, and I'd been propositioned often enough. Generally there were no difficulties. Most men are easily dissuaded, without resort to rudeness or hassle. But this Sausage King's approach set a new low in vulgarity.

"Tell the stupid bugger to piss off," I snapped: not the most ladylike way of declining an offer, but I was determined not to be misunderstood. Marko deftly and politely explained that I had no interest in becoming his gold-plated, part-time, reasonably free mistress.

I'll never forget his departure. With a face like a smacked child he stood up, kissed my hand, bowed and walked away disconsolate. "There goes Mr Moneybags," Marko said, and we both began to laugh. Soon we were giggling uncontrollably, but I wonder ... Everyone gets someone in the end, and the German certainly lacked neither determination nor self-confidence. He wanted a woman of chic, intelligence and charm - also one who would succumb to *that* approach, and never mind if they had a common language. What can she have been like? If he's reading this, perhaps he can send me a photograph.

I had an experience of a very different kind when Lila and I took a train from Rijeka. As she was between films, she accompanied me as an interpreter, and we hoped to return to Zagreb in a warm and not too crowded train. A smartly-dressed man sat opposite us, but to our horror, two rough smelly men burst into the carriage just as the train was pulling out. They were already very merry, and bottles of slivovic protruded from each pocket of their greasy sheepskin-lined cloaks. They took liberal swigs, while Lila and I sat trying to look unconcerned, and uninterested in their noisy chatter. They fished out a steel measure, and offered nips to us and the smart man, but showed no resentment when we all rather sniffily refused.

Oh, how the mighty fell! As we chugged through the heavy snow, we began to hear the unmistakable sound of the wind of the Siberian steppes, the *Borrah*, above the sound of the train. In a very short time we shuddered to a halt, and could hear the sound of voices raised in anger and fear. Lila found an inspector, who explained that we were bogged down in the snow which was blocking the line. The wind was blowing hard, compacting the snow, and he advised us to put on as many clothes as we could, because in no time at all heating and possibly lighting would be off. Fuel must be conserved for the engines, which might, hopefully, extricate us in a few hours. Men were clearing the blocked line, but conditions were so far below freezing that they could only stay out a few minutes at a stretch before having to come back on the train to thaw out.

Lila and I were reasonably kitted out for the climate. We wore oiled wool socks in our thick, waterproof boots. We were warmly clad underneath as well as on top, but even so, the icy cold began to seep through to us. As we huddled together, I noticed that the smart gentleman was turning a really dreadful colour - or to be exact, several colours, blotchy red and purple, mixed with paler spots. His teeth were chattering. He explained to us that his only baggage was an overnight bag containing toiletries and a change of shirt and underwear.

I was afraid he would have a heart attack or lose consciousness, so we sorted through out suitcases, and took out every woollen item we could find. We began wrapping his body and extremities in gloves, scarves, hoods, shawls, cardigans - never mind the fit, just get on as many layers as possible. The poor fellow soon looked absolutely ludicrous, with a hood *and* a woolly cap on his head, and two pairs of gloves stretched as best we could over his rather big hands. We draped shawls and scarves round his feet (he had only shoes and galoshes, no boots) and packed the inside of his jacket with ladies' vests and cardigans. Finally we covered his overcoat with two very fine and very expensive woolly dressing gowns, which I had bought from the White House in Bond Street because they were so light and packed into nothing. Their pale peach and pink did nothing at all for the mottle of his skin.

Nevertheless, his shivering body and chattering teeth showed signs of improvement, and when we finally felt a few tremors showing that the train was about to start moving again, his condition seemed stable. All this time the two ruffians had sat gurgling their plum brandy, but as soon as Lila and I returned to our seats they sprang into action. Off came the offensive sheep-lined cloaks, and before we could say no we were each enveloped in the smelly wool. I had imagined fleas, at the very least, living happily in their cosy recesses, but these thoughts were swept aside by the blessed warmth of them on our cold and aching bodies.

The ruffians, were, in fact, shepherds, they told us, who had been spending a few days in Rijeka having a booze-up after selling some sheep. They insisted we take a nip or two of the slivovic, and literally poured it into the no-longer smart traveller, who arrived in Zagreb safe from frostbite, but definitely tight as a tick.

It is small experiences like this that bring home to you how much you take for granted such little luxuries as hot running water, a warm room, and a bed with warm dry sheets. For millions in the east there were none of these things, and hundreds of thousands died from the lack. As a child in England I had seen some of the deprivation that followed the crash of 1929 and the depression, but that was relative proverty. However unpleasant the conditions for the unemployed or the low-paid in the British Isles, they were nothing to what prevailed in eastern Europe.

Others learnt the same lesson. Marko, the sometime sybarite of the Diplomatic Corps, never once complained at having to get up at 5.30 a.m. so as to start teaching at 6.00. A typical day for him would start with lessons from then till 2.00 p.m. Then came lunch and a brief rest, followed by more teaching from 4.00 to 9.00 p.m. This was for six days a week, supplemented by as many translations as he could fit in between. It was the only way he could earn enough to pay for the rent, the maid, and food for the household.

Lila earned very little, and spent what she made on keeping up her hair and clothes. Nada, who had a minute widow's pension, did all the shopping (with its endless queues), cooking, washing and ironing as her contribution. Fortunately Marko was fluent in six languages, so there was a constant flow of translations to be done, which paid better than the teaching.

We would usually eat lunch at 2.30 p.m., either soup with dumplings and whatever vegetables were available, or stew followed by a compote, usually of apples which Nada had stored from the summer. Then came the daily luxury and ritual; coffee beans, freshly roasted and ground. Tea, coffee and sugar were extremely expensive and hard to find, with green coffee beans the most sought-after of all. There was a black market, of course, but there the prices could be prohibitive.

I once asked Marko what a certain queue was for.

"Diana, whenever you see a queue, join it," he replied. "It means there is something to buy - soap, a roll of toilet paper, matches, aspirins, hair shampoo - something!"

So I would dutifully step in among the throng and make conversation in pidgin Croatian, French, English and Italian. My clothes marked me as a foreigner, and I took to having a few bars of chocolate in my bag in case children were waiting with their parents. I had taken boxes of small sweets, packets of Smarties and Rowntrees Fruit Gums as little treats on all my travels, but especially in winter, when my journeys might cover Christmas and New Year. The joy in the children's faces was a reward out of all proportion to the value.

Nada had an admirer, a constant companion, who had been a friend of her family for many years. Aleksander Paladiu was a charming gentleman who played second violin in the Zagreb Opera Orchestra, and though he was considered ready for retirement, his musicianship was still of such quality that he was retained on the insistence of the principal conductor. He spoke perfect French, which was useful for Nada and me, as otherwise we could only communicate by signs and a few words in German and Croatian. He made life much easier for her all round, and he would also sometimes accompany me to shops, or take me to churches, museums and other places of interest.

On a couple of occasions he came with me when I took Lila's dog for a walk. I will never forget his look of horror on the occasion when I called to him, "*Tito, Tito, vieni, vieni qui.*"

"Diana, you must not do that, you will be arrested!" Aleksander seemed in a real panic.

"Why ever not?" I turned again, and repeated my call. Fortunately the dog returned this time, and I fastened the lead.

"Come away, quickly." He hustled me out of the little park, and rushed down the street.

"What is wrong?" I noticed his pale, strained face. "Are you ill?"

At last he relaxed. "Diana, *ma chère*, do you realise what you've done?" He saw my bemused look. "You called a dog after the Marshall!"

"So?"

"It is an insult. The police could arrest you."

I couldn't help laughing. I took the dog out daily, and until that moment had never given a thought to its name. "But Aleksander, lots of dogs in England have been called Churchill or Montgomery - it's a compliment to the great men."

"Not here," he told me, "And in any case, the dog's name is Tziso, not Tito."

I'm afraid I never mastered the correct spelling or pronunciation, and 'Tito' the animal remained. I was always greeted with smiles by people who heard me call, and even the police managed a grin when we passed each other. But it shows how nervous and anxious some sections of the population remained, even so long after the war ended.

I never asked people their political views directly, but I listened avidly to all their discussions. It was surprising how much could be picked up with pricked ears, once I had a little of the language.

An instance occurred when Lila was filming, and suggested that I visit the set of Jadran Films. Having seen a Hollywood studio, I accepted with alacrity, keen to make a comparison, but I was totally unprepared for the inadequate equipment or conditions that prevailed. Only one camera, lighting at the mercy of the unreliable public supply, a studio shared between several productions, and a wretchedly makeshift wardrobe. Yet the unit made me welcome - the only fly in the ointment was the director, Branko Bauer. His name will only be known to specialists in the English-speaking world, as to the best of my knowledge none of his films have appeared with English subtitles, though they have been shown in France and Germany.

Branko Bauer was nothing less than a beast, yet I lost my heart to him, (though fortunately not my head). Although we were strongly attracted to each other physically, and our friendship has survived up to this day, it is probably because we were never lovers in the full sense. On our first meeting he made an audible aside to his cameraman that I had beautiful eyes, but little else to commend me.

I asked if he understood French, and when he replied that he did, suggested that my one redeeming feature was one more than I had been able to find in him. It doesn't sound an auspicious opening gambit, but it turned out to be the very best for this most unusual man. Exceedingly attractive, intelligent, well-read - and with a venomous tongue that he enjoyed using. Cold and remote one day, affectionate the next, he had woman after woman, and swore he'd never loved any of them.

"I despise them, Diana, and I destroy them. Why?"

The answer lay in his desire to dominate. His sarcasm made him plenty of enemies, and affected all his emotional relationships, as if he was possessed by demons intent on wrecking his life. It sank his first marriage, and even in the late fifties, his ex-wife (who was also a Party member) reported him to the Communist authorities for having allowed me into the studio without getting their clearance first. Branko was hauled over the coals for this misdemeanour, and received an official warning and reprimand. I found the whole episode ludicrous, but it could have had dire consequences if I had not been in good odour with the ruling bureaucrats.

I don't know if her action was fuelled by political zeal, jealousy or pure malice, but it shows the sort of atmosphere that 'Big Brother' can bring about in the rest of his family. It was so in Nazi Germany, and Maoist China. It is as if every totalitarian leader, whether of right or left, conceals an aspect of himself which knows how ludicrous and humourless he is, fears desperately to be exposed, and will go to any lengths to punish mockery of himself. Among the small-minded bureaucrats who serve the greater evil this aspect is foremost, as it corresponds most closely to their own emotional make-up. The fruit is repression and terror: *Kamerade* or Comrades - the word mocks itself.

I collected many sorts of information in Yugoslavia, and though doubtless much was discarded as irrelevant or duplicated, much was of value to the paymaster I had acquired through Lars (and whose name and nationality I am not going to disclose). I was an accepted informer, but life has tricks to play, even on the tricksters.

In London I collapsed with a severe haemorrhage, and was rushed to the London Clinic for emergency surgery. I had been suffering various internal problems for some years - kidney stones, minor haemorrhages, and so forth, requiring corrective surgery, but this time I needed a major operation, and my convalescence was protracted. I had to shelve my plans to return to the east.

Pam and James suggested that Mama and I spend a few months at 1018 Pamela Drive, their lovely Californian home. They promised to put the guest house at my disposal, and I was stretchered through Heathrow, to arrive at Beverly Hills three days before Christmas. There was sunshine, Pam delighted to see us, and a Rolls Royce to whisk us off to our home for the next several months.

We celebrated Christmas as quietly as we could, given the masses of gifts, flowers and good wishes that poured in, and received only a few close friends of the Masons. I spent my time telephoning my circle from bed, as I had to rest through most of the day. Altogether, our first few weeks passed in a haze of luxury. Mama and I basked in it, and chatted hilariously with Pam. She was as beautiful, witty and amusing as always, and kindness itself to us.

The shock came when we realised that her marriage to James was played out, and a split was coming. We were quite unprepared for this; when we arrived in California, we had no idea that the marriage was even in trouble. We had always kept in touch by letter, and met on the few occasions when they travelled to Europe together, though Pam was becoming less and less inclined to accompany James when he was filming. He would travel with Johnny Monaghan, and so far as we knew, the separations were simply the result of his work, not a sign of impending breakup.

In fact, neither Pam nor James had ever faced, let alone discussed, the growing rift in their relationship. When the break came, the hostility nursed over many years burst forth in a torrent of poisonous enmity. As the can of worms opened up, it was impossible for their joint friends not to take sides. Pam's children, Portland and Morgan, sided with their mother, rather than James, though he did all he could to express his care for them. I remembered my own feelings for Louis, and marked preference for Mama, so I understood, but I know it hurt James at the time. I remembered Portland from my earlier visit; now she was sweet and pretty, and getting to be a big girl. Morgan was only five, a dear little boy, already a great pool player, and bright as a button, but too young really to take in what was going on.

There was a shadow on the household, including Mama and myself as guests in it. It is never easy to play pig in the middle, and as Mama and I were attached to both James and Pam, it made for some uncomfortable moments, but this matter has already been covered in my biography of James, and I do not intend to rehash it here.

As my health and energy returned we re-started our round of visits to friends, including Knoxie, the Sinatras, the Rozsas, Judy (now divorced from Vivian), Vivian and his new wife and Red and Esther Krohn. Paul Gregory and his mother were like an extended family to Mama and me; we were so thoroughly pampered that we even considered settling in California permanently, in the house next door to Knoxie. It was the ideal size, and quite lovely, but we decided against it in the end - the Mason divorce was going too badly.

What we had hoped would be a sensible arrangement between two adult intelligent people degenerated into a series of violent and bitter scenes, culminating in open war. It was no atmosphere for Mama and me. In any case, I had decided I must spend at least half of each year in Europe if I was to continue my political researches. I was also becoming disenchanted with the political double standards of the US State

Department. They tolerated brutal and corrupt rightwing regimes in their 'own backyard', as they insultingly called Central and South America and the Caribbean, while condemning very comparable leftwing ones in Asia, Africa and eastern Europe. Roosevelt's 'He's a sonofabitch, but he's *our* sonofabitch,' (of Anastasio Somoza) sums up the attitude all too well, with its macho 'realism' which was actually as unrealistic as it was immoral.

All my old feelings of anger rose up once more, with the sense of betrayal on behalf of those who had been sacrificed at the altar of expediency. I realised that if I started to speak my mind about the administration, I would shortly become a prohibited immigrant.

Europe was our home, and so it must remain. With much regret at leaving behind so many kind and generous friends, Mama and I set off for London. We arrived just in time for some sad and unwelcome news: my father had undergone an operation for cancer of the throat, and had died a few days later.

Chapter Thirteen

Crunch Times

It was a sad homecoming, and very traumatic for Mama. Louis's death came as a great shock, though we had known his heart was in poor shape. Even Uncle Jo had been kept in the dark about the full extent of his ill-health, and had had no idea of what a risky operation he was to undergo. Loulou, his partner, had not even been told he had cancer.

I cursed the medics, who in the manner of their kind had treated the disease rather than the patient. They must have known how little chance he had, and could have allowed him a less restrictive regime in his last years.

The funeral took place at the Sacre Coeur, with the pomp and splendour of the high-class Italian style. There were choirs to sing the Requiem Mass, sumptuous wreaths on tripods, and a book for visitors to sign after they had filed past to render their last respects. For Mama the long Catholic service was an ordeal, but what she found much worse was that prior to burial, Louis's body was displayed in the funerium, for visitors to weep over the coffin.

My cousins, their husbands, sons and daughters, and various members of the de Rosso clan who had made a point of never meeting my mother, gathered with the townsfolk to make a show of public grief, which with the best will in the world can hardly have been sincere in every case. She found the whole business of the viewing deeply distasteful, and an affront and intrusion into private grief. I suppose to them she was still just an ex-mistress of Louis's, and only incidentally the mother of his child.

She returned to London as soon as the funeral was over, while I awaited the storms that I knew would break out over Louis's will.

It had been made under French law, which differs from English in that final disposition of money and property must be into roughly equal shares. I intended to see that my father's share of the business should pass to his partner, who had done tremendous work expanding the scope of the office, and received very little reward for the friendship and support he and his wife had lavished on Louis in his last years.

Half the business had already been sold to my cousin Gaby's husband, when the offices were transformed and capital was needed to finance the cost. There were not sufficient internal funds, because of Louis's gambling, I suspect. He and I had often discussed the final carve-up, and we had agreed that Loulou was entitled to the half share.

The outburst that greeted the reading of the will left the notary gasping. "It is a disgrace!" was the general cry. "What about Diana? She should inherit!" and so on. They didn't care a hoot for Diana, but they couldn't stomach the idea of a non-family person having equal control.

As I had no wish to become embroiled in such a quarrel, I let it be known that unless all the family accepted the terms as written, I would take action in the French courts for my share, and as I was not domiciled in France, I would see that every legal means was deployed to delay the hearing so that meanwhile, no one present would get a penny piece. In fact Louis had died with very little money and property apart from the business share.

All my relatives were more than comfortable, but the thought of losing what little entitlement was theirs sent them scurrying to their lawyers, who sent them back quickly enough with their agreements. As for my own position, in 1947 when Louis came to England he had given me a sum that he had put by for when I was twenty-one, or for when I married. As I was now past that age and showed no likelihood of catching or even wanting a husband, we had agreed that I should accept my dowry and not figure in the will, assuming there was anything to leave.

He bequeathed his exhibition bronzes of athletes, nudes and animals, some much-prized models, and a few special antiques to Mama. They included two grandfather clocks, some chairs, Italian glass and Lalique pieces, but when he died we found that they had all been taken from the apartment and sold. This was how he had made it 'worth his while' for Uncle Jo to look after him. Fair enough. Mama wanted nothing, and had never looked to benefit from her love affairs. Her own generosity was well known, and she knew well enough that Louis had been hurt by her refusal to return to France.

I decided to keep up the Palais Viale apartment. It was centrally located, with lovely views, four bedrooms with balconies, two living-rooms and a huge bathroom in pink marble with a tiled floor. It even had a room for a maid-of-all-work on the fifth floor. There was an old boiler in the kitchen which supplied central heating and hot water, but meant that our dear old housekeeper Marie Verrando must drag buckets of fuel up four flights of back stairs, so I arranged for it to be converted to gas.

The bathroom had been transformed into its present luxurious and elegant condition just before the war, and it was a horrid fantasy of Mama's that if the Italians invaded they might smash the marble, or worse still, Mussolini might disport himself in her bathtub, with or without Clara. Why he should choose our block, with so many luxurious hotels and magnificent villas available, was never clear, but it preyed on Mama's mind, possibly because she feared *Il Duce* would want to exact retribution from my father's recalcitrant contempt for his regime. In fact we were lucky. No such atrocity occurred, and Palais Viale suffered no damage at all.

It was to prove a fortunate decision. I was shortly to face some unexpected and unwelcome events which made my return to France unavoidable, but meanwhile I was to meet a charming English family. The fifth floor of Palais Viale had been bought by the Church of England to use as a vicarage for what I suppose one might call the chaplain to the English colony.

During my childhood it had been the home of the elderly Comte de Tilley, who had a reputation for inviting young ladies of the town to entertain him. His favourite frolic was to pursue them over the apartment armed with an epée. The squeals and scamperings were just what he needed to re-invigorate his ageing powers, and had given rise to many complaints from other residents, but Louis had taken a more sympathetic view. Even so, as a poor sleeper I was glad to find that the incumbent of the Protestant Church of St. John was more staid in his habits.

Cyril and Lina Gardner were two of the nicest people imaginable, and through them I met their son John, a delightful and widely talented man, at that time theatre critic of the *Stratford Herald*, his pretty wife Margaret, and their two children Alexis and Simon. Even at the tender age of six, Simon had all the charm and love of the ladies that characterised his father and grandfather. Cyril had an appreciative eye, as did John, for a well turned leg and shapely bottom, and this, along with his partiality for a glass of wine, endeared him to the French.

John was later to become one of the most successful popular novelists of his time, the creator of Boysie Oakes. He began his career as a naval padre, made and spent a fortune, and endured many tribulations, before settling down to write a series of spy stories and novels which has kept him among the bestsellers ever since. His autobiography, 'Spin the Bottle', is very well worth reading. He has never changed, and remains as kind and unspoilt to this day, a rare friend.

I went back to London briefly before setting off on my travels again. I was due in Vienna, for a recital at the Brahms-Salle, and from there I intended taking the Chopin Express to Warsaw, then Denmark, Sweden and the Netherlands to complete the series. I would use local pianists in eastern Europe, and Dan Kelly was to join me in Copenhagen. I completed the tour, but I had developed an aggravating cough with cold sweats, left over from a recent bout of pneumonia, I thought. Moreover, my breath control was not quite what it had been. Worse still, and for the first time, my intonation showed a disturbing waywardness. How I got through my last event, I can't say, but the critics were quick to note my deterioration as a performer.

At the end of the tour I collapsed with what X-rays showed to be viral pneumonia, which seriously damaged both my lungs, collapsing the right. The specialist was adamant that my previous lung problems had been caused by the same virus, and the damage now visible stemmed from several years of infection. Now I must face the consequences. One doctor advised me to stop singing for at least a year and preferably two. Another, more pessimistic in his diagnosis, told me bluntly that in his opinion I would do better to give up the stresses and strains of a singing career, and look for something else.

I felt he was right, but I determined to have a final fling before going back to France. A year after the disastrous Scandinavian tour, I was once again with Dan choosing a programme for a final performance at the Wigmore Hall. I went to Bruce Boyce, a tall and very handsome Canadian baritone who was teaching at the Royal Academy of Music. He and Dan nursed my voice through a not too demanding but musically quite interesting programme - Lully, Ravel, Chausson, Poulenc, Campra, Nin, de Falla, and some pretty pieces by Bellini. Bruce worked wonders, but I knew in my heart that this was the end. I must retire. My voice still sounded quite fine, but oh, the effort to breathe! I had lost my springboard, and was not prepared to go on having to make excuses for less-than-able performances, which people in dwindling numbers might attend out of sympathy.

For this reason I decided to share my last public appearance with the negro baritone, Thomas Baptiste. He and I were already firm friends, and we both hoped it would bring him to the fore as a singer. He had a fine voice, and had graduated to the stage via the Opera School receiving many good notices as a singer and even more as an actor, mainly in character parts.

As I took my final bow as a singer many thoughts crowded my mind. The period from my début to my swansong covered over twenty years.

Spurned opportunities, lack of ambition, too private and introverted a character - I had plenty of reasons for not having reached the pinnacles of fame and fortune, but had I regrets? Only one, and that was for my mother. She, I knew, would have enjoyed my success, not for any glory reflected on herself, but for what she regarded as my years of study and sacrifice having been rewarded. To me it had not been a sacrifice at all. I had enjoyed every minute. A singer's life, like that of any artist, can be solitary and demanding, but I was a loner, and I liked to work.

Piaf's famous 'Je ne regrette rien' might have been my theme. My life had given me what I wanted, even if it had disappointed Mama and those who had forecast a glittering future when I first set out.

Tom and I sang our last duets, duly obliged with solo encores, and ended the recital with 'Trot here and there' from 'Veronique'. The audience was very enthusiastic, and we afterwards held court among our well-wishers in the Green Room. Oda Slobodskaya, the great Russian singer and teacher, who had attended several of my performances, came to say goodbye and commiserate over my health. "Take a long holiday, then come back, your voice is in good shape, Diana, the Respighi songs proved it. All you need now is to rest."

Dear kind woman! Maybe a long rest would heal my lungs, but I no longer wanted a career. Mama was getting past the teatime of her life, and I wanted to spend more time with her, for the companionship which had always been such a pleasure to us both.

A curious little incident crowned the evening. A tall, good-looking man took my hand in his, kissed it very gravely, and smiled with obvious amusement at my surprised expression.

"I came to hear you, just once, and I must admit, I had no idea that you were such a fine artist - the Spanish songs were utterly delightful."

I went on gawping at him. These were not the usual words that strangers mutter backstage.

"You don't remember me, do you?"

"Forgive me, but no," I replied.

"I was your 'husband', for a brief period."

I couldn't believe it! Rodriguez etc., etc. Lopez!

He couldn't stay, he was leaving London next day. We talked no more than five minutes, and as he walked away, I thought back to those early days in the war. So much had happened, yet there was half a lifetime ahead. What might it bring? No time to ponder. Tom and his special friends, I with mine, were going off for a farewell celebration together. Tomorrow was another day.

Just as I became an old crock Mama suddenly developed a spinal pain of great intensity, which in turn affected her pelvis and her legs. I feared a diagnosis of bone cancer. She had occasionally complained of backache, and been treated for arthritis in her knees, but she was still a very healthy woman for her age, full of energy and vitality.

Fortunately Mama was found to be in no danger. She was suffering from Paget's disease, which is a progressive thickening of the bone. It's quite common, and in men often makes them need a larger hat size. It's not always painful either, though that depends on the area affected. In Mama's case it had started in several places at once, and though the specialists assured her that the pain would cease after a little while, they also expressed surprise that she had taken so long to feel severe discomfort. Paget's could affect the kidneys by putting pressure on them, and the eyes as well.

Twenty-eight Pembroke Gardens, with its many stairs, was no house for anyone suffering from even minor bone problems. You could guarantee the bell would ring just as you had reached the first or second floor. Steps to the front door, steps to the garden, all must be negotiated many times in a normal day. It was time to take stock of our situation.

John Sutherland Banks, our family doctor and a good friend, suggested moving into a flat, but how could we do that? We had a cat, two pugs, Lola the Amazonian parrot, and my aviary - two large rooms, literally full of cages, open flights and about a hundred birds of various species - canaries, budgerigars, Indian ring-necks, peach-headed and moustached parakeets, cockatiels, fire, zebra and blue finches, red cardinals and some others, at least one pair of each, and all as tame as could be. I had collected the birds over several years, and loved them all dearly, which Dr Banks said was an unwise hobby for someone with delicate lungs. He also objected strongly to my habit of feeding the London pigeons that flocked to the garden - it seems they carry a pneumonia virus or something - but the poor things were as hungry as all the other wild birds that came to feed with us.

I was unsure what to do for the best. Granted, Menton was available, we had a number of old friends still on the Côte, the climate would suit me better and so on, but to part with our old house would mean the end of my long love affair with London. How could we do it?

Two additional factors presented themselves. Sheila's husband, Bill, was having to take early retirement from Avianca because of ill health, and Sheila decided that they and their youngest daughter, Georgina, should move to Cagnes-sur-Mer. Sheila, a sun-worshipper, hoped to enjoy the Mediterranean warmth more than the grey skies of England. She also felt that the slower tempo of life would be better for Bill.

While we were still weighing pros and cons, the decisive factor appeared. Basil and Anne Appleby, and their two daughters Lucy and Suky, who were my god-daughters, were looking for a larger house. The girls were of different characters and ages, and needed a room each. Basil had quit acting in favour of production by this time, and required an office somewhere where he could entertain. Pembroke Gardens was ideal, and as there were only a few years of the lease left, I offered the place to them. It was the perfect solution. I knew the house would be well cared for, and that my old room would be at my disposal when I visited London. I gave my beautiful Brinsmead grand piano to Lucy, and the die was cast.

I set about dispersing the wildlife. Mr Yelland, curator of birds at Regent's Park accepted my offer of the smaller exotics, and I was proud to be able to hand over several varieties not previously represented. The conditions were excellent, and I felt no anxiety for the birds' welfare. The larger breeds went to Whipsnade, where again I was happy to see them installed in free-flight enclosures, with first-class care and attention. The canaries and tortoises went to Colchester, where they also had maximum freedom and proper care.

It was a wrench, but Mama's health and happiness were of paramount importance. She flew to Nice, bringing a tiny pug puppy for Paule Grenot, a friend who ran the Edouard VII restaurant with her husband, Leo. I followed in an American Ford estate car driven by our old Irish friend Desmond Jordan, currently between engagements. For additional company, I had my huge cat, Mr Tweed, and our two pugs, Biffi and Barlow, the latter so called because he looked exactly like Stratford Johns in his role as Inspector Barlow in 'Z Cars' and 'Softly, Softly'. Lola the beloved parrot was not with me - she had suffered a sudden heart attack, and died within minutes, leaving Mama utterly wretched. We never knew Lola's age, as she had been a rescue case when we took her on, but she was a great character, and very gentle - beak and all. We missed her endless chatter.

There was a lot of clutter to dispose of on the removal; music, records, costumes, wigs, librettos. I gave virtually everything that students could use to music colleges, keeping very few mementoes for myself. I didn't need pictures, press cuttings and the like. My memories were in my head, what my father used rudely to call my *appartement vide*. Indeed, in those days memory was my greatest talent. I could still tabulate dates and data with no difficulty and had almost perfect recall at that time. Now no longer; time and age have blunted my wits to some extent, but they were sharp enough as I settled down to the life of a lady of leisure - or so I hoped.

Picture if you can myself and Desmond setting out from London in a car piled high with hand-baggage, bowls, blankets and food, also two dogs and a huge Tabby cat yowling with rage in his basket. We spent the first night in an hotel in Boulogne which we had used before and knew gave good value - large rooms and bathrooms, and delicious food in its own brasserie. Our plan was to set off early in the morning and really step on it, stopping only long enough for the pugs to relieve themselves, but there was an unforeseen problem. Mr Tweed refused to use his tray before being shoved into his basket, which meant that shortly after we set out there was the most ghastly operation, as his bowels were evacuated among pitiful miaows. Inevitably, this took place without warning at a point where it was impossible to stop.

Desmond, always rather squeamish, couldn't wait to crash out of the car with the pugs, while I had to close all the windows, let the cat loose while I cleaned up the mess, pack everything in plastic bags, replace the cat in his basket, and gasp in some air tainted with nothing worse than petrol fumes. Hey ho, it was my cat, I suppose, but oh, for some air-fresheners that day!

On the second day it rained torrentially for hours on end, making driving difficult and dangerous. As a non-driver, I couldn't help Desmond at the wheel.

The final day started with another 'Operation Cat', but luckily the rain had stopped, so Desmond and the pugs could stand outside while I attended to Mr Tweed. We reached Grenoble, anticipating an easy drive to Menton, but no such luck. Our road had been blocked by a landslide, so we had to carry on by the Route Napoleon. This involves mountains, valleys, dense and unpredictable fog patches and in our case a car that suddenly developed a slipping clutch, so that when we accelerated on a steep incline we tended not to surge forwards, but slide backwards. It could have been worse. The dogs behaved in keeping with their gentle breeding, and Mr Tweed, having caused so much trouble, slept soundly.

We finally arrived at Palais Viale close to midnight, there to find Mama in bed and the pug puppy not yet handed over to the new and rapturous owner. The parquet was covered with newspaper against unwelcome puddles, and I have to confess, I greeted the little beast with less than perfect pleasure.

"He didn't take the journey very well."

Mama's lame excuse cut no ice with me. I knew she wanted to keep the little bundle herself, but within a day or two she decided that Barlow and Biffi's noses were out of joint, and they didn't enjoy being chivvied about by a miniature replica of themselves with tiny sharp teeth.

Some homecoming. Desmond remained for a few days before returning to London. Now I must adjust to life without work of any kind. It wasn't easy, but a round of entertainment, warm weather and the Casino within five minutes helped me to settle down.

For Mama it was a great blessing having no stairs to negotiate, and the pain she had borne so patiently receded. Being a very extrovert character, she was happy to take a bus to Monte Carlo, Nice, Ventimiglia, or San Remo. She enjoyed meeting people, and we passed many happy months visiting friends and eating out. St. Paul de Vence, St. Agnes, Sospel and all the places I had known in childhood were unspoiled, and having Sheila and Bill along the Côte was an added bonus.

They had an apartment overlooking the race track at Cagnes-sur-Mer, and Mama enjoyed going there and 'playing the tierce' (laying trebles) which I must add, she won on several occasions. They were usually quite large sums, that filled our dwindling coffers.

It was this aspect of matters which began to force my thoughts to the future. Mama's income had never increased, and what had been small in the twenties was totally inadequate in the sixties. My income, such as it was, would certainly not keep us, and if we started spending capital, how long would it last? Life on the Côte was no longer cheap - the 'good old days' of servants and brandy on the strong pound had gone forever - and I must face the reality of our situation. Mama was still in comparatively good health, and I, creaking door that I was, still in my early forties, and good for several more decades with care and a little luck.

I had turned to Isidore for financial advice several times before, and now I asked him to draw up a plan that would allow us an adequate income, and to keep some savings for the future. This he did very satisfactorily, and for a while we settled down to a life of comfortable indolence.

Our dear faithful Marie had finally retired, but she visited us most weeks on her way back from church. She always dressed in black, with her silver hair piled high on her head above one of the loveliest faces I've ever seen, serene and gentle. And she moved like a cat, smoothly and with elegance. Altogether, a woman in a thousand, and an unequalled cook. She had served us since I had been eleven years old, cooked, shopped, washed and ironed for a mere pittance, and never grumbled or let us down. Louis had never rewarded her after the war when she took over once again as housekeeper at Palais Viale, though he raised her wages to the 'going rate'. But she gave him far more care and attention than could ever be covered by a mere wage.

When she decided to retire Mama and I were able to see that she could afford a few simple comforts, though I know she in turn lavished them on the monks and priests in the monastery when she prepared their food on special feast days. The church was her great love, and had been her haven and comfort when her husband abandoned her with the three children, then aged six, four and two. She had worked all hours to maintain her home, and I never heard her offer an unkind word to anyone.

There were many old friendships to renew; Rosalie Catier, (née Clarke), the violinist of my childhood, her husband, Antoine (now a colonel), and their children (two boys and two girls, but now grown up) had returned to Menton from Algiers, now that his tour of duty was up. Sybil Evans, daughter of the famous 'Beauty' Payne, and now widowed for the second time was living nearby with her half Russian son and daughter. Paule and Leo were just below our block at the Edouard VII. They, with Padre Cyril Gardner and his wife, the Ratcliffes, the Bourgoints, and Peggy, another Englishwoman but married to Charles Mather, a French judge, made up our immediate circle. I also renewed some family ties, but with reservations, having little in common with Louis's relatives, and not having seen them at their best when the will was read.

An old lover of mine from Paris, Marcel Lanteri, came on the scene, according to gossip telling people that 'at last Diana will settle down and marry me.' News to me! He was a charming man, still very good looking, and I had reason to feel some genuine affection for him, but not enough to contemplate marriage. I had no desire to bind my future to anyone else's. Life with Mama was my choice, and the freedom that went with it. Fidelity was not a virtue I could claim; though I had never been promiscuous in my love life, I was not a one-man woman. One at a time (long or short), yes. My life had not been conducive to regular relationships, and if I had old men-friends and lovers scattered all over the globe, that was the way I liked it.

Anthony had parted from Esmée by this time, in favour of Vicki, a younger, prettier woman whom he later married, but meanwhile Mama invited Esmée to visit.

She arrived, beautifully groomed and smashingly turned out, and proceeded to knock 'em all dead with her wardrobe. If she changed once a day, she changed three times. I remembered a quiet, rather dowdy figure, who had startled us only with her riding stunts. Now she had metamorphosed into a gilded lily, her hair dyed a golden red, her make-up impeccable, never a crease in her clothes.

There was no way I could compete with such chic. I still tended to wear no shoes when I could get away with it, and my idea of make-up was to slap on a bit of maquillage in five minutes flat. As for hairdressers, they were my *bêtes noires*, ever since the great Mr Teazy-Weazy, no less, had said my hair was good only for lining a birds' nest. This brutal assessment of my over-fine locks was a blessing in disguise, as thenceforth I wasted no money being coiffed except for performances. On one occasion Pam took me to Elizabeth Arden in Beverly Hills to be 'styled'. Ye Gods! I came out looking like a pink-faced pig, my hair cut short, which showed my always stocky neck, and tightly curled to set off my jowls (for my figure had not survived my last convalescence) to perfection. Enough!

Esmée's visit was not an unqualified success. Most of our friends were couples, I had joined a cat rescue group, and my spare time was spent following my father's footsteps to the roulette wheel, which left Mama to entertain her as best she could. The croupiers went to great lengths to explain the different strategies, and the combinations that could (if one was lucky) win fortunes. As it happens, I was extremely lucky, so that over my first weeks I won on average something between two and three hundred pounds per visit. We used small, inexpensive restaurants, while Esmée had been looking forward to eating at the Hotel de Paris, La Bonne Auberge, the Colombière and suchlike.

I had hoped she would attract some gentleman of substance as a playmate, but instead she fastened on a croupier noted for his roving eye and propensity for one night stands. Clement had very fine blue eyes, and to my mind hideously thick thighs, which he showed off with unaffected pleasure and pride in the shortest shorts he could squeeze into. He was married to a hairdresser, who was not one to endure his peccadilloes in dignified silence. I had visions of her attacking Esmée in the Casino - I hoped only verbally. Fortunately Esmée was not prepared to accept such off-hand behaviour; she was used to far better treatment.

Other things aside, she was my guest, and I prized Louis's name in that ornate and hallowed precinct, where I was treated like royalty on the strength of it. My father was honoured among the various casinos as 'a fine, courageous gambler', much admired by the *chefs d'équipe* from Cannes to Menton. Over the years he had won and lost great sums at the tables. On the days when he lost, he would raid the safe in his office; on the good days, he would refund the business, restore his bank balance, and go back with a clear conscience.

I was very disdainful of this habit, and when he displayed to me his mass of *cartes spéciales*, which entitled him to free food and drink at all the best casinos in France, I sniffily asked him how much had each glass of Champagne *really* cost him.

He laughed ambiguously, and replied, "Little one, every glass of *water* has cost 10,000 francs." (The equivalent of £10.00 in those days.)

His love for the game was only to be reborn when I, for the very first time, sat at the roulette table and touched the green baize. A chip off the old block, wedded to the green baize cloth and the click of the wheel!

It's as well I had to leave the Côte and take up a more mundane life elsewhere. Whenever I have returned to France since then, I have gone hot-foot to the roulette tables. Now I really understand Louis's addiction, and revelled in it myself. Had I the money, I would be perfectly happy to leave it on the table each time, for winning is only important as a way of staying in the game. If I had the choice, that is how I would die - watching the ball bounce between the rim and the wheel!

Our next visitor from England was an old friend from the Indian Army, Colonel Edmund Iremonger, who took a very early retirement, spent a fortune enjoying life in Kashmir on a luxurious houseboat, and retired back to England, where he helped his brother Eardley run an hotel near Victoria. Edmund was not only a first-class bridge player, which he used to finance some of his enjoyment of the good life, he was also one of the best-looking men in London. Tall, elegant, well bred and educated, he could be the most charming of companions, but two large gins over the limit, and another side to his character emerged. He had a wickedly sharp tongue, and a degree of arrogance to put anyone's back up - including mine, when he made derogatory statements about 'niggers', and suchlike. My politics were anathema to him, liberals and socialists were the dregs, pathetic sentimentalists, and unrealistic idiots. Nonetheless, without a single trait in common, we were friends, and though he has now retired to Chichester remain so, thanks, as I often reminded him, to my liberal outlook.

Edmund's arrival in Menton caused quite a flutter among the females of the English enclave, and he basked in their open admiration for his entire stay. Another military gentleman of the old school, Anthony Squires, called on us. He was an RAF pilot who had directed the second unit aerial shots for James in 'The Blue Max'. On this occasion he spent most of his days at the poolside of the Hotel de Paris enjoying the vista of bathing beauties who collected there. Some were definitely hunting for clients, and these *poules de luxe* put me in mind of an odd little story I heard from the Menton Chief of Police.

In its early days my father's business had been owned by a Madame Amarante, who sold out to Louis and his first partner, Couregée when her husband died. When the war broke out she took herself to Paris where, as her police dossier revealed, she joined a very high-class brothel. In the early fifties she returned to her villa at Menton, and although by now into her seventies she still showed traces of having been a great beauty in her time. According to the police report which followed her (all prostitutes, de luxe or otherwise were at that time registered, for public health reasons), '*Cette vieille poule, malgré son âge, a eu grand succés pendant sa séjour à Paris*'. ('Despite her age, this old tart has done a roaring trade during her time in Paris.')

Actually she was a charming woman, and quite without embarrassment, told Mama that she had so missed the company and sexual satisfaction she gained from men, that she considered it best to go where she would be appreciated, and not be beholden to some pimp or gigolo. "You see, *ma chère*, when one is no longer young, lovers ask one for payment. I am a businesswoman, so I decided to turn my needs to profit."

I could only admire such plain, honest sense. Personally, I couldn't imagine anything more abhorrent, but I take my hat off to the old battleaxe, who in her seventies, was very well preserved and very chic. She never allowed anyone to see her without full make-up.

Mama was, as always, much in demand for luncheons, cocktail parties etc., but I noticed that for the first time her vitality had lessened. She tired easily, and needed more rest. She was now seventy-four, still full of fun, and had never lost her unquenchable interest in people and parties. Always impeccably dressed, she was famous for her hats. She had a milliner on the Côte, and another in London. Sheila and Bill invited her over regularly, and I arranged for a local taxi driver to take her to Cagnes, as the journey by bus was no longer comfortable. She never complained, but I could tell that waiting at the stop and having to climb on and off was becoming too wearing.

We had been back on the Côte less than two years when early one morning we received the news that Bill had died in the night, suddenly and without warning, leaving Sheila heartbroken and in shock. Mama duly went to her, and stayed a while. There were so many formalities to contend with, though fortunately Sheila's landlord was helpful; we were quite unprepared. We knew Bill had been unwell for some time, but with his retirement his health had seemed to improve. I think he had taken the fact that he was no longer working as a sign of failure and uselessness, which was not the case. Avianca had agreed to terminate his contract, but they had had the whip hand, and the terms had been less than fair to Bill, and I knew it rankled with him.

He had found his *raison d'être* gone. His excellent Canadian Airforce record, and his good position with a civil airline, had given him a standing in which he could take pride. Finding himself discarded at a comparatively early age on health grounds he became bored and morose. He was not a French-speaker, their daughter Georgina took up most of Sheila's time, the two older girls were married and departed, one to England, the other to America, he felt lost and useless. It was not true. Sheila adored him, and always had, and his death was a terrible blow. They say no one dies of a broken heart, but I wondered if Bill had not just turned his face to the wall. Some people require conflict and responsibility, the need to take hard and risky decisions, without which they lose self-esteem. I think Bill was one such, and he gave up.

Mama returned from Cagnes bringing with her Bill's parrot, Joe, a wretched creature that had caused much ill-feeling in the past. Joe had spent a few weeks with us in London when Sheila and Bill had been visiting the family in Canada, and when they returned Mama had been reluctant to hand him back because he was 'so happy with Lola'. It had been all in her mind. Joe and Lola loathed each her. Lola was a brilliant Amazon parrot, and probably found Joe's African Grey plumage dismal. Doubtless Joe condemned her as garish. In any case, despite their names, they may not have been of opposite sex.

Altogether, to say they were happy together was either self-deception or a large size in fibs, but Mama simply doted on Joe, who spoke very well, and laughed and sang with her far more readily than Lola. Now I could see through her tears for Sheila's loss a glint of triumph, as the taxi driver staggered into the flat bearing the huge cage, and Joe squalking such selections from his repertoire as 'Bonjour, Bonsoir, Kiss-kiss."

"I've got him," were Mama's first words, and I had to laugh. She looked like a naughty child, slightly anxious but prepared to brazen it out.

"Good!" I replied, "Sheila was always afraid of him, better he comes to us."

That was all, but Mama spent hours with him teaching him to whistle 'Pop goes the weasel', and a few less savoury accomplishments. He would sit on her shoulder even when she went for her afternoon rest. He was her creature, and he knew it. Her *familiar*!

Not long after Bill's death I suffered the trauma of losing Barlow and then Biffi, to a dreadful attack of leptospirosis. We had lost many animals over the years, but this was a particularly harrowing disease. The vet, though a good man and experienced, had none of the knowledge of new drugs that our London vet possessed, and I felt sure that the dogs could have been saved if I had been able to call on Russell. But it was not to be, we had to put them down to save further suffering, and I vowed to return to England, whatever the cost. The Côte suddenly struck me as artificial, provincial and boring. Fortunately Mama had also decided that she wanted to return to London and home, good health or not.

Chapter Fourteen

Munich

I went back to London to look for a suitable flat, and luck was with me. Roy Norton, an old friend from the BBC told me that the garden flat in his house was soon to fall empty, would I like to see it?

It was ideal, three steps down from the front garden, entirely self-contained, and with a lovely terrace, all on one level. Just three rooms, kitchen and bath - the whole thing could have fitted into half of Palais Viale, but our household was down to two people, one parrot and the cat. I took it without hesitation, and set the re-decoration in motion while I went back to Menton.

A final parting had come. France had been my first home since 1921, and then a second home, equal to England. Now we were to break the thread forever. Desmond drove out in a hired removal van to drive me back with the furniture, and Joe in his special travelling box. This time Mr Tweed was airlifted to London, there to endure quarantine, poor fellow, while Mama flew into Heathrow, and the Grenots took over Palais Viale. An ideal solution.

A year after we left, our landlord, Antoine Viale, a kind and gentle man, committed suicide. Shortly after that Michel, Mama's hairdresser, did the same. According to the superstition, these things come in threes, and so it proved, another old friend, George Helios, who ran the Helios Restaurant also ended his own life. I wondered why such tragedies should come about. My theory, perhaps rather an unfair one, was that life in Menton offered too little challenge to naturally active people. The general pettiness, with its parish-pump gossip and backbiting, ultimately made for so dreary an environment that neither the natural beauties of the Côte nor the artificial splendours of the Casino could compensate for the lack of mental stimulation.

I was relieved to be back in England, where it was easier to think in a logical manner, even if I still thought in French. What bliss to be in

London! No shortage of interesting people, beautiful parks, theatres, concert halls, museums, everything for everyone. What should be our own special contribution?

Mama and I were long-time members of the Chow and Pug clubs, and several of our old friends were now judging at the big national shows, and at Crufts. We therefore allowed two more pugs - Calvados and Bonaparte - to become our owners, and let them bring us our fun. There are *bonhomie* and camaraderie in every walk of life, and competitive showing, whether of dogs, cats or horses has plenty, as well as the more notorious envy, jealousy and sharp practice among the competitors. We had the best of it, since not being breeders we didn't care if we won or not, we just enjoyed the atmosphere. As long as the dogs didn't look too miserable we trotted off at regular intervals for a day's outing. In the process we collected dozens of cards and rosettes, and such occasional princely sums as £1.00, or even £5.00!

We spent five years in London, while I kept up my Eastern Bloc contacts, and began to research the book I had intended to write for so long. There were many pitfalls and dead ends, and old colleagues from whom I sought advice warned me again and again that I must expect the full gamut from apathy through antipathy to downright hostility. Any book bringing up the Allied disinclination to prosecute 'crimes against humanity', and the Nazi ratlines, would be regarded as rocking the boat.

There were great numbers of these, and I don't believe it is widely known how many they were, or how many sections of German higher society were implicated with them. A partial list of primary Nazi escape organisations is:

> The *Alt Aussee* Line
>
> *Aktion Birkenbaum* (The Birch Tree)
>
> *HIAG (Hilfsonganizaktion auf Gegenseitigkeit der Waffen SS)*
>
> The Odessa Line

These were all set up by Helmut Naujocks, SS Colonel Otto Bremen, and SS Lieutenant Colonel Otto Skorzeny.

Two Army Veterans' Organisations acted as cover. These were *Die Spinne*, under SS Colonel Eugen Dollman, and *Stahlhelm und Deutschen Soldatenbund.*

It was very easy in the chaotic days after the war for senior SS officers to make contact with one or other of these men, who would provide the false papers, and where necessary cash, for them to leave for South America, usually via Spain or Ireland. No one on the Allied side had much interest in stopping the flow; apart from the possibility of using them later, they had more than enough war criminals to deal with already.

Worst of all, many churchmen were active in protecting suspected war criminals from trial. These included the Catholics, Cardinal Josef Frings of Cologne, Bishop Johann Neuhaüssler of Munich, and the Protestants, Bishop Meiser of Munich and Bishop Theophil Wurm of Stuttgart. Their campaigns were the *Evangelische Helfswerk* and *Christ und Welt*, both of which lobbied for an end to prosecutions for war crimes.

I know the frustration of my Polish friends, in their efforts to trace and extradite from Germany some of those most responsible for atrocities against their countrymen. Every possible means, legal and otherwise, was used to baulk them, particularly when they tried to seek information directly in Germany. Visas were denied, permits refused, physical threats were made against them, as the 'de-Nazified minor officials' protected the bigger fish and their own backs.

I sought advice from Maurice Oldfield who had returned from the United States, and was being considered for high office within MI6. He was a delightful and kindly man, who had risen from the rank of sergeant in Field Security. Brigadier Roberts spotted him, and brought him forward. First commissioned in 1943, he was a Lieutenant Colonel by 1945, which speaks for itself. A brilliant man, always willing to listen and to help.

I think he found my rage amusing, but he offered this sound advice. "Dig too deep and you may come up with some unpleasant facts. You should also remember that you yourself may come under scrutiny. You have some questionable contacts, and your travels in the East will not have gone unnoticed."

He was right, and although I never set aside my project, I did not pursue it with the zeal that I should have shown.

In recent years I have read many slurs on Oldfield, and I have nothing but contempt for those who have tried to make capital out of disclosing aspects of his private life. If he was a homosexual, I can think of many desks in Whitehall and elsewhere that would be emptied if all the deviants were purged. As for the suggestion that he might have been susceptible to blackmail, like the wretched Vassal, that is the most contemptible insult of the lot. It comes from muck-raking journalists - the same ones who buy the stories of sexual blackmailers. Maurice would never have flunked the issue; he would have told them to publish and be damned, like the gallant soldier he was.

I have some little experience of spymasters, and I reckon Maurice Oldfield was as good as any of them - and a whole lot nicer than most.

Meanwhile, I was taking a renewed interest in another spymaster, with rather fewer pretensions to be a 'nice man'. For many years I had been fascinated by the Pullach Organisation, (named, incidentally, from a dormitory village near Munich, much used by married SS men and their families) which had become the envy of Intelligence services throughout the world. Its master was General Reinhard Gehlen, a great spymaster, who had built up his 'Org', as it was called, into a mighty security force, operating at his discretion and under his orders, like a private army, though financed by the CIA. The CIA prided themselves that Gehlen was 'their man', but I believe it was the other way about. They were putty in his hands, and if there was a conflict of interest, they got the short end.

There can be no denying that this most brilliant spymaster was a key figure in Eastern Bloc Intelligence, and his horse-trading with the US government gave rise to misgivings among some of the Nuremberg judges. For those of liberal or left-of-centre politics, Gehlen's Pullach 'Org' was a blot on the principles of democracy no less than the integrity of the trials, particularly when he re-employed SS and Gestapo men of worse than doubtful reputation. In fact, anyone who recalls McCarthy and the witch-hunts will see that expediency overruled all other considerations, including logic and decency. Gehlen incorporated into his huge networks people whom he believed would be valuable to himself and his paymasters in the United States. Millions of dollars were poured into his organisation, and in return he poured out for the US security forces all the Military Intelligence that the Germans had garnered throughout the war.

A committed anti-Communist, Gehlen had men and women in place throughout the northern hemisphere by 1950, and his power was unlimited. Chancellor Adenauer gave him carte blanche, and Allen Dulles made certain that his power was never diminished, for the benefit of the United States as well as West Germany.

I had few contacts in Germany; my visits to Hamburg, Munich, Frankfurt and Berlin had always been brief. In 1968 my attempt to set up a meeting with the great man got a polite but firm brush-off. The General would never consider an interview with a completely unknown female. The man who had sniffed out so many secrets had retired into a reclusive existence, and required the utmost privacy.

Gehlen had always let it be understood that his memoirs would not be published until many years after his death, but in 1971 he sold them, reputedly for a million dollar advance. Whether he wanted to justify his actions, rather than submit them to hostile interpretation when he was no longer around, or if he simply wanted to earn a fortune for his family, I cannot say. After he left the BND (*Bundesnachrichtendienst*:

Federal German Intelligence) in 1968 there had been considerable criticism of his activities. By this time Germany was able to turn a harsh spotlight on the Hitler Years, and this took in not only Gehlen himself but some worse than dubious characters among his employees. These included ex-SS and Gestapo, as well as a fine collection of French and 'neutral' double agents and informers.

How was I to arouse his interest? He had withdrawn from public life, and had no good reason to talk to me. But I had been lucky in the past, and I determined to press my luck again. My first idea for an approach was via the support Gehlen had given to Jacques Soustelle, Georges Bidault, General Salan and Pierre Lagaillarde when they fell foul of de Gaulle over his policy towards Algeria. The Red Hand Organisation, set up by the Colons and aided by the French Secret Service, had as its main purpose the assassination of FLN leaders. No one knew better than Gehlen how to promote undercover work and infiltration, so the OAS and their *Barbouze* killers doubtless received invaluable advice from the Org.

On the other hand, this interest might not prove a strong enough gambit. I feared it would not, as Gehlen would doubtless deny any links to the renegades, and I could never prove them. Another possible tack was the Kolberg spy ring, which had operated very successfully from 1948 to 1950/51. Colonel Gregor Kowalski, who had been on General Sikorski's staff in London, was believed to have set the ring up, along with a shadowy figure called Wlodek Kamien of whom I knew nothing. My first question would be, how had Gehlen broken the ring?

The second question must be, how had the double agent Hans Felfe so easily become Gehlen's trusted operator, and how had his final entrapment been brought about? There were conflicting stories about this, though it is not in dispute that Felfe had spent ten years spying for the KGB while in the Org's service. He was decorated by both sides for services rendered, and when finally uncovered, sentenced to fourteen years in jail, but exchanged after a few years for a number of West German spies caught in the east.

As a matter of curiosity, what caused Major General Hans Worgitsky to resign as Vice President of BND in 1967? There were several conflicting stories about this, though the most likely one is that Worgitski was after Gehlen's job. Perhaps he made his play too soon, or perhaps Gehlen saw the threat and squeezed him out.

There were two more names I could try using to open Gehlen's door. He had taken SS Brigadeführer Franz Six into his Special Force. Six had commanded a *Jagdkommando* unit, and was responsible for the deaths of hundreds if not thousands of civilians. At the end of the war he had evaded justice, and not been caught until 1948, when a US military tribunal sentenced him to twenty years' imprisonment. After four years he was released, presumably at the behest of the CIA, and joined the Org.

My last question concerned a Frenchman, Maurice Pickard, sentenced to seven years in 1968 for spying. Pickard was an old Pétainist, but after the war he had risen high in the French Security Department. He certainly betrayed French secrets to Gehlen, but how long had he worked for Pullach? There were conflicting views of this one as well.

Quite possibly none of these questions swayed Gehlen, but my German source (who has requested me not to release his name) finally came back with an agreed date. Gehlen's curiosity may have been aroused by my obvious knowledge of his career, but I believe two other factors influenced his decision to see me. He was a great lover of music, which may have disposed him favourably towards a singer. We talked about concerts as well as Intelligence, and he told me he often attended performances in Munich. I suspect boredom also played a part. A man so vital, so steeped in the world of dark secrets, must have found retirement wearisome, even though he was financially secure and free to enjoy family life. But he made certain stipulations: we were to meet for a general discussion of my queries. I must take no notes, nor might I quote from our discussion. It was to be in the nature of a confidential social call, not for publication.

It was not my intention to publish, only to gratify my professional interest in this most remarkable man. As a spymaster he had survived and conquered his past service to Hitler, sold his knowledge and expertise to the Americans, been reinstated and funded by Dulles, captivated the CIA, forging in the process the finest and most comprehensive Intelligence network. He had finally been toppled by feuding among his senior officers and colleagues.

At last I met him face to face at a private address in Munich. He was very ordinary-looking, slightly built, greying, and with only the shrewdness of his eyes to suggest he might in any way be special. They appraised me expressionlessly, as he greeted me with the formal courtesy to be expected of a Prussian officer of the old school. Over coffee he asked me a number of probing questions, which my answers seemed to satisfy. He was amused, and slightly bemused, I think, by my lack of credentials. Where had I sprung from? Who had been my Masters, my Case Officers etc? Had I any affiliations at all? What had prompted my interest in postwar Intelligence?

I gave him a couple of names, which I knew he must know already, but did not elaborate further, saying that I preferred not to disclose certain other identities. His sardonic gaze never wavered, but he accepted that I was a contact, an informer, and (not to put a fine point on it) a snoop, belonging to no organisation, and without sworn allegiance to any specific service. Then he dealt with my questions, quickly and deftly.

I actually drew a smile from him when I boldly put forward a suggestion that in other circumstances he might have welcomed me into Pullach. "A few years ago I considered knocking on your door," I said, and indeed I had, several times.

"Indeed. Your reception would have depended on your information."

"I suspect you might have considered me."

I was rewarded with a very quizzical look before he replied, "I suspect I might."

I left with a feeling that Gehlen, whatever his critics might say, had been bound neither to Hitler personally nor to National Socialism as an abstract creed. He was simply a fanatical German patriot, and determined to keep Communism outside the borders of his country. The evil deeds of his Org were only the inevitable by-product of the postwar division of Europe, with its Cold War and the ideological differences that fuelled it. A different division would only have produced similar evil deeds, though perhaps in other places and involving other people.

The more I learn and understand, the more I conclude that each and every country justifies its wrongdoing, its double standards, its outright lies to its own people and the black propaganda it spreads abroad by a single formula:

IN THE NATIONAL INTEREST

From this viewpoint there was nothing exceptional about Reinhard Gehlen, but as the most brilliant spymaster of his time, he was held to be more guilty of subversion and double dealing than the less competent heads of less successful services who failed where he succeeded. Myself, I neither condone nor condemn the Org, MI6, the CIA nor the KGB. While the world is divided economically and politically, it will be divided militarily also, unless we can learn to live at peace.

I returned to London somewhat better informed, and perhaps a little wiser than I had left it. I saw that my treasured project of a book about the war criminals and their evasion of justice was beyond my unaided capabilities. The necessary investigations would most certainly take me from home for weeks if not months at a time, and at this point I could no longer leave Mama alone for long periods.

Her sight had been failing since 1969, and London streets were increasingly hazardous for a still very independent-minded lady, who insisted on walking her dogs morning and evening. She no longer drove herself, but retained some French reflexes about which side the traffic should be on. We often went to Kensington Gardens together, but there were times when she wanted to be alone. She took a couple of nasty falls. Bones get brittle at that age, even without Paget's which increases their weight but not their tensile strength, and that decided me. I started looking for a small property in the country, where the risk from the traffic would be less.

Visiting friends in Sussex, I found a small flat with a roof garden above Grimaldi's, a tiny restaurant, near Eastbourne. It was run by a young couple who wanted to sell up, as their first baby was due very shortly. A restaurant? I couldn't cook an egg - literally. My first attempt at this feat of catering was a medium-grade disaster, with eighteen eggs boiled dry and blown all over the kitchen. I had forgotten that water evaporates. The smell of sulphur made it a whole lot worse.

For my next attempt (on a ten pound joint of finest Scotch topside) I read the instructions, and awaited the results. They emerged in the form of a shrivelled, rock-hard lump which even the rooks, jackdaws and magpies found difficult to tear apart, but I was assured that a more-than-competent lady cook was willing to stay on and take charge of the business side.

So the deal was struck, and in time I achieve some success with my sauces. The only problem was, I could never remember exactly what ingredients I had included or how I had blended them to achieve the good result. Over the years, I've learned to achieve a modicum of consistency, while keeping them unusual and delicious.

Another factor that swayed me as much as anything was the view over the village green and the pub. This was run by a charming couple whom Mama already knew. She had developed a soft spot for the landlord, a fine-looking man though of uncertain temper. Naturally, Mama only ever saw his good side.

I intended to keep the London flat also, just in case Mama failed to adapt to country life, but it was her health that failed, so that London ceased to be tenable.

The worst and saddest moment of my life was in 1974, when, after another severe fall and weeks hovering between life and death, Mama died. Anthony and Sheila were with me throughout, taking turns to sit with her through the long days and nights. The end was quiet, and we were each left to nurse our grief in our own way. For me it was the end of a lifetime's companionship, an ever-joyful friendship, and it took many years for me to regain my real interest in people or places. Events finally jolted me back to the realities confronting us.

'Us' meant myself and Anthony, whose second marriage had now ended in divorce. He had returned from South Africa without a job or means of support. Of his sons, the younger remained with Vicki, while the elder, Howard, came to live with us. It was my salvation, as I saw in the boy certain Morgan characteristics which allowed me to establish an immediate understanding and affection, which has never faded.

Beginning in 1975 other events took place that were to cause many upheavals. Isidore, with whom I was for the first time able to enjoy a friendly relationship, died quite suddenly, leaving Pam and his brother Maurice as executors of his estate. He had been badly upset by Mama's death, and his letters to me during her last weeks proved that he had never stopped loving her, for all the bitterness of their parting. I was deeply touched by his grief, and certain poignant memories that he had not previously disclosed.

Within a few months Maurice Ostrer also died, leaving Pam the whole burden of winding up an estate valued in millions on paper, but totally illiquid. There was about £500 in cash, plus the ailing textile business, which was inexorably sliding towards insolvency under the burden of its interest charges, incurred to tool up for an upturn in demand when instead demand went down.

Arguments between Pam, the surviving directors and Isidore's trusted accountants degenerated into quarrels. Pam initiated an emergency General Meeting to vote off the board all those directors whom she regarded as inefficient. This led to court action, when they tried to remove Pam and Morgan.

The quarrels spread to the other relations, who found themselves siding against each other, and a case was brought by Isidore's second wife's adopted daughter, Isabella (in her capacity as residual legatee), to have Pam removed as executrix. Pam decided not to come to court, so an order was made placing the estate in the hands of the Judicial Trustees. The lawyers, who never lose, took up their positions, licking their chops. The Inland Revenue and Capital Transfer Office took up their own positions of self-bestowed privilege on the sidelines. They knew that unless a miracle occurred, the estate would be bankrupt. Then they would be first in line for anything realised.

Against a background of gathering financial disaster the infighting between legatees only confounded the issue, and the conflict raged on year after year. Pam still tries to defend herself against the jurisdiction of the Judicial Trustee, who finds it virtually impossible to defeat her. As an American citizen she fights her case through lawyers in the United States, and to my current knowledge no settlement has been agreed between the parties. The textile company, for so many years the jewel in Isidore's crown, has been sold for a song and no doubt stripped down to a leaner and fitter concern according to strict Thatcherite principles.

Chapter Fifteen

Finale

The initial shock of Mama's death robbed me of all desire to carry on with any of the things we had done so happily together. Instead I found myself drawn increasingly to my contacts overseas, in particular my Polish and Yugoslav friends, many of whom were still pining for justice to be done against those who had wrought such havoc in their countries.

Men, women and children (now young adults) were confounded by the numbers of Nazis and Fascists who had been allowed to go free. I now realised that they were far better qualified than myself to compile an anthology of the events from 1939 to 1969 by calling on their own experiences. They had been confined in POW Stalags and concentration camps, and some had escaped from both. Others had been leaders of underground cells, or partisans, persecuted first by the Nazis, then by the Stalinists.

They were the ones who should be the basis for my research. Meanwhile I would begin to collate my own notes, study the *Livre Brun* so as to ascertain the records of bankers, judges, industrialists as well as military personnel who had not only evaded punishment but had been returned to high office in their chosen professions. The men who sat behind their desks, the 'Men in white gloves', as we called them, and consigned millions to their deaths, were just as guilty as the *Einsaztgruppen* who manned the machine guns and the mass gallows, or burned people alive. I wanted them exposed.

It would not be easy. I could understand the reasoning of the Allies who, after the first Nuremburg trials, backed off from prosecuting many well-known war criminals who, unlike the generals and politicians in Germany and Italy, were not public names. They were so many! To have treated all as they deserved would have looked like vengefulness against the entire middle class of the Axis Powers, and created a desert in the hierarchies of industry, commerce and civil service. Deals were

199

made, often to the fury and despair of those who had been detailed to prepare the charges. It caused much soul-searching among the British, American and French advocates, but they had sometimes to turn a blind eye when ordered from above.

There was no pity for the victims of Yalta and Potsdam, and the duplicity of the Americans in particular towards Germany created cynicism, and a realisation that they, who had fought so valiantly for freedom, were now to be sacrificed on the altar of expediency.

It must be said in defence of the Western Allies (principally the United States) that Marshall Aid was poured generously into the rebuilding and re-establishment of shattered Europe. However, the countries now being ground under Stalin's heel received comparatively little of the bounty. Reparation from Germany to her victims was also minimal.

Meanwhile, there was nothing for Poland, the chief sufferer under Hitler, or Yugoslavia, the chief sufferer under both the Nazis and Mussolini. What little came to Poland under the Marshall Plan was misappropriated by the Soviets. She had had her industries destroyed, her rivers polluted, her forests cut down, her agriculture laid waste. The infrastructure was in collapse, the health of the nation was at the lowest possible ebb. This last aspect was the intended result of the near-starvation diet imposed by Governor Hans Frank on the orders of Himmler - which is to say, Hitler at one remove.

From Stalin's viewpoint, a beholden and desperate Poland was the best sort of buffer state between the Soviet Union and Germany. This long-time enemy must now look east for salvation, and be grateful for what little it received. As the Cold War got colder, rather than bursting into flame, the 'battle for the hearts and minds' in divided Europe became the prime consideration. I've often heard it said behind the Iron Curtain that throwing vast sums at Communist governments was the western way of destabilising political controls. I do not dispute this.

On top of all this, to have succeeded in rebuilding the cities, the agriculture and the social fabric would have required human and financial resources far beyond what was supplied, even without the mismanagement, miscalculations, and sometimes, I think, the deliberate policies of those in power. These more than anything contributed to the apathy and sense of helplessness that pervaded all Eastern Bloc countries until very recently. Such uprisings as took place, in Hungary, Czechoslovakia and Poland, were all ruthlessly crushed, but the ensuing howls of outrage and righteous indignation from the western powers gave no comfort to populations left abandoned. As in 1939, there were only words to counter bullets and secret police oppression.

Interestingly, the earliest sign of a more humanitarian approach appeared as early as April 1956. It was little reported, and soon forgotten with the crushing of Hungary, but that year in Poland saw the summary dismissal in quick succession of General Stanislaw Radkiewiez, former head of the Security Police but by that time Minister for State Farms, General Stanislaw Zanokowski, Chief Military Prosecutor, Stephan Kalinoswki, State Public Prosecutor, Henryk Swiatkowski, Minister of Justice, and Kazimiersz Sokorski, Minister of Culture. There was then a political amnesty, which freed over thirty thousand male and female political prisoners. It proved to be a false dawn; new masters, hardly less oppressive, took the places of the old.

Many years later, in 1981 I looked out across Victory Square once again. It was a cold, starlit night, with snow falling thick and relentlessly, covering the ravages of war made worse by time and neglect. The dim lighting threw yellow shadows across deserted streets, where nothing moved but patrolling tanks and armoured cars.

Could it be true? I wondered. Had I come back only to see yet another tragedy strike Poland? I prayed that it might not be so. There was already hardly an inch of Polish soil that could not weep human blood. Surely the authorities would seek reconciliation, not confrontation, this time! But there was a smell of civil war in the air, and the lorries which brought in the hated Special Militia, or *Zomos* stood like sentinels, impatiently waiting the order to do the worst they could imagine.

It was rumoured that these were hand-picked men, deliberately debauched and brutalised with a diet of hard liquor, hard pornography and hard drugs, like the *Kapos* of the Nazi death camps. These were the regime's principal weapon against protestors, and already some of my friends had fallen foul of their batons, water cannon, and teargas canisters hurled to spread panic among packed crowds.

From my window in the Europejeski Hotel I could see the soldiers from the barracks opposite scuttling to and fro, and I wondered how these men could be feeling. Many of them were young conscripts, doing their military service, surely they could not want to take up arms against their brothers and fathers? I trembled with the pity of it all.

This brave, sad country was once again in turmoil, not because of Socialism or even Communism, but because of government ineptitude and corruption, the *Nomenklatura*, with their system of maximum privileges for the least productive, the lack of organisation in industry and agriculture (described as 'central planning'), the consequent endemic shortages of food, clothing, housing and medical care in a country beaten to its knees and left without hope.

Why had I come back? Why had I gone, day after day, to the Polish embassy begging for an entry visa at a time when virtually none were being granted? Why, finally, had they granted my request? Perhaps it was my lack of political affiliation, and my sincere love of the country and its people that swayed them, but what did a lone, elderly woman seek to achieve in Warsaw in a time of crisis?

Journalist friends had told me that getting a visa in the early days of martial law would be out of the question for someone who had no official business, but I told both the Military Attaché and Janusz Luks, the Press Attaché, that I wished, indeed needed, to speak with Captain (now Major) Wieslaw Gornicki, General Jaruzelski's aide, and Colonel Zbigniew Wiclowski of the Counter-Intelligence Service, and after a few weeks patiently waiting I was given a temporary visa for one month, though advised that I might get permission to extend my stay - 'If you keep your nose clean,' was the unspoken condition.

When I was preparing to fly to Warsaw in the early days of martial law, apart from my visa I wanted the right to take fourteen huge egg-boxes with me, stuffed with clothing donated by friends. It was all hardly worn, warm and smart. Freight charges were very high, but a Polish friend in London told me there was a special office in the embassy that dealt with parcels etc., and I should try my luck with them.

The military attaché had firmly ruled out any possibility of my gaining preferential treatment, but when I gave him my list of people I wished to speak to in Poland, I saw his eyes light on the name of the Head of Counter-Intelligence.

"Why do you wish to see him?" he asked.

I think my reply took him by surprise. "If you know who he is, you should know better than to ask such a question."

I got my baggage and boxes through as reduced-rate freight with no further trouble, and was able to give clothes, boots and shoes to numerous friends. Journalists, teachers, secretaries, etc. could no longer afford to buy them and I had some over as tips for hotel staff who trusted the currency no more than anyone else.

I had a boxful of children's clothes, which were received with absolute joy, and nowhere more so than at Laski, a home for blind children near Warsaw. It's maintained by Polish Overseas Aid and a government grant, and run by nuns and teachers. I have several friends working there, including Martha Zielinska, Beta Sawa and Madame Monawska, who is in charge of administration. They are all devoted and selfless people.

The home is a revelation, the children so independent, happy and full of fun and laughter. The education is first-class, and many totally blind youngsters go on to university and professional careers. One little girl touched my heart when I saw her on a swing. I remarked to Beta how extremely pretty she was, and Beta spoke to her on my behalf. The child told us she could still see a little, but that within a year she would be quite blind.

Her serenity was incredible. "I have no fear, I have such a happy home here, my parents love me, and so does God."

But I still cannot say why I came back to Poland. I could do very little, if anything, against a bureaucracy fat with power. My friends of all ages and of all political views were prepared to face the consequences of confrontation. They had reached the end of their tether. Only the Church stood like a beacon against the State, which had not only lost its way, but earned the contempt of its people, including many long-standing believers in Communism.

General Jaruzelski's case is typical. He is, to my mind, a patriot, a Pole whose own sad beginnings seemed virtually unknown to many who opposed him. Yet much of it is on the record; he was born in 1923 at Kurow, near Lublin. His early schooling was with the Jesuits, but in 1939 his parents were killed, whether by the Nazis or the Soviets is uncertain. He himself was sent to a Forestry Labour Camp, and thereafter trained in the Officers' School at Ryazau. He fought with the Dabrowski Polish Division, and joined the Communist Party in 1947.

He rose through the ranks to Chief of the Army Political Board (1960), Central Committee (1964), Head of the Central Political Department of the Polish United Workers' Party (1965), Chief of Staff (1965-68), elected to the Politburo (1971).

I was sure then that this beleaguered country would be liberalised, and though Jaruzelski might never gain the affection of his countrymen, I believe he will gain their respect, as de Gaulle did in France, for having clipped the claws of the hard-liners within the party and hammered out an alliance with Solidarity, without provoking an invasion from the east.

He gave a very enlightening painting to Stachu, a friend of mine (and also a Communist general), which shows a sensitive view of war. It depicts an army group in retreat through a forest, the hale helping the wounded, but all stamped with utter weariness and dejection. Stachu asked why he had chosen such a theme, and he replied, "People always see armies depicted as victorious. Rarely does anyone show the opposite, the suffering of the men, the pain of defeat."

There is no doubt that Jaruzelski loves his army, and the affection and respect are returned. Moreover, his regime has been relatively free of corruption.

I have often wondered how the West would have reacted had a Soviet general been sent to take the reins of power in Poland. There were already hundreds of thousands of Soviet troops on Polish soil, and Poland was, as always, sandwiched between historical enemies, all panting to go in and teach the upstarts a lesson. My personal view is that angry and sorrowful words, and talk of economic boycott would have burst forth like a bubble - and like a bubble, disintegrated. No one would have contemplated starting World War III over the internal affairs of the Soviet Bloc.

As for Jaruzelski, I hope history will not be too unkind to him. He did his bitter and thankless task, suffering a barrage of condemnation in the process. His own henchmen and opponents in the Party were affronted by what they regarded as his lack of zeal, his 'softness', while western governments and the press heaped him with insult upon insult. What did they hope to achieve? Civil war and a bloodbath? Perhaps.

Their belligerence depressed and angered me, but when sanctions against Poland were announced I despaired. Reagan withdrew the 'most favoured nation' status from Poland and withheld from a desperate country the vital exports of grain that the Poles desperately needed to feed their farm animals. It had to go somewhere, of course, and where did it go instead? One guess! To the Soviet Union! And at rock-bottom prices.

So much for democracy.

I knew the score, I was a very old hand by this time. Destabilisation is the name of the game, but it's not one that should be played against a courageous and persecuted wartime ally. Did British and American politicians truly believe in upholding the demands of trade unions? I think not, having seen controlling rightwingers using their own power to vitiate trade union power in both countries. You can only square this circle by assuming that they regarded Poland as an enemy, and Solidarity as a way of doing their enemy harm.

Certainly, this is how Mrs Thatcher regarded the National Union of Mineworkers during their strike. She called them 'the enemy within', and treated them as such. Scargill, for his part, condemned Solidarity as 'Catholic and reactionary'. Had anything similar taken place in the United States, I think Reagan would have called out *his* 'Zomos' - The National Guard.

The pro-Solidarity arguments which appealed to the western press were in general flawed, as was the reporting. Only a few voices spoke with the authority of knowledge and understanding. These included Neal Ascherson, whose outstanding column appears in the Observer, Kevin Ruane and Christopher Bobinski, who understood the events and the dangers threatening the Poles. Ascherson's book on Solidarity, 'The

Polish August', is especially good. Their views deserved more prominence, as did the sessions when they faced the ubiquitous and sharp-witted government spokesman, Jerzy Urban, who sat looking like Humpty-Dumpty, but with no signs of falling off the wall. Sardonic and sarcastic, but always polite, he fenced with the world's press, containing many of their questions.

In this connection I was puzzled and annoyed by the arrogance and discourtesy, amounting to near rudeness, of many representatives of the western media. I wondered if the interpreters re-worded the questions in more discreet terms. To affront the officials of a host country for no better reason than personal or political dislike gains nothing, and is not what should be expected of educated men who have been given special privileges.

After the interviews I would gather with Polish friends in the Interpress coffee bar to discuss the events of the day, and try to find a way of helping those who had openly shown their support for Solidarity. It was not a movement to bring down the government, though that was its ultimate effect, only the socialist workers' demand for a more equal society, with less privilege for the few, less corruption among Party Members and so forth.

Virtually everyone I knew supported Solidarity. Aid for those who had been dismissed from their posts came from every section of society. Journalists, musicians, actors, doctors, lawyers, academics, factory workers - all were on the breadline. I, and others like me, had to organise ways of finding money, food and clothing for these deprived people, if we could. But they were not the only deprived ones. Poverty and wretchedness persisted throughout the countryside, with large families trying to scratch a living, no medical centres for miles, no schools, no transport. These families needed immediate aid, as did the hospitals, the sick and infirm, and the surviving victims of war and the concentration camps.

I remained unimpressed with the foremost aim of the Church, which was to build a great number of new places of worship. You can administer the Sacraments and praise God perfectly well in a barn. Granted that the Poles are a religious people, with a mystical tradition, the Catholic Church is a militant church, and political in that it stands against governments that deny justice to their people. Priests and nuns were as persecuted as anyone under the Nazis, and many died in the camps. Some had gone in as volunteers, to try to relieve the suffering of the inmates. The story of Father Kolbe, now canonised, is typical of their brave self-sacrifice. More recently, Father Jerzy Popieluszko was murdered for his support of Solidarity. Even if the present Pope frowns on the activities of 'Liberation Theologians' in Latin America, he certainly upholds the views of the brave clergy of Poland. Now it seemed to me that the Church in Poland was losing sight of what should have been its main priorities, namely the physical needs of the people.

I voiced my arguments on Radio Pologna, where the English Section invited me to speak freely. I did so willingly, and suggested that not a single government of theirs since the war had treated the people decently, let alone with understanding and benevolence. I was disgusted with the rudeness of officials towards some of the older and less educated of their countrymen, the indifference of the airport and station officials to the long queues, the general and open contempt of those in power for those with none.

At the radio station in Ul Niepodlegtesci there were armed military guards, no one might enter without a pass, no one smiled and all eyes were wary and suspicious. Failure to produce a pass when ordered could mean deep trouble. It was quite different when I visited Wieslaw Gornicki at Ul Ujardowski. There the guards inside and outside the building were impeccably turned-out and scrupulously polite, while the offices, though very austere, all offered a warm welcome and greeting. It was the difference between an outpost and a centre of power, but I was also pleasantly surprised, in this period of great strife, at the frankness of everyone, at both the radio station and the government offices. My questions were answered, and my requests and criticisms were taken in the proper spirit, whether the people agreed or not. I saw no point in holding back, but I also hoped to show that what I said was constructive, and motivated by a genuine care for Poland.

My friends ranged from the extreme left to the extreme right, though most were moderate liberals. They included Jozef Szajna, the brilliant art director and producer; General Okecki, imprisoned by Stalin for seven years yet a Communist to his dying day; Mikolaj Caban, who had suffered appalling torture before escaping with a handful of comrades from Majdanek through the sewers; Tomasziewski, the painter and architect, whose life had been saved from the Gestapo by doctors switching him with a dead body; August Kowalczyk, the actor and producer, who had escaped from Auschwitz, and had helped run an orphanage for Polish children until the end of the war; Tomasz Sobanski, another escapee from four years of hell in Auschwitz, now a journalist and hunter of Nazi war criminals - my list is too long to record here, but someday I hope to write of what these brave men experienced and endured.

A dissenter who for me symbolised all the romantic heroism of Poland was Kret (not his full name - he's still very active, and I think will always be 'troublesome'), a young maverick, a Solidarity activist, but extremely leftwing, tall, dark and with the bony good looks of a gipsy. I was concerned for him; he joined open war with the authorities, challenging them to crush him. He had already been imprisoned twice, and badly beaten. "Think of your wife and child," I would admonish him, but he only laughed at me. Even so, I noticed he was always nervous when we were seen in public together, and liked to keep moving. I wished he would be more sensible.

The telephones were openly tapped now, a distinct improvement on having them covertly tapped. One knew that calls might be recorded ('earwigged', in the current slang), as a matter of course. In the old days, we had had to speak in code. Perhaps because of this, though, it was difficult to make international calls. We could only hope that things would get easier as tension reduced. Meanwhile there were queues everywhere, but coffee shops, restaurants and cheap milk bars were all packed, and so were the trams and buses. There were also more taxis than I remembered.

My doctor friend Ewa Kossowska took me to meet a group of students from Warsaw University. They complained about their physical conditions - the dirt, the cockroaches in the dormitories (what can the kitchens have been like?) the poor food, the general dilapidation. I suggested that they repair broken windows, clean and sweep the quadrangles, show a sense of pride in the traditions of their ancient university. They looked at me with pitying unbelief. How could this old bat be so out of touch with reality?

"Why should we?"

"Why should they?" I countered. "If you lounge about bellyaching, never getting off your arses, taking all you can and giving as little back as you can manage, the authorities will have no respect for you. Earn it and shame them."

The young are impatient. They were sick of being reminded of the war. Unlike their parents and grandparents they had no personal memories of the atrocities committed against their families. They saw 'freedom' in the West, and envied the high living standards, the cheap and lavish entertainment, the fashionable clothes and electronic gadgets, the comparative absence of bureaucratic controls. They knew nothing of the other side of the coin; unemployment, homelessness, the sick and old falling into want in the midst of the plenty surrounding them.

I visited Andrzej Konopacki, Deputy Press Spokesman to the Government, no less. I wanted him to try to show them some of the ills that beset our democracies. It wasn't fair to feed the Polish people pap, they should see both sides. "Reprint a few bits from the Guardian, the

Telegraph, The Times, about the problems that the Americans and the British face. Let them see that we have troubles of our own."

He laughed cynically. "What's the point? The people will believe what they want to believe." Klaudiusz Kajzer, the Press Secretary in Portland Place had been very different. Was it living in London that made him so much more understanding of the needs of his countrymen?

Konopacki seemed to see in his own countrymen a careless assumption that the West was a land of milk and honey, a childish and stupid attitude, and despised them for their readiness to accept and digest all that was fed to them by 'The Voice of America' and similar propaganda stations. For his part, as an intelligent man, he knew that his own office, like all government offices, lacked credibility and with it the trust of the people, who regarded them as Moscow's puppets. This was so widely perceived that it was impossible to still the voice of dissent. You can't imprison everybody.

The people were speaking freely, openly and contemptuously of their rulers. We sat in hotel lounges, coffee bars and private houses, but we disdained to take care in our conversation, or even to keep our voices down. The time had come to 'stand up and be counted', a phrase with less bombastic and more sinister overtones in Eastern Europe than elsewhere.

In this connection, it should not be forgotten that Lech Walesa has battles to fight with the hotheads on both his political wings. He must contend daily with those who regard his aspirations as too moderate, and himself as too prone to sup with the Devil.

They underestimate him. His circumstances compel pragmatism upon him, and the charisma of his heroism distracts attention from the wily negotiator. Other members of Solidarity fled the country, and upheld the decisions of the western powers to withhold the necessities of life from their own countrymen. An easy option. My admiration is for those who stayed behind, suffered the hardships, fought their corner.

I returned to London after two months, hopeful but fearful. If there was to be no easing of restrictions then there must be conflagration, but I hoped that the military would see the sense of offering major concessions. It has never paid anyone to rule by force for long, particularly over Poles, with their long history of repression and insurrection.

The airport was in its usual state of chaos. A few officials were bullying some elderly Polish couples at the customs desks. Departures were delayed, as no one was dealing with suitcases. My patience ran out, and much to the amusement of my companions, (Indian and Pakistani embassy staff going to a conference) I stomped off towards two staff to complain.

No joy, total lack of interest was written all over their faces, so I tried a ploy. I fished Gornicki's card out of my handbag, swearing to report their inefficiency to his office - as he had in fact asked me to.

Magic! Within five minutes customs officials of both sexes swarmed round myself and the rest of the queue, and we were all whisked onto the waiting plane. The card had worked wonders - in a selfish cause, I have to admit, though indirectly it took pressure off the Poles who were travelling too.

Before me lay Heathrow, and the Land of Plenty. Isn't it odd how your feelings alter? Since Mama died, coming home hasn't meant the same. I always used to be full of anticipation and excitement, but now my thoughts were left behind, with my friends and the danger they faced. There was nothing more that I could do for them. I was sure that political reform would come about eventually, but would it be this time around?

Since 1981 I have made several more journeys to Poland and to Yugoslavia. There have been changes, gradual but inescapable. Shortages, inflation and other ills have been as apparent as ever, but the mood has changed. The real people, as opposed to the mythical Marxist vision of 'The People', are winning, ever so slowly at first, now faster.

For those without hard currency conditions are no easier, yet the markets offer plenty of food and clothing to those who can pay the price. For the rest, life is full of petty annoyances and aggravations, having to do without simple everyday things that any sort of economy ought to be able to deliver in peacetime - and can, if you don't have centralised economic planning, whether Communist or Fascist in tone. I mean getting your car or TV repaired, being able to buy needles and thread, lightbulbs, matches, washing powder, toilet paper.

Each time I return to my own little country restaurant I count my blessings. Everything runs like clockwork, my two helpers, Helen and Rosemary, who have been with me since the beginning, are jewels, always ready and able to do whatever is necessary. They never let me down, and nor has Anthony, a helpmate I could never do without. He drives, shops, cooks and copes whenever I feel the urge to fly east once again.

Not that it was always thus. Gisela, the German chef we inherited, separated from her husband (John Debley, the local policeman) and returned home. It was an unfortunate time, as I was still dazed by the loss of Mama, and went into cooking as much to keep my mind occupied as for any other reason. Hence my early spectacular failures, and others that were less of my own making. We introduced *crudités* at dinner, and Pam sent a variety of unusual and tasty dip mixes from California, which can now be bought over here as well. I also tried garlanding the main platters with flowers, but my conservative clientele looked askance at these, perhaps fearing that the petals might harbour creepy-crawlies. I swear, not so! Everything was prepared with the greatest care and attention to detail, but one must consider customers' prejudices. I gave them up.

Mama's death also brought Oliver Rigold back into our lives. He had been living in Brighton, his mother's home town, where he felt he had roots of a sort. He and Mama would meet there regularly, either at the Metropole Hotel, or at Sergeant Yorke's Casino. Sometimes he would visit us at East Dean.

When Mama died he was grief-stricken, and his health, already undermined by malaria, yellow fever and his binges, deteriorated very rapidly. By this time he had only one sister alive, Kitty, who was much older than himself. Her children took no interest in him, so he was very lonely and hard up, and the journey to East Dean became more wearing each time. He began to walk into lamp posts during his drinking bouts, breaking his arm twice, so Anthony and I decided that he would have a better chance of surviving under our watchful eyes.

We managed to arrange accommodation for him at the Birling Gap Hotel nearby, where the Collins family, who owned it, showed him great kindness, and understanding for his somewhat eccentric behaviour. We were most grateful for their forbearance with what can only be described as an old and rather naughty child. Oliver could enjoy sitting on the Green and have the odd pint in the Tiger, with me in the background to keep him from overstepping the mark, though even so there were occasions when I had to read him the Riot Act.

Ultimately he had a very severe heart attack. We told his surviving relations, but only Anthony, myself and a kind woman who had befriended him in Brighton were there to see him through his last illness in St Mary's Hospital, where he suffered a massive stroke, and never recovered consciousness. Maddening though he could be, Oliver had the knack of making me laugh. He was one of nature's misfits, which caused great anguish to himself and those close to him, but in the end I understood Mama's attachment to him. She had an underlying desire to sustain and protect those who needed it, even such self-destructive and tragic clowns as Ollie. But then, she was a true Celt, and as she often said, "Celts see both sides of every question, and that makes it impossible to condemn."

For his part, he loved Mama, after his fashion: what more can any of us claim?

Now he is gone as have so many of my friends (and quite a few enemies!) but I still have my cats, and the wild creatures we have adopted, and who come to us for food. These include a vixen and her cubs, two fine badgers, and many kinds of wild bird. We have allegedly tame birds as well, Joe and the pretty and spiteful 'girlfriend' we got for him, a plum-headed parakeet called Tacie. They both enjoy a twice-daily hour of freedom, when we close all the windows and let them fly round the building at will. If we want to protect lampshades, books etc. from their curiosity and sharp beaks, we must be constantly on guard.

They enjoy a very varied diet, and we must spend time chopping fruit, nuts, carrots and cucumber into their seed, but it's worth it to watch them - and to listen to them. Joe speaks beautifully, in French and English, but he is unable to pronounce the letter F. This is just as well, as when we return him to his cage he makes his displeasure very obvious, and airs the ripe vocabulary that is his legacy from Mama.

For us Christmas has always been a very special day. For the last fifteen years we have had the same clients come to celebrate it with us, and we all enjoy ourselves, just like an extended family. We will miss these special dates, but Anthony and I are to retire shortly and will have done so by the time you read this, so you see, it's not all an elaborate plug for Grimaldi's! We will miss the special dates, but we won't be going far. I'm looking forward to a short rest from seventeen years of hard work.

It will be a short rest, no question. I have my planned books on Polish heroes, spymasters and war criminals to work on, but first I must make one final pilgrimage to Poland and Yugoslavia, and say farewell to all my surviving friends. I will also visit the graves of those I have loved, and who have preceded me into the Great Unknown. It will be hard to say goodbye.

Someone recently asked me if I would relive my life differently, given hindsight. I respond with an unequivocal NO. I've known hazard, illness and tears, but it has been a life blessed with more kindness and joy than I could ever have hoped for.

And what, in the end, have I sacrificed? I could perhaps have made a 'better' career for myself, by staying in Milan or America, but there's no guarantee I would have reached the top rank of diva. There are small-minded, disagreeable people who proclaim that they could have been a famous this, or wonderful that, had circumstances not conspired against them. I do not intend to join their ranks. Likewise, I do not intend to cry 'sour grapes!' I could not have been more happy.

I've been lucky as well, and even in this late stage of my life, luck has not deserted me. I have written a spy novel (as yet unpublished) which I have with my agent, Elspeth Cochrane. She had known James Mason well, and it happened that Roderick Brown of Lennard was interested in publishing a biography of James, and looking for a suitable author. Elspeth got to hear of it, and approached me. The rest is history, and though it was a hard slog, I was very glad to take it on.

James's divorce from Pam got far more attention than his happy second marriage ever did. Divorce and recrimination make far better gossip than the long happy years of a middle-aged couple, and James's own professionalism counted against it as well. The man who turned in such a brilliant performance in 'Lolita' was undergoing terrible emotional turmoil. The man who ended his life with the brilliant trio of 'The Verdict', 'Doctor Fischer of Geneva' and 'The Shooting Party' was quietly happy. I wanted to redress the balance, and I believe I did, to some extent.

To misquote Seamus Heaney, I was an idealist who became, for a while wrapped in cynicism, but now in old age I see a start towards a new world, still full of anguish, but setting out on the long slow road to peace and understanding.

For my nephews, my godchildren, and for the sake of children everywhere, let us hope that as the dramas of the twenty-first century unfold, they will see an end to conflict, starvation, cruelty and all the destructive forces that could otherwise wreck our planet.

Coda: 1991

Twenty years ago the possible collapse of Communism would have been seen as a pipe dream by idealists or wilful self-deception by politicians seeking a new order in Europe.

I, for some years, had foreseen a gradual liberalisation within the Eastern Bloc if only as a means of allowing the Soviets to maintain their domination of countries alienated by history, traditions and war. Yet today as the dramas unfold and liberty seems within the grasp of many countries, I feel like Cassandra calling her warnings of doom and disaster. Why? Should I not be rejoicing? In my heart I do, but my head is full of foreboding.

My years as an 'assessor' of conditions in countries allied to the Warsaw Pact have led me to the opinion that the words 'democracy' and 'human rights' have little real meaning. The desire to achieve these ideals is genuine enough but the attainment will not happen at a stroke. Like peace, democracy must be paid for, fought for by new systems which have to prove that they can work for the benefit of all the people. The rich must not grow richer on the backs of the have-nots, or fresh revolutions will convulse the countries now seeking salvation from want and persecution. I fear, and view with scepticism, the role of the Western powers in their dealings with the inexperienced leaders of these newly-detached countries. Unless these leaders can satisfy the needs of their people havoc will ensue.

There are formidable problems to overcome. Massive foreign debts and the closure of factories and businesses will result in hitherto unknown unemployment, with no established social services to afford the necessary solutions. Ill health and inadequate medical care abound and there have been environmental disaster to cope with. Worst of all there must be a period of belt-tightening which will hurt the most vulnerable and poverty stricken members of society.

Nationalism, racism, sectarianism are already raising their ugly heads, not least in the Soviet Union itself, and if the seeds of freedom are to be nurtured and flower the West must prove its worth, not by words or hard-nosed bargaining, but with long-term generosity, understanding and trust, to ensure that democracy puts down indestructible roots.

There are lessons to be learned and consciences examined, not only by the Communist regimes. The Western policies of materialism, the free market philosophy and financial affluence are not the sole necessities of life. The Central and South Americas bear witness to the poverty and deprivation which exist in the free world. If we ignore the needs of those people whose standard of life is below even that of the Communist states, we do so at our peril, and a cauldron of discontent will overflow bringing disaster and even greater disharmony to an already troubled world seemingly bent on self destruction.

The recent war in the Gulf has highlighted the horrors of scientific warfare, the collapse of the infrastructure of Iraq, the pollution of Kuwait, the plight of the Shias and the Kurds, all presage further political upheaval and discord, and it is the people who suffer not the rulers.

Much of the turmoil must be laid at the door of the Gulf States for having maintained Saddam Hussein's power base and some responsibility also must lie with the Western powers who turned a blind eye to Iraqi excesses whilst viewing Iran and Syria as the 'enemy'.

The intransigence of Israel with her repression of the Palestinians, her invasion of Lebanon, her brutal reprisals against thousands of men, women and children, has been allowed to pass with the minimum of criticism and without sanctions or clear demands that the rules of the United Nations be applied and upheld.

If peace is to be established, then Justice must be seen to be even-handed, not slanted for reasons of political expediency or the 'self interest' of individual countries.

If stability is to prevail, ideological and commercial interests must be re-thought and not used, as in the case of Vietnam, Cambodia, Cuba, Mozambique, Angola, Nicaragua and many others, to disrupt and destabilize governments whose policies we disagree with. To deprive populations of succour by withholding aid, will not breed peace; and if revolution, civil war, disease and starvation are to be overcome and over-population eradicated, a far-reaching and concerted effort will be demanded by all countries and governments, irrespective of political bias.

The remarkable efforts by Save the Children, Medicin Sans Frontiers, Oxfam, CAFFOD to name by a few, can relieve but not cure the world's ills. Loans to corrupt regimes must be stopped, the sale of arms prohibited, sanctions taken to enforce the demands of the United Nations, and above all the determination to bring about the brotherhood of man before worldwide chaos engulfs the future generations of every continent.

The reality of failure is too painful to contemplate, the survival of this planet depends on our actions as we go forward into the twenty-first century.

I will not live to see what I believe can, and must, be achieved. Social justice, war on want, freedom of choice, both political and religious, education, health care, housing for all, a basic standard of living and the greatest necessity – PEACE.

Index